The Favored Circle

THE MIT PRESS | Cambridge, Massachusetts | London, England

The Favored Circle

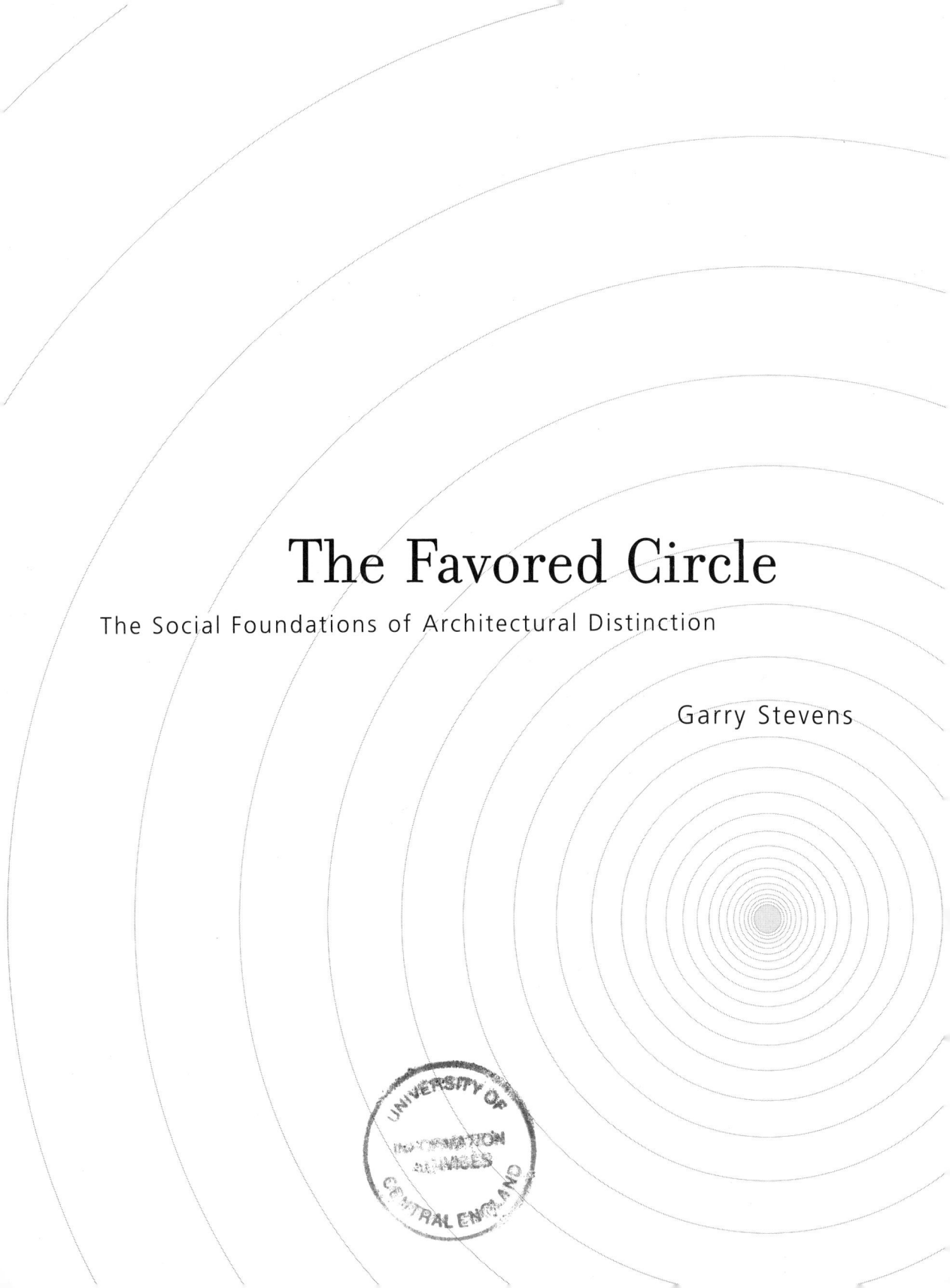

The Social Foundations of Architectural Distinction

Garry Stevens

© 1998 Massachusetts Institute of Technology

All rights reserved. No part of this book may be reproduced in any form by any electronic or mechanical means (including photocopying, recording, or information storage and retrieval) without permission in writing from the publisher.

This book was set in Filosofia by Graphic Composition, Inc., and was printed and bound in the United States of America.

Library of Congress Cataloging-in-Publication Data

Stevens, Garry.
   The favored circle : the social foundations of architectural distinction / Garry Stevens.
       p.   cm.
   Includes bibliographical references and index.
   ISBN 0-262-19408-2 (hc : alk. paper)
   1. Architecture and society.   2. Architecture—Social aspects.   I. Title.
NA2543.S6S67   1998
306.4'7—dc21   98-29297
                                                                            CIP

CONTENTS

1 Targeting the Favored Circle 2
"Dangerous, Mischievous, Subversive and Offensive" 2
My Puzzled Career 4
Quest for Genius: The Psychological Approach 8
Architecture and the Social 11
   Sociologists Are Critical 11
   Architects Are Not Socially Minded 13
   Architectural Discourse Avoids the Social 14
   A Sociology of Architecture Is Redundant 15
Sociological Studies of Architecture 17
   Studies of Practice 18
   Historical-Theoretical Studies 20
Studying Architecture as a Profession 23
   The Sociology of the Professions 25
   Defects in a Sociology of "Profession" 27
Changing the Sociological Study of Architecture 31
   Reformulating "Profession" 31
   Abandoning "Profession" in the Social Study of Architecture ... 33

2 The Sociological Toolkit of Pierre Bourdieu 36
Introducing Bourdieu 36
   Bourdieu in the Intellectual Field 37
   A Very French Sociologist 38
   Bourdieu and Other Thinkers 42
   Bourdieu and Architectural Theory 46
Overview of Bourdivin Theory 47
Bourdieu's Formal Sociology 49
   The Central Problem of Sociology 49
   Bourdieu's Resolution of the Central Problem 52
   Linking Practice to Structure 56
Bourdieu's Model of Society 59
   Symbolic Power and Culture 59
   Symbolic Capital 62
   Strategies of Investment 64

Social Space and Class Structure 65
Historical Movement in Social Space 67

3 Architecture as a Field 68

What Culture Does 68
- Culture as a Battlefield between Classes 69
- Taste 71

The Field of Culture 74
- Fields 74
- Field and Habitus 76
- Functions of the Field of Culture 78
- Ensuring Closure through Culture 80
- Outline of the Structure of the Field 81

The Field of Architecture 83
- Basic Structure 83
- Forms of Capital 88
- The Quest for Autonomy 91
- A Semi-Autonomous Field 94
- Priests and Prophets: Conflict within the Field 98

How the Field Works: Three Examples 103
- From Modern Movement to International Style 103
- Attacking the Field's Autonomy 105
- Decon Comes to Town 112

4 The Field through Time 122

A Threefold Social Space 122

A Study of Architectural History 125

A Portrait of the Architect 130
- The Architects' Nationalities 133
- The Architects' Buildings 133

Historical Growth of the Architectural Community 137
- Temporal Limits 137
- Per Capita Growth 140
- The Two Communities of the *MEA* 143
- Growth of the Major Sector 145
- Growth of the Minor Sector 147

Historical Dynamics of the Field 151
   Dynamics of the Major Sector 153
   Dynamics of the Minor Sector 159

5 Understanding Architectural Education 168

The Field's New System of Reproduction 168
   The Critique of Architectural Education 170
   Britain: Articled Pupilage 174
   France: The State Certification Model 179
   Germany: Research Enters the Universities 182
   The United States: An Uneasy Synthesis 184

How the Schools Socialize 187
   Favoring the Favored 189
   Longevity of the Studio System 204

Architecture as a Discipline 204
   The Discipline in the Field 206
   Structure of the Discipline 207
   Architecture and Related Disciplines 210

6 Contemporary Transformations 212

The Expansion of the Subordinate Sector 212

The Permanent Crisis in Architectural Education 214
   The Critique of the Intellectually Dominant 215
   The Critique of the Professionally Dominant 216

Transformations of the Field 217
   The New Market for Credentials 217
   New Trajectories 218

Explaining Some Puzzles 220

Notes 224

Index 246

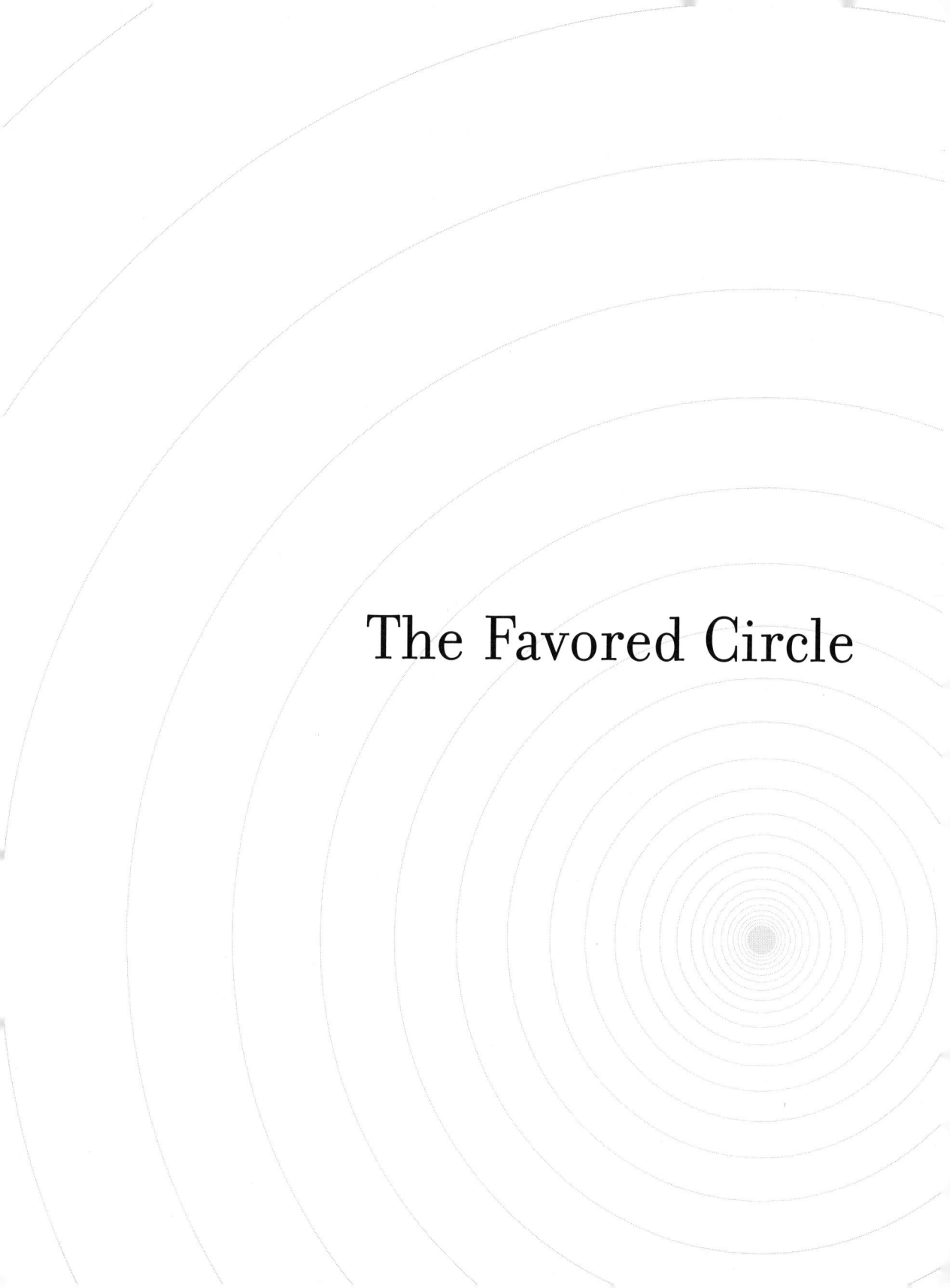

The Favored Circle

Targeting the Favored Circle

"Dangerous, Mischievous, Subversive and Offensive"

What I have to say in this book is extremely simple: *there is a social basis for intellectual development*. By this I mean both the development of the individual over the course of a single life, and the development of an entire arena of thought—architecture—over a period of five hundred years.

Put so baldly it would hardly seem possible to object. Yet, as the French sociologist Pierre Bourdieu—from whom this work adopts much of its fundamental analytical apparatus—has found, a full development and exposition of the proposition arouses the most intense antagonism from those to whom it is applied (as in the heading to this section, a quotation from a colleague after a lecture I gave on this book). When the subjects upon whom this apparatus is turned realize the logical consequence of holding forth that there is a social genesis to architectural creativity, namely, that their success owes *at least* as much to their social background and to the social structures within which they are embedded as it does to their native talent (or, as Bourdieu puts it, as much to the unchosen determination of their social milieu as to the undetermined choosing of the application of their gifts), they find the very concept an insult to the exaltation of genius that has been so much a part of the field's discourse since Vasari or before.

It is for this reason that I, like Bourdieu, find that in order to state my case at all, I have to overstate it. With this comes the converse danger, that of being misunderstood by the reader as holding that there is no such thing as talent or genius, that such individual qualities are entirely reducible to the social environment. This is clearly not the case. I make a case in this book that one of the prime functions of the system of architectural education is to produce cultivated individuals; that the central function of the discipline of architecture is to produce instruments of taste; that efflorescences of architectural creativity at the highest levels can be most readily explained simply by the existence and particular structure of master-pupil chains. However, with all these claims I *do not* intend to deny that architectural education also imparts skills, that the discipline does generate knowledge, and that talent is necessary to occupy the highest reaches of architectural genius.

To say that this book is a social study of architecture is ambiguous. Such a statement could refer, first, to an examination of the artifacts that constitute the built environment: how people use and have used those buildings called "architecture."[1] This book is a social study of "architecture" in a second sense, taking that word to refer to the individuals involved in the construction of artifacts, the immediate social structures within which these individuals are embedded, and the discourses they participate in.

I use the term "social study of architecture" rather than something like the "social study of architects" because in this book I am going to attempt to persuade you that to concentrate attention on the members of the *occupation* of architecture, as so much previous work has done, is to ignore important aspects of a much larger social entity, the *field* of architecture, which structures the entire social universe of the architect and of which architects are only one part.

My Puzzled Career

I cannot and do not pretend to be a disinterested analyst of architecture. Like other sociologists tackling their problems, I have a personal stake in the analysis, and I believe that there is a dilemma in need of resolution. Fifty years ago most sociologists would have claimed to be disinterested scientific observers of society, as detached when studying their own social milieux as physicists can be about electrons. Few make the assertion today, recognizing—as I shall discuss later—the impossibility of studying objectively the very social world in which they are enmeshed. There is, then, a normative and critical element in the sociological enterprise.

So: this book grew out of my attempt to understand and explain the fratricidal warfare between the two main factions at my old Faculty of Architecture at the University of Sydney, a university cast very much from the Oxbridge mold. I spent almost twenty years there as a student and a lecturer. In a situation unusual in the English-speaking world, the staff was divided into two cumbersomely named departments: the Department of Architecture, Planning and Allied Arts (DAPAA), and my own Department of Architectural and Design Science (DADS), corresponding to the division between the humanities and the sciences. The former is responsible for history, design, professional practice, and construction; the latter for the environmental sciences, building services, structures, and computing. Although this constitutes a clichéd divide, its history goes back to lectures by T. L. Donaldson, the first professor of architecture in the English-speaking world.[2] The DAPAA is staffed largely by people with degrees in architecture, and DADS by a mixture of individuals, some with architecture qualifications, but also some with backgrounds in engineering and the physical sciences.

DADS has few counterparts elsewhere. The department is a product of the enthusiasm for bringing science into architecture that swept the British Commonwealth in the 1950s. Where most schools the University of Sydney's size—with its three hundred students—will have just a few people teaching in DADS's area, or even rely entirely on adjunct instructors (casuals), DADS has a staff of fifteen. Not only do the architectural scientists at Sydney enjoy a considerable autonomy as a result of having their own department, but this autonomy has allowed the development and expansion of this side of architecture to a degree uncommon elsewhere: DADS has a thriving postgraduate program, an international research reputation, and a large say in the development of the professional architectural curriculum.

The two departments always coexisted uneasily, relations varying from bare tolerance to outright warfare. That tensions should exist in an architecture school was nothing unusual, of course. Academics, with the luxury of tenure, do not suffer from the restraints that commercial tact imposes on those in the private sector, who can only voice pugnacious dissent at risk to their employment. But the stresses at Sydney were of a different kind from those present at other schools, where conflict between the humanists and technologists is only a minor eddy amid the vortices generated by the everyday discord among the design staff.

A Note on Terminology

This book describes and analyzes the field of architecture as it exists in modern English-speaking nations. I have used examples from North America, the United Kingdom, and my own country of Australia to carry on the argument. The examples also illuminate some important and interesting differences between the three nations.

A few words on terminology will prevent confusion later. I will often refer to the professional associations in those countries: the American Institute of Architects (AIA), the Royal Institute of British Architects (RIBA), and the Royal Australian Institute of Architects (RAIA). In Australia, the academics that North Americans call "faculty" are just called "staff." In my country a Faculty (always capitalized) is an American School or College, and only the most senior academics receive the title Professor—all the rest are lecturers. Undergraduates are the same everywhere, but a North American graduate student is called a postgraduate in Australia. In the U.K. and Australia, a master's degree is a research degree, and never a professional one. In those countries, a Ph.D. is the lowest doctorate and rarely requires coursework. The higher doctorates, such as a D.Arch., are usually honorary awards to distinguished individuals, while in the U.S. they can be professional degrees ranking below a Ph.D.

When the only representatives of the sciences and technology are perhaps one or two professors or a few casuals teaching everything from structures and fire safety to acoustics and lighting, it is hardly possible for them to threaten the dominance of the design teachers and historians. Where other schools are vaguely aware of the differences and disagreements between the humanistic and technological components of architectural education, at Sydney one could experience them at their most intense. DAPAA and the local profession regarded DADS as at best an irrelevance, and at worst as a parasite leeching DAPAA of money and resources. The undergraduates would have concurred, adding that DADS's courses were boring and occupied too much of the curriculum. The proper role for the technologists, all would have agreed, was to provide the occasional lecture, to act as desultory consultants in the design studio, and, in short, to assume the properly subservient role they had in other schools.

Over twenty years of academic infighting, DAPAA never succeeded in freeing itself of the succubus. This failure was partly the result of DAPAA's political ineptitude: where DADS's staff was capable of maintaining a solidarity of purpose unusual for academics, the machinations between DAPAA's internal factions constantly diverted their attention from the common enemy. There were, of course, other reasons. For while DADS had a dismal standing among the architectural community, its research reputation was excellent and, to the university, that is what counted most. It was one of the world's top five CAD (computer-aided design) research centers, and had an international reputation for its work in lighting, acoustics, and thermal studies of buildings. The flourishing postgraduate programs, the constant flow of books and papers, and its success in attracting research funds ensured that it was never in danger of dissolution.

When the warfare was discussed—as it often was—its existence was attributed to the fact that one department perversely refused to acknowledge the other's greater virtues. DADS could not understand why DAPAA failed to recognize its superior standing in the academic community. Was not research, after all, the veriest raison d'être of the academic? DAPAA was at a loss as to why DADS could not see that its only mission was the teaching of undergraduates. Each dismissed the vices attributed to the other. If students questioned the relevance and competence of DADS courses, the subjects of their derision replied they did not know what was good for them. If DAPAA did not churn out abstruse papers and books, it was because this had nothing to do with designing buildings.

The whole state of affairs was put down to academic politics: once certain recalcitrant, arrogantly ambitious, or grossly incompetent individuals were removed, all would be well.

In my early years I would have agreed. I took the superior performance of my own department as an article of faith, and adopted the appropriate air of condescension to contrary expressions of opinion. In my teaching, whether the topic was fire safety or structures, there were always some students who would ask, "Do we really have to know this?" I always patiently replied in the affirmative—of course they did.

The possibility that there were other, deeper and more subtle processes operating in architectural education than the ones we thought were going on became evident to me after I started studying sociology in the embers of my youth. As I slowly acquired what has been called the "sociological imagination," I became suspicious that the entire quarrel was miscast and that the altercations—which usually ended up as debates about the degree to which architecture was artistic, scientific, or professional—resulted from disputes about the wrong questions altogether.

Other architectural scientists, I discovered, were in similar positions in their own schools. Sydney's tensions, it transpired, were more intense than most, but they were certainly not unique; and if they were not unique, they could not be the result of personal contumacies. As Templer pointed out, the whole discipline of architecture is ruptured into scientific (or, if you will, scientistic) and humanistic domains.[3]

I had also come to notice that the students who had a few years before avoided and most disparaged as irrelevant our supposedly fact-filled courses were now, as recent graduates, the emerging bright lights of the profession. Those who had been most enthusiastic about the environmental sciences were languishing in the lower rungs of firms, usually trapped before a computer screen. Moreover, they were always the same sort of student—right from their first year, it was possible to pick which was which just by looking at them. Why was this so?

Quest for Genius: The Psychological Approach

Psychological literature is the obvious place to start an attempt to explain the puzzles of my academic life. Perhaps the quarrels between the academics, and the different career paths of my students, could be understood best by examining the psychology of the architect.

The *locus classicus* is Donald MacKinnon's study conducted nearly forty years ago.[4] He asked 120 architects to submit themselves to an entire weekend of psychological testing. One third were invited on the basis of their extremely high creativity, another third were chosen on the basis of exhibiting considerable but not first-class talent in design, and a final third were selected randomly. The last group was taken to be average in creativity.

Dozens of personality and intelligence measures from ten instruments were derived for the three groups. Those in the creative group scored as more feminine,[5] flexible, and happy with themselves than the lesser lights, and less sociable, responsible, self-controlled, and concerned with giving a good impression. They were also assessed as intuitive and introverted. A test of interpersonal behavior revealed them to be distinctly uncommunal: they had little desire to be included in others' activities, nor to include others in their own. When obliged to interact with others, the test showed they had a strong desire to control group activities and a distinct reluctance to submit to others' control. The creative giants also valued aesthetic and theoretical values higher and economic values lower than the control groups. The control groups believed that satisfying the client was quite important (ranking it eighth out of fifty statements describing a variety of skills, work habits, interests, and values), and the creative group did not (ranking it thirty-fourth). The average architects also felt some responsibility toward their profession, while the creative felt virtually none at all. Self-descriptions showed the creative group to favor autonomy, change, and aggression.

Finding more than a hundred architects willing to be subjected to hours or even days of psychological testing is no mean logistical feat. Since MacKinnon's time most of the psychological work has been directed at analyzing creativity in architecture students, a population more accessible and easier to cajole.[6] (At least testing students has the laudable aim of improving selection procedures into architecture schools.) So far the results have been uniformly unpromising. One psychologist had to admit that "all efforts to identify the successful or unsuccessful student met with little success."[7] Others found that the General Aptitude Test Battery was unable to distinguish poor from good students with any reliability, misclassifying almost forty percent of their sample.[8] Another group of psychologists had as little success, although they bravely claimed progress.[9] Had their suggested selection procedure been followed, their university would have rejected 110 of the 178 students who did in fact graduate. Not surprisingly, some relationship had been found between various spatial ability tests and academic performance in architecture, although the correlations were quite small.[10] In its study of advanced architecture students, one research group also found only a modest correlation with a spatial ability test, and none with standard academic measures.[11]

The grand aim of the psychological enterprise is to discover the personality characteristics that determine architectural creativity, but to date the results have been unimpressive. As another, more critical, psychologist pointed out about MacKinnon's work, the only substantial difference between his creative and mediocre architects was the former's indifference to economic concerns.[12]

Despite meager results, the psychological approach remains the dominant one among social science studies of architecture. The quest for some simple formula to explain genius attracts researchers, and the laudatory profiles they produce of their subjects only encourage architects to participate in the studies. Moreover, since psychology, by definition, directs its attention to the individual, the nature of the enterprise finds ready acceptance in the ideology of the artistic genius that is one of the fundamental axioms of architectural thought.

This is not to say that psychological studies are without value. My main criticism is that *by its nature psychology precludes a social explanation— a sociogenesis—for architectural creativity* in favor of a purely individualistic explanation. It is one of the main arguments of this book that this is not so, and that there are greater social forces operating to produce architectural genius.

A Psychologist Describes Architects

It would seem that professional psychologists have a particular affection for architects, a feeling no doubt reciprocated by the objects of their eulogies. I must admit that I am irked by the psychologists' attitudes, which vary from the disingenuously uncritical to the positively fawning. In a paper written for the official publication of the American Institute of Architects, the *AIA Journal,* for example, Donald MacKinnon concluded by saying:

If I were to summarize what at this stage impresses me about the genus Architectus Creator varietas Americanus *it is their openness to experience, their freedom from petty restraints and impoverishing inhibitions, their aesthetic sensitivity, their cognitive flexibility, their independence in thought and action, their high level of energy, their unquestioning commitment to creative endeavor and their unceasing striving for creative solutions to the ever more difficult architectural problems which they constantly set themselves.*

D. W. MacKinnon, "Genus Architectus Creator Varietas Americanus," *AIA Journal,* September 1960, 35.

MacKinnon seems not to have missed any opportunity for compliments:

The invited architects responded courteously and even warmheartedly [to our invitations]. Their sentences were grammatically formed and felicitously expressed and their letters were typed with novel arrangement on letterhead stationery of their own design so aesthetically pleasing as to make their letters seem even more friendly acceptances of my invitation than they may have been intended to be.

D. W. MacKinnon, "Genus Architectus Creator Varietas Americanus," 32.

These remarks were not simply an effort to be polite to architectural readers. Writing for the professional psychological press, his descriptions become even more Olympian:

The creative architect thinks of himself as creative. . . . Above all else he thinks of himself as imaginative; unquestionably committed to creative endeavor; unceasingly striving for creative solutions to the difficult problems he repeatedly sets for himself; satisfied only with solutions which are original and meet his own high standards of architectural excellence; aesthetically sensitive; an independent spirit free from crippling restraints and impoverishing inhibitions; spontaneous; forth-right; and self-accepting. He has a sense of destiny about his career as an architect.

One is struck by the accuracy of self-perception, by the degree to which architects see themselves as they really are, and by the remarkable consistency with which they conform in their thought and in their behavior to the type of person they see themselves as being.

D. W. MacKinnon, "Creativity and Images of the Self," in *The Study of Lives,* ed. R. W. White (New York: Atherton Press, 1963), 276.

Architecture and the Social

Although psychology and sociology are usually regarded as sibling sciences, their adherents usually find little in common to talk about. Sociologists cannot conduct experiments in the ways that psychologists can, so their methodologies differ. Psychology has always been strongly tied to the biological sciences, and especially medicine, while sociology has closer relations to economics and political science. No one ever debates whether they should see a consulting sociologist rather than a psychiatrist. Everyone could bandy about a few psychological terms—id, ego, Oedipus complex—but few understand the meaning of social role, contradictory class position, or habitus.

To move from the psychological to the sociological realm is therefore a greater step than might be thought at first. One problem attendant to social writing about architecture is that the field itself has not been receptive to sociological input, nor to sociological description and analysis. This produces an antagonistic air the very opposite of the warm feelings surrounding the psychologist-architect relationship, and does nothing to assist the sociologist's task. Four reasons may be suggested for this:

1   Sociologists are critical.
2   Architects are not socially minded.
3   Architectural discourse avoids the social.
4   It is thought there can be no sociology of creativity.

1   Sociologists Are Critical

First, while the psychologists seem to have nothing but good things to say about architecture,[13] the few sociologists interested in the field are much more critical. The psychological study of the architect is the quest to ascertain the determinants of genius, a condition admired and aspired to by all. It seems to be left to the sociologists to analyze rather than simply adore genius, and they are not nearly as flattering. Sherry Ahrentzen and Linda Groat, for example, support their work with these remarks from female architectural academics:

> The star system is definitely male dominated and excludes the female. The field encourages hero-worshipping and the heroes are all male. I've gotten rather tired of this myself! . . . History of architecture focuses on building and design as activities of "great men." Textbooks tend to be sexist by omission or language—even when good in other areas. Significant effort is required to counteract this, and most faculty seem unaware of the sexism and therefore do not work to counteract it.[14]

It must be admitted that to outsiders a lot of sociology appears to comprise nothing but carping criticism. To quite a few, the discipline seems little more than an infestation of Marxist jeremiahs. This has something to it: sociologists tend to be quite liberal politically. However, while Marxism remains a significant theoretical tradition in sociology, much of its significance derives from the many important theoretical positions that have been created in reaction to it (such as Pierre Bourdieu's). The appearance of rampant leftism also perhaps arises because sociologists do see problems everywhere—it is one of the reasons they become sociologists. Moreover, they usually have ideas about how to solve these problems, about what society should be. Having strong opinions on what society *ought* to look like, sociologists often say things the profession is not very interested in hearing. The doyen of architectural sociology, Robert Gutman, for example, argued that the natural market for architecture was the design of monumental buildings, that there were simply too many architects for this market, and that the profession ought to reduce the number and size of firms, and cut the number of graduates and schools.[15] In another place he sniped at "the tendency of architects to leaf through books on social science and philosophy, looking for phrases that express their personal views and lend an imprimatur to their design work."[16] In a similar vein, Herbert Gans, a fellow sociologist, launched out with, "Architects are generally not accomplished philosophers in the first place; the statements they want to make are often half-baked or cliched even when the architecture itself is good."[17]

All the architectural sociologists referred to here believe that architects do not pay much attention to the social, to the needs of the people inhabiting or working in their buildings. They tend to dislike any tendency toward architectural formalism and away from functional considerations. Being interested in the social they also dislike architecture's fixation on the individual. In consequence, they were usually unsympathetic to (or even quite hostile to) the formerly dominant avant-garde position of deconstructivism. None of these things endears them to contemporary architects.

2   Architects Are Not Socially Minded

Second, the psychology of architects is not socially receptive. Architects do not seem to be very communally minded individuals. In the psychological literature cited above, a definite tendency is seen for architects, particularly the more eminent, to be most unsociable. All three of MacKinnon's groups regarded the architect's responsibility to society as unimportant. His most creative group was not really interested in interacting with other people at all, and when they were obliged to deal with others they preferred to be giving orders to them. As the sociologist Dana Cuff found in her interviews with some eminent New York architects, they conceived of people as beholders, not willed agents. Fundamentally social notions such as community, family, friendship, or work relations were ill-defined

---

Why Sociologists Aren't Objective

The eminent American sociologist Stephen Cole put it like this:

A sociologist, for example, might select a problem because of the biographical experiences that he or she has had. Thus, I became interested in teachers' unions—the subject of my doctoral dissertation—because my mother was a militant member of the union and had participated in the first strikes, not because the research site was a compelling one for answering urgent theoretical questions. Or a sociologist will decide to study marriages between blacks and whites because she is involved in an interracial marriage. . . . When feminists study the cause of gender inequality most are not doing so primarily because the topic is of theoretical significance but because they want to show that the inequality that is "bad" is a result of discrimination that "should" be eliminated. These political and social goals are very often more important to investigators and audiences in sociology than are cognitive goals.

S. COLE, "Why Sociology Doesn't Make Progress Like the Natural Sciences," *Sociological Forum* 9, no. 2 (1994): 146, 151.

among them.[18] People, it seems, get in the way of architects and architecture. Take a look through any of the glossy architectural magazines showcasing the talent and one cannot but be struck by the absence of *people* in the photographs. It may be impossible to clear the streets of New York to photograph the latest skyscraper, but wherever possible it seems the photographers vacate the buildings and surrounds to present the building as a pristine objet d'art, uncontaminated by users, clients, and inhabitants.

3   Architectural Discourse Avoids the Social

From this follows a third point, noted by Bill Hillier some time ago.[19] He described the central problem in the theory of architecture as the determination of the abstract principles underlying built form. Once discovered, it is believed, these principles allow architects to design good architecture. Since Greek times it has seemed self-evident that these principles must be mathematical in nature. Sometimes the mathematics has been numerical, and sometimes geometric. The former leads to proportional and modular systems. Taking the latter route entails asserting that architecture must emulate the underlying geometrical order of nature, and tends to produce schemes for the analysis of finished forms. In either case the quest is for a naturalistic order, derived from the structure of the world, and profoundly suprahuman.

The point is that theories of architectural form have never been *social* theories. Even when they have purported to be, the reality has been rather different. On the Modern movement, for example, Spiro Kostoff remarked:

> Modernist rhetoric waxed eloquent about the needs of users. It represented architecture as the vehicle of social welfare and set public housing issues as the highest priority of architecture. But there was no question of consulting with the user of the housing estate during the course of their design. . . . Users did not know what they wanted or, more importantly, what they should have. Their collective needs, interpreted by the architect and the sponsoring agency, would be codified in the "program"—as had been the case with hospitals, schools and prisons in the past. The fit might not be comfortable at first. The setting might appear alien to our habitual ways. The fault was with our habits. We would learn

to adjust to the new *Wohnkultur* because it was based on rationally derived standards. . . . Architectural revolutions required the redesign of humanity.[20]

So not only are architects personally not very social animals, neither are their theories.[21]

The history of architectural theory could be written as a cycle of formalistic theories, followed by a crisis of confidence, a search for external values to base a theory of form on, then slowly increasing introversion and formalism. Architectural theory has also historically aligned itself with philosophy rather than with any of the social sciences. Academic and critical debates take place on the high ground of aesthetic theory. They are more congruent with the general cultural studies that the French do so well than with any form of Anglophone sociology, or even Anglophone philosophy; architecture has thus looked to Europe for almost its whole history to ground its intellectual content. Taking the postmodern as their own fond invention, architectural intellectuals have contributed enthusiastically to the now vast literature on that topic.[22] Notions of "text" and "discourse" and the like pop up quite frequently, aligning architectural theory with Francophone literary studies more than anything else. Since, as the American sociologist Randall Collins has pointed out, sociology is an underdeveloped discipline in France, architectural theory there is also sociologically impoverished.[23]

4   A Sociology of Architecture Is Redundant

This brings us to the final reason for architecture's lack of interest in the social. The general response from philosophers and theorists to any sociology of art has been to deny the validity of the whole enterprise.[24] Ever since Kant, philosophy has worked with the idea of art as autonomous, and its central problems have been how one may distinguish art from non-art, or how one can determine aesthetic quality, or just what beauty is, and so on (so-called postmodern theory notwithstanding). By holding art to be essentially transcendental, aesthetic philosophers, art historians, and critics rule out the very existence of a sociology of art ("ontologically gerrymandering" it into oblivion[25]), save for the relatively harmless investigation of the linkages between social forces and art movements.

Sociologies of architecture necessarily conflict with several important assumptions of aesthetic and architectural theory. There are four presuppositions among philosophers and architectural theorists with which the sociologist must take issue:

- Great buildings, qua works of art, are unique. The sociologist must instead address observable regularities.

- Great buildings are executed by a single creator. Art theory has always centered on the individual. To cope with the great new art form of the

Postmodern Theory and Why It Isn't Here

You won't find the word "postmodern" used much in this book, because the theorists most associated with that term don't really have anything to say to us. The French philosopher-kings have no interest in the body of results accumulated by sociology but, since sociological themes cannot be avoided, they keep inventing their own amateur sociologies. This has exasperated some Anglo-Americans (including me). Randall Collins, one of America's foremost sociologists, expressed his peeve against Parisians such as Foucault like this:

The amateur sociology of the Paris philosophers and literary theorists is impressive mainly to people who lack much grounding in what sociology has achieved. It is hardly necessary to tell sociologists that social conventions are arbitrary and are historically constructed. . . . Where the amateurs have made useful contributions, it has not happened by theoretical breakthroughs so much as by taking ideas that parallel existing sociological ideas and applying them to fresh empirical materials. It is in this respect that Foucault's contributions, for example, are valuable. . . . Foucault was primarily an historian of psychiatry who saw the connections between his specialty and other institutional spheres. The historical detail and the new understanding of psychiatry are welcome contributions, but they do not constitute any great theoretical departure. In Foucault's efforts to theorize, he hit on a more modern sociological theme, the relationship between microprocesses and the macro structure of power. Again, bravo; but frankly, it is an amateur's performance.

R. COLLINS, "Cumulation and Anticumulation in Sociology," *American Sociological Review* 55 (1990): 462.

twentieth century, the cinema, for example, it had to invent *auteur* theory, which holds that a movie may be a collective effort, but all save the director are mere day laborers. Sociology is concerned with the collective.

- Aesthetic value is inherent in the great building. The sociologist must determine instead how and why society comes to valorize some works and consign others to oblivion. A sociology of art (usually) denies essentialism.

- Architecture is the expression of the creator's singular genius. The aesthete would hold that a sociology of architecture is therefore redundant, since it ignores the resulting unanalyzability of the work.

Sociological Studies of Architecture

The little sociological work conducted on architecture falls into three broad areas: studies of practice, historical-theoretical studies, and gender studies.[26] The entire literature could be read in a day. The lack of material might seem unusual, as architecture intersects two sociological specialisms—sociology of professions and sociology of art—and should therefore be the subject of attention to researchers in both. Yet in both cases architecture seems to slip through the cracks. While there is any amount of art or architectural history that one might look on as socially informed, the sociology of art, properly speaking, is a relatively recent focus of attention in the English-speaking world, only attracting interest since the 1960s.[27] Even today it accounts for only about two percent of the sociological literature.[28] It has only a slightly longer history in Europe, and this mainly from a group of sociologists belonging to what is known as the Frankfurt School, or from other Marxians.[29] In general, Marxian analyses have not been received well because, in trying to explain everything in economic terms, they have seemed simplistic and reductive.

Within this small subfield of sociology, the arts of interest to social scientists have been painting, sculpture, music, and opera.[30] Architecture has attracted only passing interest, no doubt because the other arts are simpler cases in the sense that they seem less contaminated by nonartistic concerns, and are therefore easier for the sociologist to make sense of. Architecture has also been little studied by those interested in the sociology of professions: law and medicine are the typical objects of research. Again, these areas have seemed better "developed" as professions and hence more interesting objects of research.

Studies of Practice
Such as it is, the majority of empirical research in the sociology of architecture has been squarely focused on what architects would consider the traditional and certainly the most desirable form of earning a living, the private sector firm. Work in this area has conceived of architecture as consisting of individuals grouped into practices, which supply services to various forms of clients. The questions of interest center on the nature of the market for these services, and how this market has been changing. There is usually a strong pragmatic cast to these studies, and some are written as guides to firms, offering advice on how to navigate their way to happier and healthier practice.

Robert Gutman's *Architectural Practice* describes in detail the profession as it existed in the United States in the mid-1980s or so.[31] Gutman summarized his findings by posing five challenges to the profession. First, it had to adjust the number of individuals in the field to fit the potential demand for their services. He noted that law and medicine had succeeded in restricting enrollments in the schools, and suggested that architecture follow the same course—although this would remove the supply of cheap labor in the form of recent graduates that firms were used to having.[32] He also suggested the development of some sort of stratification system, as in medicine, where interns, residents, nurses, and other paramedical occupations are controlled by full members of the medical profession.

Second, Gutman challenged the profession to develop a philosophy of practice that corresponded to the demands of the building industry. He criticized architects, and especially their professional organizations, for failing to develop consist policies with respect to other occupations in the industry. He described the community of architectural firms as fragmented and lacking leadership from the AIA.[33]

Third, Gutman called on the profession to maintain a secure hold in an increasingly competitive market. He proposed the establishment of specialized training programs within the schools, so that architects could acquire expertise in other areas of construction. As an alternative he suggested a retreat into the core of the architect's role, that of artistic design. The fourth challenge was the need to keep firms profitable. His final challenge was to find ways to improve the morale of the young architect, and to motivate firms to produce good work.[34]

Further extensive descriptive work has been carried out by Dana Cuff, who conducted participant observation research in several architectural firms, generating a description of the typical life career of an individual through architecture school, graduation, and work life.[35]

Judith Blau, who has investigated various aspects of the art world, also studied the world of architectural practice.[36] In 1974 she surveyed 152 Manhattan firms, with a view to determining various organizational traits and their evolution over time. As she reported in her book *Architects and Firms*, there were no structural characteristics separating failed from surviving firms. A pattern did emerge, however, when firms were classified into one of three categories: successful, merely surviving, or completely failed. She found that similar types of firms either failed or succeeded, and such firms were different from the mere survivors. Blau concluded that what was most critical in staving off disaster, in simply hanging on through a depression, was sufficient size and a stream of corporate commissions. Smaller firms, though, were balanced on a fulcrum of risk: properties such as organizational flexibility, nonlocal commissions, freedom from constraint by a parent firm, and reliance on a referral network could spell extinction as much as growth.

A final descriptive study worth noting is that of Magali Sarfatti Larson et al.[37] Her team surveyed one in twelve of the American firms listed in the AIA's *Profile of Architectural Firms* for 1978. Among other results, they found that there were strong ecological linkages between the size of the local construction industry, the number of firms, and the number of schools. Firms seemed to be founded by architects trained in the same state, and to recruit most of their qualified personnel locally.

Historical-Theoretical Studies

A second type of sociological research seeks to explain the development of the architecture profession and how it has come to be the way it is. Such work is of necessity both historical and theoretical.

Very few sociologists have turned their attention toward theorizing specifically about the architecture profession. The first was Magali Sarfatti Larson, who constructed a theory of historical development based on her earlier work in the sociology of the professions.[38] The occupational role of architecture, Larson holds, depends on two sets of social relationships. The first is that between those who conceive the building and those who execute that conception, or between *telos* and *techne*, as she calls them. Architects only exist when the execution of construction is separated from its commission. The second social relationship exists between patrons, who define the functions of a building, and those who mediate between patrons and executants (builders). The architectural role has arisen several times in certain historical circumstances when a special group of builders (such as master masons) or exceptional individuals (as in the early Renaissance) appear and mediate between the elites who commission buildings and their stylistic conventions.

Through the Middle Ages the architect remained largely anonymous. As Larson puts it, the charisma of great building was instead appropriated by the patron. In the Renaissance, architects were able to turn the tables on their patrons by displacing the charismatic properties of building into an abstract and theoretical discourse about architecture. The passage of the occupation into an increasingly academic and official phase began in the late Baroque in France, where the monarch increasingly controlled monumental building programs. The establishment of the Royal Academy of Architecture in France allowed architects to affirm official control over the symbolic and aesthetic dimensions of architecture. After a brief dissolution during the Revolution it reemerged as the Ecole des Beaux-Arts, thus carrying the conception of the architect's role as a specialist in the elaboration of stylistic codes right through the disintegration of the ancien régime into the modern period.

Larson continues by noting that the Industrial Revolution brought new tensions to the role of architect. As specialists in the aesthetic, architects were faced with the increasingly difficult problem of giving adequate expression to the novel and different types of building that industrialization was demanding. While they attempted to resolve these problems in eminently symbolic and theoretical terms, engineers were inserting themselves more and more into building construction. The architects' attempts to theorize their way to relevance began to seem trifling when faced with the engineers' undoubted competence in building execution. Moreover, their theorizing, hitherto conducted in historical terms, was confounded by the rise of science and positivist ideologies. The classical tradition had nothing to say about factories, warehouses, or railway stations.

Like professionals in many other occupations at the beginning of the nineteenth century, architects embarked on what Larson refers to as the professionalization project. This involved two lines of attack. First, defining and controlling a protected market for architectural services that must be distinguished from the services offered by competitors such as builders or engineers, and defended in terms of competence and the benefits bestowed. Second, attaching social status and concrete socioeconomic privileges to the fact of membership in the professional category. This points toward some sort of institutional means for self-definition and corporate defense, and the need to find adequate ideological justification for the exclusion of competitors. It also implies the creation of standardized competencies among its practitioners to distinguish their services from alternatives. The sanction of the state and formal education and credentialing can satisfy these requirements.

Larson thus explains the formation of professional associations of architects in the first half of the century as attempts to define the architect and exclude mere builders. The replacement of articled pupilage by formal education is seen as the method undertaken to standardize architectural skills. The fundamental problem plaguing the profession was then and still is its inability to construct a monopoly market. As she puts it, since the products of architects and non-architects are functionally indistinguishable, the profession has never been able to construct an ideological justification sufficiently convincing to persuade the state to allow it to monopolize the design of buildings. Appeals to aesthetic and theoretical grounds have never succeeded in a society in which cultural plurality is acceptable in a way that, for example, medical heterodoxy is not.

Larson's market monopoly theory was criticized by David Brain in his study of the development of the architecture profession in the United States in the nineteenth century.[39] He argues there that Larson's theory is unable to explain why the aesthetic dimension, specifically, emerged as the key component of the architect's role, and proposes a model that focuses on the nature of architectural rhetoric. Larson is indifferent to the actual content of professional knowledge, seeing it as simply a resource to be wielded in the contest for monopolization and legitimation. By examining the process of architectural professionalization toward the end of the century, Brain discerns the evolution of a rhetoric of style that was able to unite many practitioners over a large number of dispersed work sites into a cohesive profession. The central threat was the eclectic stylism that supplanted the previously dominant Greek style in the second third of the century. With a panoply of styles in use and no theoretical justification for any of them, architects could find little to distinguish themselves from builders. They found a solution by adopting the Beaux-Arts stylistic system. This enabled the profession as a whole to justify itself by the nature of *how* it did what it did. As he further elaborates the process, Brain shows that the Beaux-Arts regime provided a rational design method that could be formally taught in schools; a practical foundation for its routinization in large offices; and a coherent disciplinary framework within which a market for unique services could be sustained.[40] It could link the small-town practitioner to the big-city designer, and show how the design of a city hall or a small cottage followed the same principles. It allowed the profession to construct a coherent theoretical base, which could encompass problems that had hitherto threatened to pass to other occupations for solution.

In later work Larson shifted theoretical ground by moving to examine the role of discourse in the construction of architectural practice.[41] She went on to study the decline of Modernism and the rise of Postmodern architectural styles through a study of *Progressive Architecture*'s annual awards.[42] These prestigious American awards were judged by eminent architects. By analyzing the jurors' discourse Larson showed how judgments of architectural quality reflected normative conceptions of the architect's social role. The rise of the Postmodern was, she thought, a return to a formalism and "architectural supremacism" that denied any place to the social. Larson followed up her interest in discourse by showing, in a later paper, how architectural competitions reaffirmed central values in the ideology of the profession.[43]

Studying Architecture as a Profession

Almost all the sociological work focused on architecture has been conducted firmly within the framework of the sociology of the professions. Most readers of the architectural literature would probably accept something like these three characterizations, one from an article in *Architectural Record*, the second from the *Journal of Architectural Education*, and the third from a collection of essays on contemporary practice:

> First, that a profession is intellectual, and requires a professional to exercise judgement and to deal with a substantial body of knowledge. It also requires a life-long commitment to learning. . . . Second, the profession must be practical—its knowledge needs to be applied to reality and real concerns. Third, a profession has techniques and skills. . . . In a true profession, however, these techniques are secondary to the body of knowledge underlying their proper application. . . . Fourth, a profession must be organized into associations and/or groups of practitioners.[44]

> What is distinctive about any professional group is that its members must deal with uncertainties and they do so on the basis of long formal training followed by supervised informal training, such as apprenticeship or residency programs. This is the classic distinction between occupations and professions.[45]

> First, there is a professional claim to exclusive and expert knowledge. Moreover, this assertion is corroborated by prescribed education and training requirements. Second, the competence and skill of all professionals are explicitly guaranteed. . . . Third, and perhaps most significant, the profession claims to serve society.[46]

Together, these accounts from the architectural literature stand firmly in the Anglo-American tradition of conceptualizing one group of occupations—professions—as somehow quite different from others, as being in some sense "higher," nobler, and more prestigious. People consider that it is better for one's occupation to be a profession than just a job: the

Gender Studies

One of the themes of this book is the manner in which hidden forms of domination operate in the field of architecture. There is no doubt that women particularly suffer from these mechanisms, but I do not treat women separately in this text. This book looks more at the general instruments that operate at the level of class on all persons, male and female. As far as I know, there are few others studying this topic in architecture. Conversely, there are several groups conducting valuable empirical and theoretical work on gender studies in architecture. I concede the floor to them.

For example, Kingsley and Glynn conducted two surveys to ascertain the degree of gender discrimination in architecture. One survey was of female graduates, and the other of a sample of male architects in the profession. They found lower pay for equally skilled female graduates, a tendency for women to leave the field, and a general feeling of frustration among female students, graduates, and professors. Ahrentzen and Groat attacked architectural education as profoundly sexist: propounding a view of architecture's history as one of Great Men; encouraging the notion of architectural masters; portraying design juries as battlegrounds; and promoting sexual harassment. Frederickson provided quantitative support for their work by showing that female students were interrupted more often in design juries and that female jurors spoke less often and for shorter times than men.

See K. Kingsley and A. Glynn, "Women in the Architectural Workplace," *Journal of Architectural Education* 46, no. 1 (1992): 14–19; S. Ahrentzen and K. H. Anthony, "Sex, Stars, and Studios: A Look at Gendered Educational Practices in Architecture," *Journal of Architectural Education* 47, no. 1 (1993): 11–29; M. P. Frederickson, "Gender and Racial Bias in Design Juries," *Journal of Architectural Education* 47, no. 1 (1993): 38–48; L. Groat and S. Ahrentzen, "Reconceptualizing Architectural Education for a More Diverse Future," *Journal of Architectural Education* 49, no. 3 (1996): 166–183; and L. Groat and S. Ahrentzen, "Voices for Change in Architectural Education," *Journal of Architectural Education* 50, no. 43 (1997): 271–285.

name has a symbolic force. Like John Cullen, when Anglophones think of "profession," they take as their exemplars the Anglo-American law and medical professions, regarded as the most successful, powerful, and prestigious of their kind. Other occupations are taken to be striving toward this ideal form. Architecture is often measured against these ideal types and found lamentably wanting.

Some of both the sociological literature proper and the architectural literature seeks to diagnose and remedy this situation, hoping to elevate the profession to its rightful place. In one of the most widely read professional journals of the time, the late *Progressive Architecture*, for example, the senior editor cited several major problems affecting the profession.[47] As Thomas Fisher saw it, the basic problems were enduring high rates of un- or underemployment, intense competition for work, and stagnant or declining incomes. The sources of these, he believed, were increasing productivity caused by the widespread use of computing, an erosion of the traditional client base, competition from other professions, and a general public disillusionment with architects. For possible solutions or "models of action" Fisher looked to other professions, ones he considered much more successful. Medicine, he thought, could teach architecture about specialization. Architecture's structure is almost the opposite of medicine's. In the latter, general practitioners coordinate the efforts of highly paid specialists, who act as conduits for the transmission of research results to patients. Architecture was full of expensive generalists and low-paid specialist employees. The medical profession showed how it was possible to incorporate more and more expertise into one occupation. The expansion of the legal profession since the turn of the century could also teach architecture about how to expand markets for services. From engineering, Fisher thought, architecture could learn how to develop a research base of developing knowledge.

The Sociology of the Professions

As it developed from the 1930s through the 1960s, the sociology of the professions saw as its main task the explanation of how some occupations had been able to acquire material and symbolic rewards that eluded others. As the sociologist Andrew Abbott explains it, the focus of interest was on the organizational pattern of profession, how this had originated and developed.[48] Professions were characterized as organized bodies of experts who applied specialized and esoteric knowledge to the cases brought to them by clients. This knowledge was acquired over a long period of formal training in an elaborate educational system. Clients' interests were safeguarded by a code of ethics, more or less regulated by the state, and a modicum of altruism presumed not to exist in lesser occupations, whose members were taken to be motivated by more mercenary concerns. The empirical diversity of professions was explained by assuming a continuum of professionalization, with occupations at various points of this continuum, à la Cullen.

One sociologist of professions, Eric Freidson, identifies this as the folk concept of professions, since the description so closely matches the professional's self-image and, indeed, is almost apologetic for it, acting simply to regenerate common wisdom.[49] I would also add that it is particularly sanctimonious and self-serving, attributing to certain occupations a moral superiority over others because they "serve society" while the rest of us just grub for money.

Freidson and Larson semi-independently developed a much less flattering model of the professions, the market monopoly model.[50] The professions were not bands of trusted experts, giving to clients the benefit of a wisdom acquired through many years of self-sacrifice in the gloomy halls of academe. They were organizations attempting the intellectual and organizational domination of important areas of social concern. Professions were monopolies that had succeeded in convincing others to hand them that monopoly, justified or not.

Both sets of theories worked with much the same conception of "profession," and both knew what one looked like when they saw it. In brief, a profession had these elements:

• A white-collar, nonmanual occupation, ideally consisting of self-employed practitioners.

• Long, formal education in a university, providing a rigorous and extended theoretical basis.

• A set of self-regulating organizations for association and for control of work, regulating access to the profession, and sanctified by the state.

- A monopoly on the profession's work, granted to the profession by the state.

- Autonomy—from the state, and from the judgments of clients as to excellence.

- A relative homogeneity, practitioners differing in their skills and competencies, but otherwise more or less interchangeable.

Defects in a Sociology of "Profession"
It is now generally accepted by sociologists that this is a parochial conceptualization, one strictly limited to the English-speaking world. Europeans have had difficulty understanding the whole concept. In German, for example, one may talk about *freie Berufe*, in which one refers to self-employed practitioners, or about *akademische Berufe*, referring to the old university educated professions of the clergy, divinity, law, and high school teaching, but there is no single phrase for our "profession."[51] The word is used in other languages strictly as a technical sociological importation.[52]

In our tradition professionals identify themselves by what work they do, and their status and prestige flow from their membership in this corporately organized occupation. Non-Anglo-American individuals whom *we* would label professionals often do not think of themselves as such. In Japan individuals' status and identity are dependent first on the company they work for, then the position in that company, *then* the sort of work they do. In Europe, in general, status is bestowed by graduating from one of the elite state universities or schools, regardless of what one has specialized in (as, for example, to say one is a Yale or Cambridge graduate is much more impressive than to say what one studied there). One then identifies with the entrepreneurial class if one is self-employed, or as having a certain rank in the civil service. The content of one's work (designing buildings or healing the sick) is less important than whom one does it for (the state or individuals).[53] In the Benelux countries, for example, an architect must register as either a principal, salaried, or a government employee, and must inform the authorities if his or her status changes.[54] An Anglo-American is an architect first and foremost, but a European is a graduate of such-and-such a school and member of a certain class, *then* an architect. Our concept of grouping certain occupations together as "the professions" makes less sense in the context of this mentality.

It also makes less sense when viewed historically. Modern Anglo-American professions arose from groups of people doing similar work in a capitalist marketplace. Group identity was centered on common work. The arena in which they battled for a right to monopolize certain work was ultimately that of public opinion. The only part played by the state was to sanction and embed in law a monopoly on that work. The European professions arose mainly from the civil services of the industrializing nations in the early nineteenth century. Their closest models were the aristocracy and the structure of the military. In France and Germany until the middle of the century, most professionals—doctors, lawyers, engineers—were employed by the state and organized into bureaucratic hierarchies. Identification was based on one's employment as a civil servant and on the fact that one had graduated from an elite state school, such as the French *grandes écoles*, not on the work one did. In France, a state engineer who graduated from the Ecole Polytechnique did not think of himself as having much in common with an engineer in private practice who had not.

The notion of a state profession is alien to Anglo-Americans. Only teaching comes close, and though they are usually government employees, few teachers would actually think of themselves as in the service of the state. Perhaps the closest analogue in the English-speaking world would be the gulf that an Ivy League MBA working as an executive in a large corporation believes separates him or herself from the owner of the local bar or pub, though the former is salaried and the latter is not, and both are classified occupationally as "manager."

In Germany, the organizations we believe to be fundamental to professional identity, associations and societies defined by occupation, did not appear until the 1870s. The first national organization, the Bund Deutscher Architekten (BDA), was not formed until 1903, about eighty years after its English equivalent.[55] Today, what we would regard as the one "profession" is divided in two, the high-status civil service architects tending to belong to the BDA, an elite organization that requires sponsorship by an existing member for entry, while the lower-status architects in private practice belong to the Vereinigung Freischaffender Architekten (VFA).

In Italy architecture functions more as a mechanism for entering a cultural elite than as anything else.[56] Where the United States and the United Kingdom have 120 to 150 architecture students per million population, Italy is educating a staggering 1,700 per million. The 97 percent or so of architecture graduates who never enter practice no more think of themselves as belonging to a profession of architecture than a Bachelor of Arts graduate in the English-speaking world thinks of himself or herself as belonging to a profession of "arts."

From the first, European professions were occupations defined and controlled by the state. Those whose training was the ancient province of the *grandes écoles* in France or the universities in Germany, and whose members were destined for the service of the state, had and have the same sorts of social status that the Anglo-American professions have. Those trained by the provincial universities or the German polytechnics did not and still do not.

To talk of simply the "profession" is, then, to ignore several important problems. First, there are substantial differences between the same occupation in different countries. The way of conceptualizing the occupation may entirely differ. Further, the content of the work handled by the occupation may be strikingly different. Architecture's jurisdiction varies from country to country, and hence its relationship to other occupations in the building industry also varies. In France, architects rarely prepare construction drawings, and may never set foot on site. In Australia and other Commonwealth nations, the measurement and costing of large buildings is conducted by quantity surveyors, an occupation totally independent of architects. Norwegian architects also invariably handle town planning. Not only does the division of labor vary, but also the sort of client handled by the architect. In Italy, almost all small-scale construction is handled by the *geometria*, whom we would consider surveyors, and the division of labor between architects and civil engineers is very indistinct.[57] Spanish architects deal with highly technical buildings, such as industrial plants, that English-speaking architects tend to leave to civil engineers. Similarly, architects in the Benelux countries produce technical drawings that in the U.K. or U.S.A. would be handled by engineers. The jurisdictions covered by architects, civil engineers, landscape architects, interior designers, project managers, planners, and facilities managers vary considerably from place to place.[58]

That the term "architect" is not a simple label easily transferred from one nation to another can be seen by examining data for the numbers of architects per capita.[59] In some countries we find extremely high numbers: Japan, Italy, and Greece each have over 1,300 architects per million inhabitants. Is there really that much more building design going on there than in, say, Chile, the U.K., France, Australia, or Hungary, each with around 500 architects per million? Could Canada, Poland, Russia, and Korea—all of which have fewer than 300 architects per million—really find work for all those other architects if their numbers were quadrupled to Italian proportions?

Within a given country, professions exhibit diverse patterns. The folk concept of profession does not help us explain why doctors have a higher professional status than nurses, even where both require university training, nor why architects who never went to university have the same status as those who did. In countries with the British legal system, why are all the many sorts of medical specialists thought of as belonging to one profession, but solicitors and barristers thought of as belonging to two? Or, in the English-speaking world, why is the architect who only does small-scale residential work thought of as belonging to the same profession as one who only does large commercial commissions, when in Italy they are different occupations?

When Thomas Fisher looked to engineering and medicine to remedy architecture's problems, he took for granted that all professions are more alike than not. But are they? Structural engineers really make a living by producing the certificates of safety that the state demands for most structures, and the everyday general practitioner earns his or her way mainly by issuing temporary licenses to members of the public to enable them to buy drugs. The specialist doctor spends his or her life in hospitals, huge concentrated work sites, in which he or she commands the daily services of a large number of practitioners in other health occupations. Do any of these modi operandi bear much resemblance to the way architects work?

But, most important, *to think of architecture as a "profession" is to gloss over its relationships with other elements of society,* and especially to discount the importance of its mechanisms of reproduction, that is, the educational system. A preoccupation with the body of practitioners relegates other social actors of importance to architecture to marginal positions, when they are better thought of as constituting a system in which practitioners are but one component.

Changing the Sociological Study of Architecture

After her work on the monopoly market model of the professions, Magali Larson later admitted that she had exaggerated the importance of protected markets, and virtually omitted the European professions from her analysis.[60] The trend among sociologists today is to abandon the parochial Anglo-American-centered concept of "profession."[61] There are two alternatives: reformulating the concept, or abandoning it altogether.

Reformulating "Profession"

The most successful attempt at reformulating the concept of profession has been that of Andrew Abbott.[62] He takes issue with two points about all previous analyses. First, he argues that the focus on professional *structure* is inappropriate because it studies the form rather than the content of professional life. The nub of professionalism is what *work* people in these occupations do, and one should study who is doing what to whom and how, not looking at association, or licensure, or ethics and so on. The essential phenomenon of professional life is the link between a profession and its work, what Abbott refers to as its jurisdiction. The study of the professions should be the study of how this link is created and how it is anchored by formal and informal social structure.

Second, he argues, it is pointless to study one profession at a time. The driving force in the history of the professions is the competition between them, competition to establish jurisdictional boundaries. New professions arise when jurisdictions become vacant and die when they are taken over by other groups. Their histories are therefore interdependent, and a major task of a sociology of the professions is to show how the interplay of jurisdictional links between occupations determines the history of individual professions themselves. One must study the entire *system* of professions, not isolated examples.

Abbott differentiates professions from other occupations by characterizing them as applying (somewhat) abstract knowledge in their work. He argues that only a knowledge system governed by abstractions can redefine its problems and tasks, defend them from interlopers, and seize on new problems to increase its jurisdiction.

He determines the basic tasks of professional work to be diagnosis, inference, and treatment. Diagnosis assigns to a problem subjective properties that are then related to various conceptual dimensions in the profession's discourse. Diagnosis reinterprets a problem in terms of this discourse, admitting and rejecting information. A profession becomes more open to competition from other occupations if it severely restricts the type of evidence considered relevant. Architecture, for example, historically has not been interested in matters of structural safety, and very little in environmental systems. As soon as separate occupations appeared to handle these matters in the mid to late nineteenth century, architects discarded them as quickly as they could. As buildings have become more complex, the problems they have posed have generated more information, but the strict relevance rules of architecture have tended to dismiss this information, leaving it to other occupations to interpret.

Treatment is organized around a typological system that classifies together problems amenable to similar remedies. A profession must avoid too close a mapping between diagnosis and treatment, as it then opens itself to routinization. As David Brain points out, such a dilemma occurred in the middle of the nineteenth century in the U.S.A., when architects found themselves in competition with builders using imported pattern books to design buildings.[63] A builder had simply to select which style (treatment) was available for a given building type (diagnosis), and produce it for the client. The efficacy of treatments must also be relatively easily measured by outsiders. A profession becomes redundant if no one can tell if a treatment has worked or not. This is one of the most significant problems affecting architecture. Within the field, architects often argue about the quality of a building, whether it is successful or a disaster in aesthetic terms. Moreover, their assessment of the success of a treatment (building design) is often at variance with the assessments of others. The supposed experts cannot agree, and the public often cannot agree with the experts. In such a situation it is little wonder that architects design so little of the built environment.[64]

Abandoning "Profession" in the Social Study of Architecture

Abbott's work is useful in extending the concept of profession beyond the Anglo-American parochiality to which it has been confined the past thirty or forty years. His work will be cited several times in the coming pages for the insights it provides into architecture.

Useful though it may be, a reformulated concept of profession only goes so far in helping us to understand the sociology of architects. Those who have devoted the most time to its study look on the architectural field as a profession that has somehow failed to achieve the glory of its sister occupations of law and medicine, no doubt because of all sorts of inappropriate ideological baggage about the occupation's being an art. From their writings architecture emerges as a quirky and slightly retarded but lovable occupation.

Any attempt to study architects in terms of the usual concept of profession has several defects:

- It leads to an inappropriate concentration of effort on the capitalist marketplace and the structure of firms in the private sector. It has little to say about those countries, such as Portugal, where most architects are employed by the state.

- It concentrates on the *products* of the occupation. It completely ignores the possibility that architects may have functions other than designing buildings, thus inappropriately disconnecting the study of architects from their social milieu and the systems within which they are embedded.

- It ignores internal stratification, particularly the social stratification of individual architects. There is all the difference in the world between someone like Stanford White, who strutted through New York's social scene in the late nineteenth century, and someone working in a small country town doing small additions. Occupational titles may be similar at different work sites, but what individuals with the same title actually do, and their locations in society, may differ vastly. Does an architect with ready access to a national leader have that much in common with one who can barely persuade his or her local building authority to approve a roof alteration on a suburban cottage?

- Finally, all conceptions of "profession" take the deployment of specialized knowledge as central to its definition. This rules out of court the notion that what may be most important is not *knowing* something so much as *being* something. In the coming pages I want to suggest that a focus on knowledge-content is not necessarily the best way to conceive of architecture, and that it diverts us from examining the importance of social being in defining the occupation.

For all these reasons I argue that it is best to abandon any analysis of architecture solely in terms of "profession," and hereafter the word will be used simply to denote the body of practitioners, without implying any of the connotations inherent in the old Anglo-American sociologizing.

The Sociological Toolkit of Pierre Bourdieu

Introducing Bourdieu

It always seemed to me that the old Anglo-American sociology of the professions was a poor tool for analyzing architecture; a rather crude instrument which, by treating architecture as a particular social entity, a profession—differing merely in the content of its work from other occupations of high prestige in the Anglo-American world (law, medicine, engineering)—misled the analyst more than it aided.

The old sociology is still popular among amateur analysts of the profession—it is, after all, in accord with the "commonsense" views that professionals have of themselves. Very recently this rather old-fashioned approach has begun to fade in favor of more sophisticated ones.[1] The theoretical perspectives informing this new approach come not from the old Anglo-American sociology of the professions nor of art, but from a European intellectual tradition that has long been concerned with the study of culture and society. Prime among these influences is the work of the French sociologist Pierre Bourdieu. He has nothing to say about the professions per se, and regards their description as but one component of a general sociology of occupations. His importance to this book is in his exceptional work in the areas of culture and of education, and in his construction of a formidable toolkit of sociological concepts. These are tools of some power: as Scott Lash writes in the introduction to a volume on modern cultural sociology, "Bourdieu's general sociology of culture is not only the best, but it is the only game in town."[2]

In this and the next chapter I present a selection from Bourdieu's toolkit and show how it can be used to provide a sociological description of architecture far richer than previous models.

Bourdieu in the Intellectual Field

We must start with the man himself. Bourdieu is most insistent that what one says and what one does are always affected by one's social position and location in the field, and that this certainly applies to what sociologists do and say. No one develops theories in a social vacuum—there is always some personal motivation behind one, and one must always be aware of this. Any attempt by the theorist to claim a godlike objectivity is worse than naive, it is dangerously misleading, disguising what may be strong personal biases with a facade of scientific neutrality. Many sins have been committed in the name of "objective science," and one way to prevent these is to admit from the start that the researcher is not and cannot be a neutral observer and analyst. One cannot discuss the theory without discussing the man.

Bourdieu is not a name the architectural reader is likely to have encountered in the way that one encounters other French intellectuals such as Foucault or Derrida or Barthes, although a poll of French intellectuals ranked him among the ten most influential of their kind.[3] Well known in France, he has only had significant influence on the Anglo-American field in the past fifteen years, since the translation into English of his book *Distinction*.[4] In that time, "he, more than any other comparable figure, . . . has come to personify the continued value and vigour of a distinctly French intellectual tradition within the social sciences."[5] He is not a great traveler and, because he has eschewed the North American literati circuit, is not well known outside of sociological circles. In France he is considered a partisan, a political and polemic intellectual, a champion of the disadvantaged against the ruling classes, perhaps a little like Noam Chomsky. None of his political activities has impinged on his reputation elsewhere, and among Anglophone social theorists he is regarded as one of the great living sociologists, a notable contributor to the sociologies of education, culture, and art.

Translations of his work tend to appear five or more years after their French publication. To date there are only four significant monographs by English-speaking writers—and a few collections—devoted specifically to his work.[6] Yet over the past fifteen years he has established himself as the flag-bearer of the distinctive Gallic tradition in the social sciences once borne by Louis Althusser, Roland Barthes, and Michel Foucault. Long overshadowed by other French intellectuals with more public personae, he has achieved in the 1990s a respectable place in the English-speaking intellectual world.[7] In particular, he has exerted a great influence on those interested in how and why individuals act as they do, how these actions are related to social structures, and how culture and society interact.[8]

A Very French Sociologist

The first problem any reader of Bourdieu must face is that of his style. His writing is long-winded, discursive, convoluted, formal, and rhetorical; so much so that, when one can understand him at all, it is easy to take him as arguing from positions he is strenuously opposed to. His theoretical formulations are scattered and diffuse, rendering it difficult to give precise references to a particular idea. For these reasons, direct quotations from Bourdieu will appear infrequently in this book. One must also contend with the sheer volume of his work: one bibliography lists some 160 items authored, coauthored, or translated from 1958 to 1991.[9] Reading Bourdieu is like watching a Peter Greenaway film: beneath the tortured rococo exquisiteness one can make out that he really has something profound and important to say, but it is often difficult to determine just what it is. One perseveres as one perseveres with Derrida or Foucault, for the stylistic theatrics that are part of the repertoire of every French intellectual are crucial to the content of their thought. Comparing the intellectual communities of the English-speaking world, France, Germany, and Japan, Johan Galtung writes about French sociological prose:

> I think the gallic [sic] approach is certainly a stringing-together-of-words, but not necessarily deductively. The words connote something, they carry conviction. . . . [This] power of conviction is due less to logical structure than to a certain artistic quality that gallic social-science prose often possesses, particularly when spoken and written by its true masters. Persuasion is carried, perhaps, less by implication than by *élégance*. Behind the *élégance* is not only the mastery of good style as opposed to the dryness of German social-science prose, often bordering on drabness, but also the use of bon-mots, double entendres, alliterations and various types of semantic and even typographical tricks.[10]

The French sociologist Charles Lemert emphasizes the clublike and hermetic nature of French intellectual life:

> Those of us exiled to life outside the Parisian literary world are often confused and put-off by the secret codes which seem to govern those who write from within. What we gain in cheaper rents and fresh air, we lose in our ability to decipher what we read. Intricate sentences seduce us by their magnificent form, but we often are left limp for want of detectable substance. Arguments take place on these pages, and we are befuddled non-persons. We are invited to dinner and end up dumbly overhearing without understanding the hushed conversations of the real guests. Thus enticed, we crave a meagre footnote and are given the stalest of morsels or, worse, nothing at all.[11]

Since, in France, to be an intellectual is to be literary, the writer who wishes to be noticed must have a style worth noticing. Bourdieu's is most charitably described as mannered. Bourdieu does not so much write

Why French Intellectuals Are Difficult to Read

Over the past fifty years, architectural theory has been subtly but pervasively influenced by several generations of the sort of public intellectual that France prides itself on producing. Unfortunately, when their ideas cross the Channel or the Atlantic, they are ripped from the context in which they were born and developed. The meaning and import of these ideas in their new homes is often quite different from their intent in the heart of Paris. This applies as much to Derrida and Foucault as to Bourdieu.

I think it is important to remember the social origins of these ideas. Using one of Bourdieu's key concepts, for example, Charles Lemert describes the Parisian intellectual scene as a *champ,* a field. Here the word is intended to connote both a field of force in which its members are held—and hence a place in which certain practices take place—and a battlefield, in which its members strive to obtain power and prestige, and in which struggles occur. Parisian intellectuals are engaged in an intense battle within the confines of the City of Light:

Before "all Paris" authors face the scrutiny of an ambitious reading public created, in large part, by a perversely dense and imploded structure of publishing houses, reviews, newspapers, radio and television commentators which mediate between writers and readers. The struggle involves writers' desire to be read, and readers' needs to be well-read. . . . In France, tout Paris is tout. Thus, among intellectuals in Paris, it is very difficult and frequently embarrassing not to have an opinion on what has been or is being written.

. . . Paris—as literary capital, and as intellectual champ—is a field whereupon ideas and their authors arrive, conquer, hold the centre for a moment, then inevitably fall. As Bourdieu puts it, "Epistemological conflicts are always, inseparably, political conflicts." Knowledge and writing involved the protection of one's theoretical territory in a field of constantly changing boundaries. . . .

[French sociology] is very often shaped in and by a literary space unknown to most foreigners. This is the space between the surface of the published text and the social deep structure of the tout Paris debates which exert pressure on the author. This is why—now from the point of view of the reader—many of us are frustrated by that large portion of French writing in the human sciences which makes constant—though often uncited—reference to what others are saying and writing. We search for frequently non-existent footnotes in order to identify opponents alluded to in the surface text. The Parisian author, unimpeded by the Anglo-American empiricism of the footnote, often finds documentation superfluous because "everyone knows" that the reference is to Sartre, or the humanist marxists, or to Aron, or to whomever.

C. C. LEMERT, "Literary Politics and the *Champ* of French Sociology," *Theory and Society* 10 (1981): 646, 647.

as declaim. His most often-used translator, Richard Nice, has managed to capture the baroque nature of the French quite well, although Bourdieu has chided him for trying too hard to reproduce rhetorical effects. After a while, I must admit, the theatricality of it all grows on you and, thanks to Nice, there are more than enough elegant turns of phrase to keep you interested. Here's one example from *Distinction:*

> Whereas the holders of educationally uncertified capital can always be required to prove themselves, because they *are* only what they *do*, merely a by-product of their own cultural production, the holders of titles of cultural nobility—like titular members of an aristocracy, whose "being," defined by their fidelity to a lineage, an estate, a race, a past, a fatherland or a tradition, is irreducible to any "doing," to any know-how or function—only have to *be* what they *are*, because all their practices derive their value from their authors, being the affirmation and perpetuation of the essence by virtue of which they are performed.[12]

Bourdieu would probably cite as justification for writing the way he does that it constantly reminds us that he is a particular individual within a particular field, with his own interests and goals, shaped by the forces within the field. He would argue that the virtues that the Anglo-American sociologist would applaud in writing—clarity, neutrality, objectivity—serve only to disguise their personal interests.

In a critical and polemical discipline, Bourdieu is more polemical than most. He is a critical theorist in the technical sense of someone who not only has ideas about how society does work, but also about how it should work. Bourdieu is an angry man, his works "pounding with the rhythms of philosophical doom,"[13] propelled by a tide of deep passion motivated by the conviction that modern society is riven by profound iniquities, iniquities the greater for being camouflaged and received as perfectly acceptable and natural practices. One gets the distinct feeling that his provincial background has left a legacy of resentment toward the Parisian patricians, and that in some way his whole sociological enterprise is his revenge on that society.

The notion that in society things are not as they seem; that society operates in some sense beyond the control of the individuals it comprises; that social patterns can be produced and persist even when the people in them are unaware of their existence and do not want them, is not unique to Bourdieu—it is a commonplace of sociology. But Bourdieu's attempts to unmask the realities behind the surface appearances of our everyday experience give his work an especially strident tone, which his baroque style does nothing to ameliorate. Are these polemics necessary? Within his theoretical framework they certainly are, just as they are for Derrida and Foucault.

As further defense of his idiosyncratic style, Bourdieu might argue that, as the sociologist Ian Craib has also pointed out, social theory involves something we know about in intimate detail already—our own social life.[14] Theory attempts to explain our everyday experience of the world, our own closest experiences, with concepts that are not so close, often in terms of things we do not and cannot have any direct experience of at all. Bourdieu might argue that the language of the social sciences must distance itself from everyday language, because everyday language is by its very nature predisposed to reflect the existing taken-for-granted social world. One cannot usefully describe a social world in the normal language that is generated by that social world, so the sociologist must at every turn make the reader aware that he or she is using language in ways different from the everyday. His or her language must make a break with the everyday.[15] I think that we must accept Bourdieu's rationale for adopting an unusual style, but that nonetheless an exposition of his theories can be done in English in ways that do not completely overwhelm the reader nor obfuscate one's argument.

Bourdieu and Other Thinkers
Bourdieu's closest affinity is perhaps with Michel Foucault. Like him, Bourdieu addresses issues of power throughout his work, and the two would agree that power is a product of relations *between* people, not quality inherent *in* them, and that it often lies concealed in the unquestioned ways of seeing and describing the world. They would also agree that the exercise of power does not have to be conscious, or the result of explicit decision-making. But Bourdieu would find fault with Foucault on three matters. First, he argues that power does not necessarily operate through discourse or formalized bodies of knowledge. Instead, relations of power come to be

Bourdieu on His Critics

The British sociologist Richard Jenkins lambasted Bourdieu's style in Bourdieu's book *Homo Academicus* for its obscurity. It is worth quoting Bourdieu's reply, to show both his style (and this is from an interview, not a carefully prepared text), and why he objects to plain writing:

[When Jenkins] goes so far as to excoriate me for an expression such as "the doxic modality of utterances," he reveals not only his own ignorance ("doxic modality" is an expression of Husserl that has not been naturalised by ethnomethodologists) but also and more significantly his ignorance of his own ignorance and of the historical and social conditions that make it possible.

If, adopting the mode of thinking suggested in Homo Academicus, *Mr. Jenkins had turned a reflexive gaze on his critique, he would have discovered the deeply antiintellectual dispositions which hide themselves behind his eulogy of simplicity, and he would not have offered in such* plain *view the naively ethnocentric prejudices that are at the base of his denunciation of my stylistic particularism. . . . He might have asked if the cult of "plain words," of plain style, plain English, or of understatement (which may lead the virtuosi of this rhetoric of antirhetoric, such as Austin, to mimic in the title of their books or articles the naive simplicity of children's ditties), is not associated with another academic tradition, his own, thus instituted as the absolute yardstick of any possible stylistic performance. And if he had understood the true intention of* Homo Academicus, *he would have found in his disconcertment, nay his disgust at my writing, an opportunity to question the arbitrariness of stylistic traditions imposed and inculcated by the various national school systems; that is, an opportunity to ask himself whether the exigencies that British universities impose in matters of language do not constitute a form of censorship, all the more formidable in that it can remain almost tacit, through which operate certain ignored limitations and mutilations that school systems inflict upon us all.*

THE ORIGINAL CRITICISM IS IN R. JENKINS, "Language, Symbolic Power and Communication: Bourdieu's Homo Academicus," *Sociology* 23, no. 4 (1989): 639–645, of P. Bourdieu, *Homo Academicus*, trans. R. Nice (Stanford, CA: Stanford University Press, 1988). Bourdieu's reply is in P. Bourdieu and L. J. D. Wacquant, *An Invitation to Reflexive Sociology* (Chicago: University of Chicago Press, 1992), 169.

internalized within us, in our taken-for-granted beliefs. This mechanism allows him to overcome Foucault's second perceived flaw, his inability to explain the subtler forms of domination that arise through sheer belief. As will be shown later, Bourdieu's notion of the "habitus" is meant to explain how cognitive schema of perception, appreciation, and action come to be subtly inculcated in individuals and groups. Third, Bourdieu argues that power is concentrated in certain institutional sectors and parts of social space rather than diffused throughout all society.[16]

Among Bourdieu's antecedents is the group of sociologists known as the Frankfurt School, whose best-known members were Theodor Adorno, Max Horkheimer, Herbert Marcuse, and Jürgen Habermas. Like Bourdieu, they were concerned to reveal how culture and consumption practices contribute to the reproduction of social inequality.[17] But where they were abstract and philosophical, Bourdieu is thoroughly empirical. He dismisses them as aristocrats, unwilling to dirty their hands in the empirical realities of field work. Adorno's notion that avant-garde experiments in artistic form could change or subvert the social order Bourdieu derides as a fantasy only intellectuals could have by refusing to admit that they only talk to themselves, their discourse circulating among a tiny circle of the elite, the readers of academic journals such as *Tel Quel, Partisan Review,* and so on.[18] The Frankfurt School argued that culture performs its ideological function of legitimating the existing class structure by preventing any recognition of class differences. If we are all middle class, then of course there are no classes at all. Culture mystifies and obscures the real class relations pertaining to people. Bourdieu argues that far from purporting to *obliterate* class by preventing recognition of class, culture operates to *legitimate* class by fostering misrecognition. Culture becomes a system of class symbols that reveal one's class position at every turn.

Several writers have compared Bourdieu to Thorstein Veblen, the eccentric, brilliant, and caustic turn-of-the-century American economist and sociologist. There are similarities with Veblen's idea of conspicuous consumption, but Bourdieu argues, against Veblen, that there is no element of *rational choice* involved here since our choices are largely determined for us by our habitus (a concept discussed below).

Bourdieu is a bitter opponent of Heideggerianism and its associated aesthetics, once dominant in architectural thought via deconstructivism."[19] He accuses the whole school of an intellectual dishonesty and a philosophical aristocratism hiding behind a facade of radicalism, much along the same lines as Diane Ghirardo's attack on Derrida's most devoted follower in architecture, Peter Eisenman, as constituting a "bogus avant-garde."[20] Following the old French tradition that "once an opponent is named, he must be dealt with in no uncertain terms,"[21] Bourdieu reserves a particular venom for Derrida and his cohorts:

> [There is] a vision of philosophy, especially through the exaltation of the works of Nietzsche or Heidegger, that leads to an aestheticism of transgression, to a "radical chic," as some of my American friends put it, that is extremely ambiguous intellectually and politically. . . . The critique, not of culture, but of the social uses of culture as a capital and instrument of symbolic domination, is incompatible with the aestheticist entertainment often concealed behind a scientific front. . . . Of those French philosophers who have taken the degree of aestheticizing of philosophy to a degree hitherto unequalled, Derrida is, on this point, no doubt the most skilled and the most ambiguous in so far as he manages to give the appearance of a radical break to those semi-ruptures which extend the game of iconoclast destruction into the realm of culture. His analyses always stop at the point where they fall into the "vulgar."[22]

Bourdieu is, in general, contemptuous of Parisian "proletariod intellectuals" who, he holds, are always careful to maintain all the privileges that attach to their membership in the Brahmin caste that is French philosophy while purporting to denounce them. He is particularly resentful that philosophy denounces the social sciences while borrowing from them:

> In fact, it seems to me that the philosophy labelled postmodern (by one of those labelling devices until now reserved for the artworld) merely readopts in a denied form, certain of the findings not only of the social sciences but also of the historicist philosophy which is, implicitly or explicitly, inscribed in the practice of these sciences. This masked appropriation, which is legitimised by the denial of borrowing, is one of the most powerful strategies yet to be employed by philosophy against the social sciences and against the threat of relativization that these sciences have held over it. Heidegger's ontologization of historicity is, indisputably, the model for this operation. It is a strategy analogous to the "double

jeu" which allows Derrida to take from social science (against which he is poised) some of its most characteristic instruments of "deconstruction." While opposing to structuralism and its notion of "static" structure a "postmodernized" variant of the Bergsonian critique of the reductive effects of scientific knowledge, Derrida can give himself the air of radicalism. . . . [Yet his] implied critique of the institution remains half-baked, although well-done enough to arouse delicious shudders of a bogus revolution.[23]

Bourdieu and Architectural Theory

Bourdieu is only now appearing in architectural theory. One of his most famous concepts, that of cultural or symbolic capital, is popping up in various places in the works of socially minded theorists.[24] The only article in the architectural literature proper that discusses Bourdieu at length is one by John Snyder, in which his interest is in Bourdieu's opinion of Heidegger.[25] Among sociologists of architecture, Magali Larson and David Brain have taken on board some of his most important concepts, and that recently.[26]

The reasons for this architectural indifference are not hard to identify. Unlike other French luminaries Bourdieu has never claimed the robes of a philosopher-king, garments especially alluring to architectural theorists. Unlike Derrida or the late Michel Foucault, he has never courted the media, and he has conspicuously avoided the voluminous and verbose debates that constitute the discourse of postmodernism.[27] While one can hardly find any academic writing on architecture that fails to take postmodernism as central to its argument, Bourdieu has only ever referred to postmodernism in order to dismiss it as intellectual faddism.[28] He may, perhaps, have found an audience twenty-five years ago during architecture's brief flirtation with the social, but contemporary theory and writing, being a sort of Heideggerian *nouvelle cuisine*, has no place for someone so unpalatably left-of-center. Theorists preferring their seers to be, like their architects, gifted with a unique, personal, and solitary prophetic vision would find Bourdieu's extensive empirical studies unappealing, and be disillusioned to find that his work is collaborative and collective, and relies on the efforts of his coworkers at the Collège de France.

Architectural theorists would therefore find Bourdieu hard to digest. He stands at a considerable philosophical distance from other recent French imports into the English-speaking world, his intellectual forbears the social thinkers Max Weber and Karl Marx more than the philosophers Martin Heidegger and Edmund Husserl. He positions himself squarely in the field of sociology, declining the title of philosopher. When poststructuralists—architectural theorists included—invoke the social, they do so only as a weapon in their battle to advance the interests of the humanities against the sciences. By asserting the socially constructed nature of the world they deny the efficacy of science, and especially of positivism, and its self-proclaimed role of producing reliable, true knowledge. Their only use of the sociological is to *deny* its use.[29]

Overview of Bourdivin Theory

Finding a starting place to describe Bourdieu's work is complicated by its diffuse and convoluted nature.[30] Several points should be made before plunging into the depths. First, three formal matters:

- *Bourdieu demands engagement.* He is not putting forth ideas for armchair theorists. If you accept that what he says is true, or meaningful, then you become committed to certain practices, just as if you believe in what Marx or the Bible says, you become committed to living your life in a certain way and trying to effect specific changes in society.

- *His work is reflexive.* His methodology demands that the sociologist constantly be aware of his or her own position in his or her own society, and how this affects studies of that society.

- *There is a constant interplay between the theoretical, the methodological, and the empirical.* How one does sociology has an important bearing on the sorts of theories one devises about society. Get the methodology wrong and the theories, he argues, will necessarily be inadequate. Moreover, theories are there to be used and discarded if found wanting. They must be constantly tested against empirical data. But the methodology determines what data will be considered relevant. Bourdieu is unusually open in inviting the reader continually to criticize the processes linking theory, methodology, and data.[31]

In substantive terms, Bourdieu's themes are sevenfold:

- *Power and domination.* Bourdieu's work has been described by one of his most dedicated followers as a "generative anthropology of power." He is preoccupied with the mechanisms that generate, mask, and help perpetuate domination.[32]

- *The symbolic world.* These mechanisms of domination, he argues, are largely effected through symbolic means, that is, through culture. He strives to uncover the specific contribution that symbolic forms make to the construction of inequality by masking its political and economic roots, how culture reproduces social structures that maintain inequality.[33]

- *Misperception of practices.* Symbolic means of domination work so well because they are misperceived. Many social practices are portrayed as, and genuinely believed to be, disinterested or natural or objective, when in fact they work to promote the interests of some privileged members of society at the expense of others. This misperception legitimates them.[34]

- *Culture is used to reinforce the stratification system.* The net effect of this is that symbols and culture are used to perpetuate the existing class system. Cultural signals and practices are therefore important means of maintaining the privilege of certain groups.

- *Symbolic and economic capitals.* Symbolic and economic interests are distinct and irreducible. Nonetheless, the symbolic world operates economistically, in that people try to accumulate symbolic capital as they do economic capital, and one can speak of rates of return and investment strategies on such capital. The two forms obey different logics of accumulation and exercise, but they are partly interconvertible.

- *Practices can be understood economistically.* Sociology then becomes a study of the economy of practices. Its main task is to clarify the historical and structural logic of social action by classifying and positioning agents according to their individual, group, and class struggles to accumulate symbolic and economic capital.[35]

- *Society is a relational space.* Society can be thought of as a space occupied by people and institutions. The most important way of thinking of this space is relationally: people always stand in some relation to all others, whether it be superior, inferior, or equal. As one person or group's position changes, its relations with all others necessarily change, and hence so does the whole social space.

Bourdieu's Formal Sociology

Of central importance to Bourdieu's thought is the fact that he intertwines his theories about society with those about sociology. In recent years he has been interpreted in English mainly as a social theorist, but he may well see his most enduring contribution as methodological, as constructing a craft of research practice in sociology.[36] Here he is out of step with other poststructuralist thinkers, for he tends to be a methodological universalist in a world of theoretical relativists. Although English-speaking writers more and more are taking on board his theoretical work, they are tending to ignore the fact that while he is intensely theoretical, he is also eminently empirical: visitors to his offices are most often struck by the sheer quantity of fieldwork being done.[37] His theories are intended to be a set of sociological tools, to be used and tested, on real-world situations.

The Central Problem of Sociology

Sociology has, since its inception, been bedeviled by a fundamental problem that every major sociological theorist has had to tackle at some time or another: that of agency and structure. The problem arises from the observation that society seems to consist of two distinct types of entity. First, there are individuals, *agents*. They are intentional and reflexive: they have wants, needs, desires, and goals, and they can reflect on these and alter their actions as they will. But societies do not consist only of agents. Every agent lives in some sort of relationship to other agents, and every society is therefore constructed of relationships. The patterns of these relationships tend to be reproduced through time, enduring beyond the lifetime of any individual. Moreover, the agents engaging in the relations are often unaware of them or do not want them. There must, therefore, be other sorts of entities beyond just individual people, and these are traditionally known as *social structures*.

The fundamental problem of sociology is how to construct theories that encompass both agents and structures. The particular resolution of this problem generates, first, an ontology—a theory about the nature of social entities. Second, it generates an epistemology—a theory of knowledge, and of what sorts of explanation are held to be meaningful. This task has proved enormously difficult, as the existence of numerous hostile schools of sociology, each with its own solution, attests to.

As the British sociologist Ian Craib points out, theories devised to address structures must offer descriptions and explanations of a certain kind.[38] Descriptions must be intelligible and analogical. Explanations must deal in causes, showing not only that x causes y, but how it does so. Causes are not seen as single events or things, but as residing in particular arrangements of relationships.

Theories of human agency or action must also incorporate causation, but in this case causes are teleological. An action is explained by its end result, by the fact that the agent was trying to achieve something. Where one seeks for causal mechanisms when trying to explain structures, one must look for forms of thinking inside people's heads to explain actions. Fitting both sorts of explanation into one theory is not made any easier by the fact that there is no simple relationship between individuals' intentions and actions and their effects on larger structures. Nor do structures affect individuals in a completely deterministic way.

Grand sociological theories have tended to favor one sort of entity and explanation over the other, privileging either agents or structures. These viewpoints can be labeled as subjectivist versus objectivist. The former is a view from below and emphasizes the importance and value of what individuals know and their capacity for making up life from moment to moment. The idea is to understand the world from the point of view of the individual. It assumes that, first, it is possible to arrive at such an understanding and, second, the individual's apprehension of the world is a more or less adequate form of knowledge about it. This is the path taken by the phenomenological and ethnomethodological schools of sociology. The latter, objectivism, seeks to describe the overarching relations that structure individual practices, elucidating the structures that govern us but with which we have little direct experience. The really important things in society are taken to be independent of agents' minds. This is the position taken by structuralists and structuralist Marxists.[39]

The position one takes on the subjectivist-objectivist continuum will decide one's response to four important questions:[40]

- *What aspects of social life can be scientifically grasped?* Objectivist position: in general, that of the natural sciences, of positivism. Only those matters that can be operationalized, and preferably given a mathematical or quantitative treatment, can be studied. Subjectivist position: Qualitative descriptions and narratives capture the important realities of social life.

- *What is the relative epistemological status of the sociologists' and the agents' conceptions?* Objectivist position: agents' ideas about what is going on are inadequate and of limited use. Only the outsider can produce an unbiased description. Subjectivist position: the agents know better than the sociologist what is going on in their society, and the sociologist must build up his or her theories from them.

- *Are explanations mechanical or teleological?* Objectivist position: people are viewed as respondents to structural factors, largely trapped by forces vastly greater than themselves (similar to behaviorism). Subjectivist position: people act rationally or at least voluntaristically for teleological reasons.

- *What is "in" individuals and what is outside them?* Objectivist position: there are structures that exist above and beyond the particularity of the individual. Subjectivist position: ultimately, everything comes down to the contents of people's minds.

As both Ian Craib and Malcolm Waters point out in their resigned reviews of modern sociological theory, theories at any point on the subjectivist-objectivist continuum have so far been defective.[41] Theories emphasizing agency tend to be analytic and descriptive and weak on assigning causes to processes. Society is reduced to the totality of people's behaviors, and becomes a sort of vast jelly of congealed action. One ends up more with a social psychology than a sociology. On the other hand, theories at the objectivist pole tend to lose sight of people altogether, individuals often ending up as actors caught in some sort of play they have had no part in writing.

Bourdieu's Resolution of the Central Problem

Bourdieu refers to his particular resolution of the subjectivist-objectivist (or agency-structure) problem as "constructivist structuralism" or "structural constructivism."[42] By this he affirms, first, that there exist in the social world itself, and not just in symbolic systems, objective *structures* that are outside the minds of people or agents. Second, that agents nonetheless *construct* the world themselves. The social world is not just an empirical given ready to be studied by neutral researchers, but is actively constituted by practices and beliefs. Others have called his approach "generative structuralism," a name that emphasizes his idea that objective structures are generated by the day-to-day practices of people.

Bourdieu agrees with those at the extreme end of the subjectivist pole, the phenomenologists and ethnomethodologists, that people do have an active apprehension of the world, and they do construct their own vision of it. But where these schools would argue that this is about all there is to the social world, Bourdieu asserts that the subjective construction of reality is carried out under the constraint of objectively existing structures. This has an important consequence for his methodology, for it implies that the sociologist cannot take at face value the descriptions that individuals give of their own social life. An excellent example: most Westerners say they are middle-class when asked, regardless of the realities of their circumstances. Except for well-off Americans, wealthy people modestly place themselves below their true economic place. Poor Australians, in contrast, are most reluctant to admit they are at the bottom of the economic pile, and locate themselves a few notches higher than their financial standing would imply.[43]

Being bound unaware by structures that have conditioned their behavior and beliefs, people will give false or partial descriptions of their social lives. Talking to the sociologist, they are likely to provide normative responses to questions, saying what ought to happen in their social world, rather than what does. Their discourse will also be self-consciously semi-theoretical, as the subject attempts to impress his knowledge on the observer.

To Bourdieu, the analysis of everyday life conducted by the ethnomethodologist is but the analysis of how people conform with the constraints laid down by unseen structures. He describes it as "a depoliticized form of the analysis of conformism," content to catalogue the predicaments of social life without attempting or wanting to do anything about them.[44] This comment resonates with the views of that sociologist of the built environment, Bill Hillier, who pointed out in a throwaway remark some time ago that the phenomenology imported into architectural thought tends to appeal to right-wing mystics.[45] Bourdieu likewise characterizes the hermeneutic thinkers as aristocrats who have mistaken a mode of thinking typical of the privileged classes as a universal description of human thought. Donald Schön's influential phenomenologically based work on the architectural studio and education, for example, would be taken as an attempt to impose the mentalities of the upper classes on the architecture student.[46]

A final objection to the in-depth interviewing characteristic of subjectivist sociological method is that the observer necessarily brings with him or her all the mental baggage from his or her own social world. If it is true that people actively construct social reality, then sociologists also construct their own reality, and this must influence their study of society. One of the crucial aspects to Bourdieu's methodology is that the sociologist must approach any act of observation reflexively, self-consciously reflecting on how his own preconceptions are affecting his practices. Architectural scientists do not spend time worrying how their social prejudices affect wind tunnel studies of buildings. Architectural sociologists *must* concern themselves with how their own position in the academic field affects their descriptions of their object of study.

Bourdieu inverts the conventional anthropological method of immersing oneself in the society under study. No such immersion is ever possible, because the observer is not an authentic member of the society under study, if only because the observer *is* self-consciously observing and analyzing. Rather than pretend that it is possible to immerse oneself in a society while simultaneously analyzing it, the sociologist should take the opposite step and distance him or herself from the subject: the subject must be objectified. But a second step back is needed, that called for by insisting on reflexivity. One must scrutinize one's own scientific stance toward the initial act of objectification, and the effect of adopting such a stance on the resulting sociological analysis. To the whole process Bourdieu gives the unlovely name of "objectification of the act of objectification."[47]

This insistence on reflexivity distinguishes his work from all forms of sociology at the objectivist end of the continuum, those that model themselves on the natural sciences or claim to operate positivistically, such as French structuralism or the old American structural-functionalism.[48] He argues that the accounts they produce are remote, distant, and theoretical, purporting to be disinterested descriptions of social reality. He is particularly critical of the structuralists and their attempts to discern rules of social life. People do not run their lives by adherence to rules. Daily life is a lot messier, full of tactical improvisations and strategic vaguenesses.

A constructionist stance has become popular in the past fifteen or so years in the sociology of science.[49] Here it has manifested itself as the attempt to describe the detailed workings of scientists in laboratories, investigating how they produce "facts." Since constructionism is premised on the notion that all reality is constructed by people, that there is no greater reality "out there," it holds that scientific knowledge is just another such construction, and not at all the ever more accurate description of underlying reality that both common sense and positivism hold it to be. Both Bourdieu and these sociologists of science have been important conduits of the constructionist perspective back into mainstream Anglo-American sociology in recent years.

Constructionism has some affinity to deconstruction (the similarity of name is unfortunate). Yet they differ in two respects. First, the Derrideans fixate on the literary, on language and on signification, where the constructionists have a much wider interest in physical objects and other nonliterary matters. Second, where the Derrideans try to demystify by showing the emptiness of discourse, the constructionists try to dethrone science by showing the nitty-gritty of how it is actually built, bringing to light all the behind-the-scenes activities that are never discussed in scientific papers.[50]

Bourdieu's form of constructionism differs both from this form and from the variety of approaches commonly labeled postmodern in one important respect. Flying straight in the face of the now common notion that we cannot know anything with any degree of certainty, that scientific enterprise is a hangover of the Enlightenment project, Bourdieu strenuously upholds the ability of sociology to produce true, objective, and reliable knowledge about the social world. Contrary to the massive counterreaction to positivist science that European intellectuals have been promoting for the past fifty or so years (one writer called it "the revenge of the humanities"[51]), Bourdieu stands in full defense of the viability of science, and especially of social science, to achieve meaningful results.

Bourdieu on the Validity of Science

Far from leading to a nihilistic attack on science, like certain so-called "postmodern" analyses, which do no more than add the flavour of the month dressed with a soupçon of "French radical chic" to the age-old irrationalist rejection of science, and more especially of social science, under the aegis of a denunciation of "positivism" and "scientism," this sort of sociological experimentation applied to sociological study itself aims to demonstrate that sociology can escape from the vicious circle . . . and that in pursuit of this end it need only make use of the knowledge which it provides of the social world in which science is produced, in order to try to gain control over the effects of the social determinisms which affect both this world, and, unless extreme caution is exercised, scientific discourse itself. In other words, far from destroying its own foundations when it brings to light the social determinants which the logic of the fields of production brings to bear on all cultural productions, sociology claims an epistemological privilege: that conferred by the fact of being able to reinvest in scientific practice its own scientific gains, in the form of a sociological increase in epistemological vigilance.

P. BOURDIEU, *Homo Academicus*, trans. R. Nice (Stanford, CA: Stanford University Press, 1988), xii.

Linking Practice to Structure
Practice and Doxa

Any resolution of sociology's central problem must explain the mixture of freedom and constraint that is social action. We are willed agents, but we are not completely free to do as we choose. Bourdieu starts by asking just what "practices" are. He rejects as ambiguous the structuralist notion that our behaviors are determined by sets of rules, whether explicit or implicit. Structuralism does not make clear whether such rules are produced and explicitly understood by agents themselves, or whether they stem from objective, exogenous constraints or simply from the explanatory concepts of sociologists. He replaces the notion of rule with that of strategy, a general orientation of practice.[52] Practices rarely arise from rational calculation, and Bourdieu is particularly critical of those theories—some derived from economics—that depict people as running their lives by pursuing self-consciously calculated strategies of utility maximization (rational action theory).[53] We do not act like miniature economists, choosing the best from the numerous possibilities open to us through life.

But, although people are not coldly rational, they are reasonable. Most of life goes on without intellectual calculation but through a process of practical construction. Bourdieu sometimes likens it to a game or set of games we are involved in, and which we have learnt to play by watching and participating, not by reading a book of rules. Bourdieu assumes a fundamental link between actions and interests in that our actions are determined by our interests, but not in an intellectual way. Our interests determine which games we want to play (parent, employee, doctor, executive, mechanic). Some games we have no interest in. Since all the games have no explicit rules, we are obliged to construct our own logic of practices to get us through life, a logic that is polythetic, able to sustain a multiplicity of confused and often logically contradictory meanings.

Central to Bourdieu's ideas about human actions and practices is that most of them take place in a *doxic* environment. By this is meant the uncontested acceptance of the daily lifeworld, the adherence to a set of social relations we take to be self-evident.[54] Bourdieu lists three important aspects of the doxic experience: *naturality, misrecognition,* and *arbitrariness.*

First, the "natural order of things" is seen as somehow universally right and normal. The whole idea of challenging it just never occurs to anyone, neither the powerful nor the powerless. So, for example, in medieval and early modern Europe it was taken as absolutely natural that an absolute monarch should govern absolutely. Only the most tremendous upheavals, such as the American and French revolutions, could show that the taken-for-granted did not have to be.

Second, this perception of naturality is a *mis*perception, or, in Bourdieu's terminology, *misrecognition*. As fish in water, individuals in societies move through the taken-for-granted symbolic order that structures the whole of lived experience, but that structures it so completely by precisely *not* being seen to structure it.

From this follows the third characteristic, the *arbitrariness* of the doxic order: it could be other than it is. Only people not embedded in the particular social order see that it is not natural, but just one particular way of doing things. To those vast numbers of us who are not part of the haute couture industry, the ten thousand dollar creations of high fashion are more ridiculous than anything. To those who are, it is life itself.

Habitus

The mechanism by which the experience of doxa is produced is also that which Bourdieu uses to link practice to structures. Bourdieu uses the term *habitus*. By this he refers to a construct that is both psychological, since it is in people's heads, and social, since one may refer to a group or class as having a habitus. The habitus is a set of internalized dispositions that incline people to act and react in certain ways, and is the end product of what most people would call socialization or enculturation. To a large extent we do not choose to be what we are, but receive from our family a way of looking at things and of doing things, a habitus, handed down from previous generations. In a very real sense, habitus is a social analogue of genetic inheritance. This identity is modified as we pass through the educational system and as we encounter other individuals throughout our lives. Nonetheless, the possibilities for change are circumscribed by our own history, the history of our class, and the expectations of the groups with which we identify. We may make our own history, but not necessarily in the circumstances of our own choosing.

Habitus, in Bourdieu's formulation, seems to be acting as a sort of feedback loop between social structures and personal practices, and is

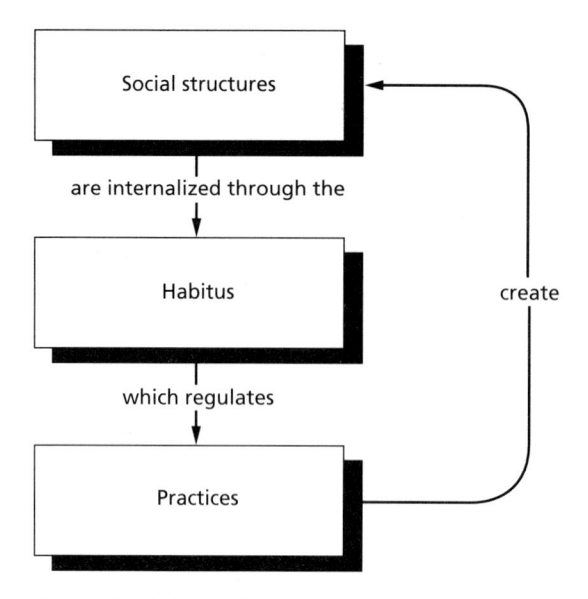

```
Social structures
         │
are internalized through the
         ▼
      Habitus ─────────► create
         │
which regulates
         ▼
     Practices ──────────┘
```
(arrow from "create" loops back to Social structures)

Figure 2.1 Relationship of the habitus to structures and practices (after Bourdieu).

the vehicle by which he links the two (fig. 2.1). It is this linkage by which the social order is reproduced—and reproduced so efficiently—through time. Everyone has his or her own habitus, inculcated from birth but modified by experience. But groups and classes also have a habitus, and thus one's personal set of dispositions and practices is a variant of one's class dispositions. Bourdieu thus sees the family as the key link between class and the individual, transmitting the class habitus to the child.[55]

One's habitus generates perceptions, attitudes and practices. It is at once the filter through which we interpret the social world, organizing our perceptions of other people's practices, and the mechanism we use to regulate our actions in that world, producing our own practices. In this sense it is a *structuring* structure. However, the habitus must not be conceptualized in the structuralist sense: it is not a passive collection of knowledge, a set of rules we apply to social situations. It is an active, unconscious set of unformulated dispositions to act and to perceive, and much of its power to structure our lives without our realizing it derives from the thoughtlessness of habit and habituation that the habitus produces. The habitus provides us with a practical mastery of social situations, telling us "instinctively" what to do.

Habitus does not determine, but it does guide. It provides the feel of the game.[56] Individuals are both completely free and completely constrained as is, in Bourdieu's metaphor, the good tennis player, who, though completely governed by the play of the game, nonetheless completely governs it.[57] Where our habitus is correctly adjusted to the social game we are playing we feel comfortable, natural, at ease—we know how to react, we feel at home. When we move to another game—a plumber attending a high-society do, a socialite on a building site—our habitus may be inappropriate to cope with the situation, and we feel uneasy, not quite knowing what is the right thing to say or the right way to behave, not quite liking what is going on.

Habitus is also a *structured* structure, since Bourdieu sees it as an internalization of the structures of the social world.[58] Since its enculturation starts from birth, it is a product of the material and symbolic conditions of existence of our family, conditions shaped by one's class and therefore by the large-scale structures of society. In a very important sense, then, habitus is an embodiment of the entire social system, and each of us carries around in our heads the whole history of our social space. But this history is obliterated and manifests itself as a self-evident order. It is this that generates the doxic experience, the feeling of ease in playing the games of society, because we have effectively internalized the play of those games in our heads, without ever explicitly learning any "rules" of them. Also, in this sense, our habitus imprisons us in the doxic experience, precisely because we live in the illusion that we are free to do as we want, as fish in water feel free to swim where they wish, never knowing that others may also walk, or climb, or fly.[59]

Bourdieu's Model of Society

Symbolic Power and Culture
The starting point for Bourdieu's model of society is the unremarkable assumption that all societies are distinguished by competition between groups to further their own interests. These struggles operate at many different levels: between individuals, families, classes, and all sorts of other collective entities. It is also obvious that some groups succeed in furthering their interests better than others—they control more resources.

Not only do they have control but they keep control, and this is only possible by denying these resources to competitors. This fundamental social fact means that in the many intersecting fields that society comprises some groups are dominant and some are subordinate. The control of resources both requires and gives power, and it is with power that Bourdieu is primarily concerned—how it is exercised, who wields it, and for whose benefit.

In common with other European thinkers, such as Foucault, Bourdieu regards as inadequate the usual Anglo-American sociological definition of power as control. For Bourdieu, power is the capacity to impose a specific definition of reality that is disadvantageous to others.[60] The most obvious sort of power is physical force, but only a few groups use physical force. It is inefficient, and most societies grant the monopoly on the use of legitimate physical violence to the state. A second type of power is economic. The importance of this is obvious. Marxian theory holds that economic power is the only sort of power, and that all groups can be placed in some sort of social hierarchy, their places contingent on the amount of economic capital they control. One of Bourdieu's major contributions to modern sociological theory has been to extend Max Weber's sociologizing and decisively demonstrate that this is not so, that there is a third, more potent and more pervasive form of power—the symbolic. Symbolic power involves the wielding of symbols and concepts, ideas and beliefs, to achieve ends.

At the highest level, that of society as whole, we call the field in which symbolic power operates "culture." It is Bourdieu's contention that the logic of the cultural field is such that it operates to create, legitimate and reproduce the class structure, a system of inequality. For this reason culture is at the center of Bourdieu's substantive—as opposed to formal—contributions to sociological theory. Like many (if not most) sociologists, Bourdieu believes that the class structure of modern societies is iniquitous, denying to some what could be theirs, while ensuring that others are granted privileges they do not deserve. Much of his work is dedicated to unmasking the mechanisms by which this takes place.

Prime among these is the inflicting of what he calls *symbolic violence*, the use of symbolic power to achieve what would otherwise have to be accomplished with force. The essence of the concept is that an individual or a group wields symbolic power over others by simply convincing them that this should be so. Its key characteristic is that it is not perceived as power per se, but as a legitimate right to make demands on others. A good examplar would be, say, the class structure of medieval Europe. Individuals then thought of society as structured into spiritual and temporal domains, with more or less elaborate hierarchies in each. People were inculcated from birth into a doxa that maintained that every individual was born into a certain position of the temporal order, an order ultimately grounded in religious beliefs. To be born a peasant or serf was to mean that one accepted that position in the order, accepted one's place on the feudal estate, accepted that one worked for the local lord, accepted taxes and impositions and drafts and requisitions. Likewise, to be born noble was to accept unquestioningly that one had the right to live off the labor of others.

Symbolic power operates so much more effectively than physical because it convinces those who benefit least from it to participate in their own subjection, to be active accomplices. Poor Americans may defend the most deeply held beliefs in American society about, say, individualism, though such an ideology works against them, to deny comprehensive health care or welfare benefits; the worst-off of the British lower class may yet still feel a natural deference to a member of the peerage, a distinct unease, and a sense of being in the presence of someone of greater worth than they. It is much easier to control resources if a group can simply convince competitors that it should control them. No need to carry a big stick if all your rivals are flagellating themselves on your behalf. No need to cajole if people voluntarily comply. Symbolic power is therefore essentially misperceived (*misrecognized* in Bourdieu's terminology) as perfectly legitimate and completely natural. These qualities conceal the power relations that actually exist between the dominating and dominated groups. Symbolic power, operating in the field of culture, is used by the dominant classes in society to maintain their dominance. Economic power is not enough, nor is physical. The groups that benefit most from society do so with minimal social conflict because the cultural system of that society is constructed to make their dominance appear natural. Only when the naturality and legitimacy of the cultural order collapses do the dominant classes find themselves in grave trouble, for then the arbitrariness of that order is exposed, and alternatives become thinkable.

Symbolic Capital

As economic power flows from the possession of economic capital, so symbolic power flows from the possession of symbolic or cultural capital. Just as, in all societies, groups—from families to organizations to classes—compete in the economic arena to increase their economic wealth, to maximize their economic capital, so they also contend in the cultural arena to maximize their cultural capital.

This notion of cultural capital is a second important Bourdivin contribution to social theory, from which four basic forms can be distinguished: institutionalized, objectified, social, and embodied.[61] Three are quite straightforward. *Institutionalized* cultural capital is constituted by academic qualifications and educational attainments, knowing things, and being certified as knowing them. *Objectified* capital consists of cultural objects or goods such as works of art, or any of the many symbolic objects produced in society. *Social* capital consists of durable networks of people on whom one can rely for support and help in life. Such capital is most useful in those areas of social life that the state has not bureaucratized, where formally certified skills count for less than social ones. Naturally, the more capital vested in the particular members of one's social network the higher the value of that network, and thus the privileged classes have an inherent advantage over the lower classes, simply because their social capital is so much higher. Moreover, upper-class individuals have more "weak ties" to others than do the less privileged. That is, they have bigger networks of acquaintances, people who they do not know very well, but who can be of invaluable assistance in business.[62] Further, this lets the upper classes get by with less of the other forms of cultural capital—they need fewer formal qualifications, and they invest in fields where they can most skillfully deploy their social capital.[63] Knowing the Queen of England or the President of the United States will not get you a job as a computer programmer in a bank if you cannot program, but it could get you onto the bank's board if you knew nothing about finance.

The fourth form of cultural capital is much subtler, and is the element that makes Bourdieu's notion of cultural capital so important. It is obvious that one does not have to have a private art gallery or a slew of diplomas to be considered cultured, and it is entirely possible to possess vast amounts of cultural goods and a degree or two, yet be considered vulgar, crass, and boorish. Possession of goods or qualifications is one way to own cultural capital, but there is another way to possess it, by simply being cultured. This is *embodied* cultural capital, by which Bourdieu means that it exists within individuals, as attitudes, tastes, preferences, and behaviors. How we talk, walk, and dress, what we like to read, the sports we like to play, the car we like to drive, the sorts of clothes we wear, the entertainments we prefer, all the multitudinous ways in which taste and attitudes are manifested are markers of embodied cultural capital. As one sociologist has remarked, part of Bourdieu's importance is in perceiving that the most apparently trivial and natural practices—the clothes we wear, the foods we like, the friends we make—are all crucial.[64]

The peculiar potency of this sort of capital lies in the fact that—to reiterate one of Bourdieu's phrases—owners of the other forms are only what they *have*, whereas the possessors of embodied capital only have to be what they *are*. Perhaps the most familiar and readily accepted example would be the concept of a "gentleman" or a "lady." Anyone, rich or poor, can be a gentle (to use the nonsexist but archaic term). You do not have to own anything, or to declare the fact by any other means than by simply being one.

The possession of economic capital allows consumption of economic goods by the mere fact of its possession—everyone knows how to spend money. Symbolic goods can only be "consumed" if one has the right mental schemes of appreciation, if their meanings are understood. Symbols are always codes of one sort or another, and must always be decoded. An accountant looking at an Eisenman house sees something very different from an architect.

Since the ensemble of dispositions that allow one to consume symbolic objects is part of one's embodied capital, it follows that embodied capital affects the rate of return received from the other symbolic capitals. Moreover, since embodied capital is not perceived as capital, it operates surreptitiously, covertly. One has different reactions upon hearing that Donald Trump has purchased a Renaissance engraving than that Gore Vidal has: the amount of symbolic capital that we perceive Trump as receiving by this purchase is rather less than the amount that Vidal receives. Why should this be? Because we understand that Vidal is a cultivated person, and that Trump is not. Vidal can appreciate the engraving, Trump cannot.

Cultural and economic capital are quite distinct forms, although interconvertible in different ways at different rates of exchange. For example, the educational system allows cultural capital to be converted to economic capital by giving access to high-paying sectors of the labor market; or, the old-boy network converts social into economic by providing business contacts. As the exchange rates are quite arbitrary, they are an object of struggle between different groups, each trying to maximize the rate of return on the particular sorts of capital they have. A hundred years ago, an American architect whose only formal education was a few years at the Ecole des Beaux-Arts was set for a rapid rise, as the existence of the elite Society of Beaux Arts Architects and the careers of Richard Morris Hunt and Charles McKim attest.[65] The cachet so obtained would have been rather less in the 1960s, just before the Society's closure.

Strategies of Investment

All individuals try to increase the goods they have, whether economic or symbolic. To this end, throughout their lives they pursue strategies of investment in both economic and cultural capitals. It is in this sense that Bourdieu argues that symbolic capital can be thought of in economistic terms. But not in *economic* terms. The symbolic is not directly reducible to the economic, as Marxians would have it. We do not all valorize the same symbolic capitals equally. Attaining an architecture degree is a worthwhile objective for one person, but not for another. People pursue those strategies that they believe will yield them the highest returns, symbolic or economic.[66] The fields they decide to enter (carpentry or architecture), their stage of entrance (when young or old), and what they do there (salaried or private practice), depends on their perceived chances of success. We all adjust our aspirations and goals to the situation we find ourselves in by virtue of our place in the social structure. *People attempt what they think is possible.* We show our practical acceptance of the realities of social life by excluding ourselves from areas where we do not think we can be successful. Thus the disadvantaged eliminate themselves from those fields that they know are risky, those dominated by the dominant.

To see the power of this effect one has only to consider the proportion of people from each social class participating in higher education

Social class	Australia	U.K.	U.S.A.	Sweden	Poland
Top third	33	18	75	23	21
Middle third	15	5	27	8	7
Bottom third	12	5	25	4	7

Table 2.1 Percentage of each social class participating in higher education. (Source: D. Anderson, "Access to University Education in Australia 1852–1990: Changes in the Undergraduate Social Mix," *The Australian Universities Review* 33, nos. 1 and 2 [1990]: 37–50. Figures for the United States are slightly inflated because the U.S. definition of higher education includes forms excluded by the other nations.)

(table 2.1). A variety of nations have been shown to demonstrate the universality of the effect. In the U.S.A. one would expect the cost of higher education to work against the lower classes, but similar patterns hold for other nations. Australia's removal of all university fees in the 1970s, the United Kingdom's red-brick universities, Sweden's democratic socialism, and Poland's communism have not altered the fact that the most privileged classes are vastly more likely to send their children to university. By saying, "This is not for me," the disadvantaged exclude themselves so much more effectively than any economic penalty could.

Social Space and Class Structure

Bourdieu uses the notions of economic and cultural capital to model society as a two-dimensional space in which individuals, groups, and classes can be located (fig. 2.2). He operationalizes the concept of class in a manner fundamentally different from Marxian theorists. In Marxian terms a class is defined by its relation to the means of production and is motivated by some sort of recognition of identity. In Bourdivin terms a class is a group of people occupying similar positions in social space.[67]

Classes are defined relationally, as being above or below each other in terms of the capital they have. Since it is always better to have more than less, and those with more can further their interests better than those with less, society naturally divides into subordinate and dominant classes. In a sense there are as many classes as there are distinguishably different points in social space, but a broad division into three can be made. The *subordinate class* consists of those with little of either form of

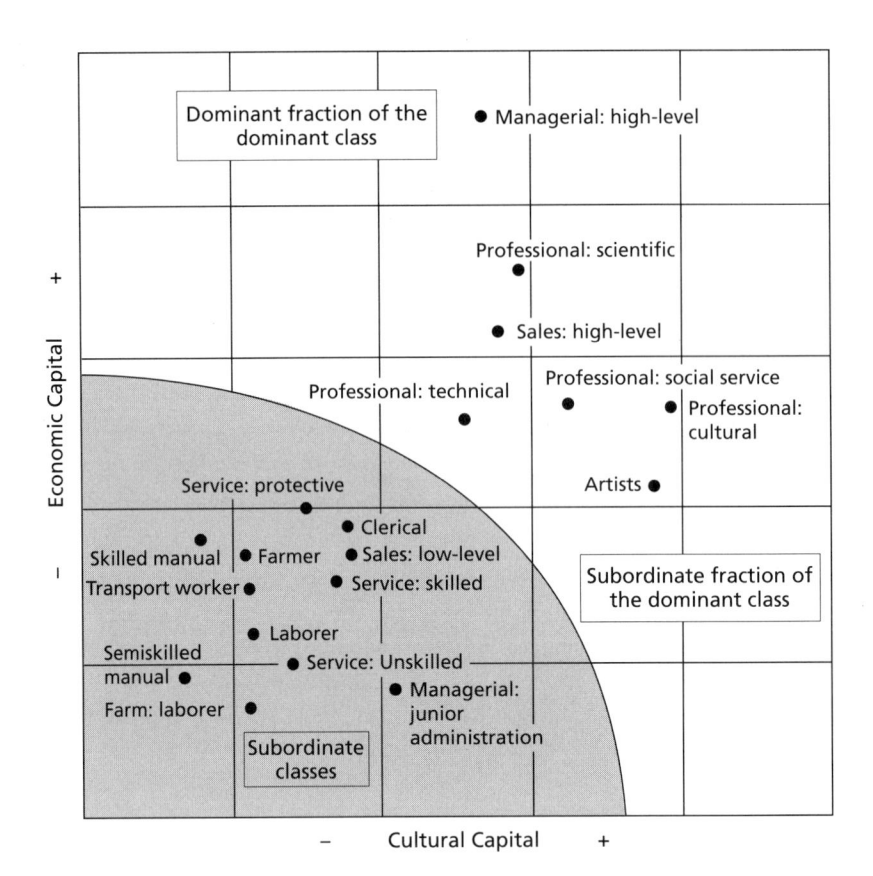

Figure 2.2 Social space in the United States, mapped as occupations. (Author's analysis, based on data from P. DiMaggio and M. Useem, "Cultural Democracy in a Period of Cultural Expansion: The Social Composition of Arts Audiences in the United States," in *Art and Society: Readings in the Sociology of the Arts,* ed. A. W. Foster and J. Blau [Albany: State University of New York Press, 1989], 141–171; and R. A. Peterson and A. Simkus, "How Musical Tastes Mark Occupational Groups," in *Cultivating Differences,* ed. M. Lamont and M. Fournier [Chicago: Chicago University Press, 1992], 152–186.)

capital. Since, in the last resort, economic capital dominates cultural capital, the *dominant class* itself divides into a dominant and subordinate *fraction*: the dominant are those with most economic capital—entrepreneurs, managers, and so on—the subordinate consist of those with more cultural capital: intellectuals, artists, professionals. The former are responsible for the production of material goods. The latter, as will be discussed in the next chapter, are responsible for the production of symbolic goods.

Historical Movement in Social Space

Individuals are not defined completely by their present location in social space. They carry around the history of their class and group in their habitus, and so the practices they engage in depend not only on their current position but on how they got there, their past position.[68]

Movement in social space is not easy, nor as common as some would believe, but it does occur and is not random. Bourdieu describes as *trajectories* the potential positions one may move to in society. To a given volume of cultural and economic capital there corresponds a group of more or less likely trajectories, the field of possible positions. Such trajectories apply to individuals and to classes, which are linked by the family. The space of possibilities is constrained, not only by one's initial volume of capital, but by the habitus, acting to generate the strategies of investment one pursues. Few children from the families of rural laborers end up as manufacturing magnates, or vice versa. But, of course, some do. The system lets just enough people—Bourdieu calls them *miraculés*—rapidly migrate from the lowest to the highest social strata precisely so they can be used as evidence that society is in fact meritocratic.

The trajectory that an individual or a family has followed to arrive at its social location will define its social being as much as the quantities and types of capitals it controls. There is all the world of difference between an aristocratic family that has lost its fortune and a farming family that has just gained one, though they may have the same wealth. The Beverly Hillbillies are not the Rothschilds. Though individuals within the two families may have identical capital and similar positions in social space, this trajectory effect produces a *hysteresis* between the habitus generated by the individuals' previous social existence and that required for their new lives. Bourdieu has argued that significant social pathologies can be produced when entire classes experience this hysteresis: a group that is downclassing will be unable to fulfill the expectations that its previous class position allowed it to have, and the resulting discontents of its younger generations can result in social upheavals.

ARCHITECTURE AS A FIELD

What Culture Does

Architecture and architects are embedded within the field of culture, a field that has been one of Bourdieu's preoccupations. His interest is in how culture is made to serve social functions. The basic argument is that culture is used to conceal the true nature of the power relations between groups and classes. In modern capitalism classes have increasingly taken the form of what one of sociology's founders, Max Weber, called status groups, founded on distinctive lifestyles; and not—it would appear—on dominant positions deriving from power and privilege. With the collapse in credibility of communism as a way of running a country, rhetoric from aging socialists about class conflict seems silly in Western societies where "everyone is middle-class." Despite the belief among some that people in the underclasses just do not want to help themselves, modern societies appear to be meritocracies, rewarding talent and enterprise. The evident unequal distribution of material and symbolic rewards is explained as the outcome of an unequal distribution of natural talents in individuals.

This explanation, common enough in everyday life, but especially characteristic of conservative political thought, disguises the true nature of the social structure, Bourdieu would argue. Against the idea that individuals succeed or fail on their natural talents one must weigh the fact that there is extraordinary continuity in the dominant classes from generation to generation. Were one to take snapshots of the dominant families in a given society at, say, fifty-year intervals, one would find the same names appearing. If success were strictly a personal, individual matter, then one would expect to find a good deal of social mobility between strata. The evidence is that while there is considerable mobility between the various levels within the middle strata of society, there is very little social mobility into and out of both the lowest and highest strata.[1] If you are born very poor or very rich, your children and their children will probably be the same.

How, in a society where the educational system is supposed to ensure equality of opportunity, can the persistence of this class structure be explained? Drawing heavily on Weber, Bourdieu argues that predominance is maintained by the use of symbolic power, by cultural means. The dominant class maintains social closure and transmits power and privilege through the generations by erecting symbolic boundaries around itself. These take the form of distinctive lifestyles and tastes. Tastes, lifestyle, culture, and class are intimately linked—a fact known to advertisers for quite a long time.[2]

Culture as a Battlefield between Classes

As the British sociologist Richard Jenkins put it, culture is something *with* which people fight, *about* which they fight, and the ground *over* which they fight.[3] The essential arbitrariness of symbols, of cultural goods, is what allows them to be the object of struggles, in which groups try to convince others to value their own capital more than that of their rivals. If cultural goods were not arbitrary—in the sense that money is not arbitrary (it is nonsensical to argue that my one hundred dollars is worth more than your one hundred dollars)—there would be no possibility of competition. Everyone would agree that an architect-designed home is better than a project home and that is that. We all know this is not so: although their fees are only a tiny part of the total cost, architects are used by very few individuals outside the upper classes to design private homes. I suspect that this situation would not change even if architects worked for nothing.

Culture is a structuring structure in that, being arbitrary, it cannot reflect reality, but instead helps to *define* what is real. Society's symbolic system valorizes some cultural objects and practices and deprecates others; it defines what is good and worth having, and what is bad and not worth having. Groups that succeed in achieving their own symbolic system, their own tastes, lifestyle, and culture, defined as socially worthy and as worth emulating and acquiring, are those that dominate society. Classes struggle, then, to impose their own symbolic systems on others and to impose their own vision of the social order that these systems help to create.[4]

In the class struggle over symbolic ground, the very nature of the battle is concealed from those fighting it in a way that would be impossible were the conflict economic. If the wealthy lobby the state to reduce taxes on the rich, it is seen as a naked act of class interest and could be expected to meet some resistance. But if the wealthy subsidize opera or dance companies, or build a new museum of art, then these things—though they are overwhelmingly the cultural province of the privileged, rarely visited by the lower classes—are seen as selfless acts, benefiting the whole of society. So the culture of the dominant becomes that which all others should support; the wealthy can promote the interests of their class under the guise of promoting society's.[5]

There is, therefore, a dominant culture that valorizes certain cultural goods and persuades society to accept this evaluation. Some analysts criticize the notion that there exists a single dominant culture in most Western countries, holding that the truth is closer to the Frankfurt School's notion of culture as mass reification.[6] Others, like the American sociologist Judith Blau, insist that the gap between high and popular culture has eroded, that there is a standard culture participated in by all.[7] This criticism has been most stridently voiced by conservative American researchers, who find Bourdieu's theories pessimistic and outdated. I suspect that this is in part because American intellectuals are somewhat embarrassed to be intellectuals, as one sociologist discovered,[8] and have fond illusions that while Europe may still be the class-ridden quagmire it always was, the United States is a cultural as well as a political democracy. In fact, in the United States we find that there are great differences in the class participation of different cultural activities.

It would, perhaps, be better to refer not to a dominant culture, which implies a simple correspondence between a given cultural practice (such as opera) and class, but rather a dominant cultural regime, by which

I mean to connote a more complex situation. Members of today's upper classes in the English-speaking nations differ from the lower strata in both the quantity and range of cultural forms they consume. They are omnivores (elitist inclusivists, who accept many practices) rather than snobs (elitist exclusivists, who reject certain practices). The privileged show their class not by enjoying opera instead of rock, but by liking both: their cultural knowledge is broader, deeper, and more encompassing than that of others.[9] In her study of the American middle class, Michelle Lamont has also made the point that moral boundaries figure as much as cultural ones.[10]

It is true that there is a greater commonality of material culture between classes than Bourdieu would be prepared to admit, but even this may be more illusory than real. Bourdieu points out that showing a similarity in material consumption patterns between classes may mask the different uses to which such items are put.[11] For example, although the rate of ownership of televisions and VCRs is similar in both the lower-middle and upper classes, it still means something that in the former, life is lived with the television always on in the background, tuned to certain channels and certain programs, or else showing rented videos, whereas in the latter, the VCR is used mainly to record programs for later viewing.[12]

Taste
Taste is the prime mechanism by which privileged groups can maintain their cohesion and separate themselves from outsiders. Bourdieu defines taste as a certain propensity to appropriate, materially or symbolically, a given set of objects or practices.[13] It functions so much more effectively than other means of exclusion for three reasons. First, it is misrecognized. No one would like to think that they smoke cigarettes, drink Moët, or attend the opera because these are implicit demands of membership in their class.

Nor would people like to think that their tastes are the product of their upbringing, of the inculcation of their habitus. To the contrary, it is held deeply that taste is a perfectly personal, natural thing—I just happen to have certain tastes. This is the second property, naturality. Nothing is more effective in denying that culture is a social weapon than simply as-

Percentage attending	College graduate	High school only
Ballet	65	13
Classical music	63	15
Opera	62	19
Theater	58	17
Art museums	48	17
Science museums	34	40
U.S. population	14	74

Table 3.1 Percentage of people in the United States participating in various cultural activities, by level of education. (Source: P. DiMaggio and M. Useem, "Cultural Democracy in a Period of Cultural Expansion: The Social Composition of Arts Audiences in the United States," in *Art and Society: Readings in the Sociology of the Arts,* ed. A. W. Foster and J. Blau [Albany: State University of New York Press, 1989], 141–171.)

Different Cultures in the USA

Table 3.1 and table 3.2 illustrate the cultural divides between classes in the United States. Table 3.1 shows the proportion of Americans attending various cultural activities, divided by level of education. Those with the least education avoid ballet, classical music, opera. We should pay particular attention to the fact that the lower classes do find science museums worth attending, for scientific expertise has never been a mark of upper-class cultivation in the way that, say, classical musical expertise has been.

Table 3.2 shows the musical and artistic preferences of Americans, divided by the occupation of the respondent. Architects belong to the category of "Professional, Cultural."

Those in the wealthiest occupational group (high managerial) or in any one of the professional categories, are much more likely to participate in certain leisure activities than those in the worst paid occupational categories. That economic reasons cannot explain this is clear when we examine the data for free or nearly free cultural forms, such as art museums, or when we recall that a ticket to a rock concert costs about the same as the opera, or that a night at the bar or pub listening to a local rock group costs about the same as an evening at the theater. Nor can economic reasons explain why, for example, smoking is more common among the lower classes than among the upper.

Occupation	Average income ($)	Percent attending				Percent preferring	
		Opera	Plays	Dance	Art museums	Classical music	Country and western
Managerial, high	45,500	10	23	7	39	10	20
Professional, scientific	39,900	18	26	7	45	18	13
Professional, sales	36,500	11	24	8	41	11	20
Professional, social service	33,400	19	32	14	48	19	7
Professional, technical	32,500	8	22	9	37	8	23
Professional, cultural (including architects)	32,000	29	38	11	59	29	9
Artists	29,500	24	28	12	57	24	12
Clerical	28,000	3	14	6	25	6	21
Skilled manual	27,000	1	6	2	14	3	36
Laborer	23,000	1	6	1	15	0	21
U.S. population	28,000	7	13	5	24	7	23

Table 3.2 Participation in arts activities and musical preference, by occupational group. (Source: R. A. Peterson and A. Simkus, "How Musical Tastes Mark Occupational Groups," in *Cultivating Differences,* ed. M. Lamont and M. Fournier [Chicago: University of Chicago Press, 1992], 152–186.)

serting that our tastes are purely natural, and that if I have superior taste to yours, it is just because I *naturally* have better taste. The original meaning of the phrase *De gustibus non est disputandum* was not, after all, an affirmation of the plurality of taste, but a statement of its irreducible naturality, affirming that one cannot contest the taste of those who have it. Nor can one contest my taste if it is believed to arise naturally from my inherent worthiness, not from my class position and upbringing.[14] When Royston Landau, writing from the elite Architectural Association school in London, said that "it is [the] agreement as to what is important that permits such distinctions to be made between 'high culture' and 'low culture,'" he must have had no doubt that the people who did the agreeing included only those with the education and competence—that is, the taste, the right social being—to make such judgments.[15] Or, as César Daly, founder of one of the first architectural journals, the *Revue Générale de l'Architecture*, said: "In a democracy as in an aristocratic monarchy, it is always the elite that truly guide the crowd, ostensibly or not."[16]

Third, taste is embodied. Taste is acquired very slowly and from earliest youth, by an immersion in practices of taste. You cannot acquire taste by reading books or attending a lecture course, a fact that has served as the basis for the plot in every movie comedy descended from Shaw's play *Pygmalion*. It is simply part of your social being, and manifested to others in attitudes and dispositions, by a thousand subtleties that cannot be codified. If taste could be codified it could not serve its function of exclusion, for then any parvenu could acquire it. Hence the hatred that the most eminent (which is to say, the most tasteful) architects have of all the petty building regulations the state imposes on them, since to be bound to written minutiae is the very antithesis of their social being.

Perhaps these properties of taste explain one of the great puzzles of the architectural persona: the extraordinary lack of humour and priggish self-righteousness noted in the great architects. Read through the biographies of the Masters to find a jocular, whimsical, earthy soul, and you shall be disappointed. From my own experience, the more eminent the architects, the more they regard themselves and their works with the most sober solemnity. An innocent quip about their work will be met with a maiming glare from the cooler patricians or a tirade of abuse from the more mercurial; for to attack one's taste, one's aesthetic judgment, is to attack the whole person, one's entire embodied cultural capital. To criticize a Master's works is to assault his or her very being.

The Field of Culture

Fields

The arena in which competition between the classes operates is that of culture. Bourdieu conceptualizes this arena as a *field*. I have used the word "field" loosely so far to refer to architecture and other social areas, but Bourdieu uses it as a specific technical term. As one sociologist summarized it, a field is a mutually supporting set of social institutions, individuals, and discourses.[17] Society is constructed of a number of overlapping fields: the fields of education, religion, class relations, and so on. As a first approximation, we might consider the field of architecture to consist of architects, critics, architectural academics, builders, all the forms of clients, the part of the state concerned with construction, financial institutions, plus architectural discourse and building regulations, among other things.

From this catalogue one might feel that "field" is a word of great vagueness and little analytic power. A field is not, though, a nebulous social background or environment, nor simply an enumeration of relationships. Bourdieu uses the term to describe a veritable social universe with definite properties.[18] The word is meant to connote both a *battlefield* and a *field of force.* In the first sense, it is a place of struggle. Individuals in a field compete for control of the resources and capitals specific to the field. In architecture, for example, architects compete for status as great creators, a form of symbolic capital of no worth in the field of, say, religion.

In the second sense, a field is a place in which forces operate on its members, and in which each member exerts a force proportionate to the composition and nature of the capital specific to that field that he or she controls. The position of an individual in a field cannot be defined in absolute terms, but only relationally. A field's capital only has meaning in that field, so its value depends on the state of the whole and is liable to devaluation or revaluation as the state of the field changes. Architectural history provides excellent examples. After the 1893 World's Columbian Exposition in Chicago, the cultural capital represented by knowledge of the canons of the Beaux Arts was valued much higher by architects and their patrons than the ideas of the American progressives. The story of the Modern movement is precisely the story of the avant-garde's ultimately successful attempts to devalue completely Beaux-Arts capital in favor of its own.[19] Thus, the location of an individual shifts as her position is affected by the totality of the lines of force operating in the field.

The structure of the distribution of capital between individuals structures the field, and so every individual's position depends on the other positions in the field. One interesting consequence of this way of looking at fields is that individual positions do not exist without a field to exist *in.* This or that particular architect exists because we have constructed a field of architecture. To create a social role and to give it a label—"architect"—is to conjure into existence a particular field.[20]

The Beaux-Arts example illuminates one very important characteristic of fields. Bourdieu views fields as occupied by people trying to maximize their forms of capital.[21] In this sense every field operates according to an economistic logic. But competition for economic capital is quite straightforward in that economic capital is monolithic: money is money. Struggles over symbolic capitals are more complex, for the value of the capital as a whole is set by the field, and, being arbitrary, can change through time. An individual can therefore improve his or her lot in two ways: either by increasing the total quantity of capital, or by having it revalued. The decline in standing within the American architectural community of the great Beaux-Arts firms of the late nineteenth century arose not through a decrease in the quantity of their symbolic capital—represented by design of admired Beaux-Arts structures—but through the wholesale collapse in value of that capital. Struggles in the symbolic realm are therefore twofold: to maximize capital, and to change its value. People compete to impose on the field their definition of what is symbolically worthwhile, or, in Bourdieu's terms, they attempt to impose a *principle of domination*.

Field and Habitus

Another way of looking at any field is that it is a social space in which a game is played. To call it a game is not to trivialize or belittle it, but to emphasize certain aspects of its working. The game is always played for stakes specific to the field, irreducible to those of other fields. To outsiders the game may not seem important, but those playing it are united by the fact that all believe in the game and the stakes for which it is played. Players are not free to play as they like, but do so according to their place in the structured set of positions, and according to how their habitus dictates. Harker *et al.* encapsulated the relation between habitus, capital, field, and practice by the pseudo-equation below (reformulated as fig. 3.1):

$$(\text{Habitus} \times \text{Capital}) + \text{Field} = \text{Practice}^{22}$$

All practices take place in some field or other. One's habitus unifies all one's behaviors, so the particular practices an agent carries out in a field depend not only on their position in the field but on their habitus. Their chances of winning or losing a particular game depend on more than

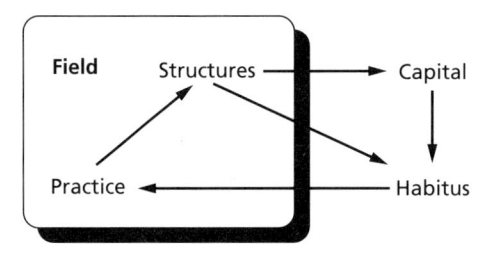

Figure 3.1 Practices take place in specific fields.

the amount of capital one has. One may be rich in the right forms of capital, but one may find that success in a field is denied because one's habitus generates inappropriate practices. This is the fate of all parvenus, those who suddenly achieve the means to enter a desired field late in life, but who find that—not having been brought up with the game from early age—they lack a natural feel for it. Finding their habitus betraying their origins at every turn, they discover a surreptitious closing of ranks against them, never quite knowing why they are not accepted.

The children of the privileged can get by on less institutionalized capital than others because their habitus provides them with an intuitive feel for the game they want to play—their embodied capital more than compensates. Where the newcomer must struggle to understand all the subtle, covert, taken-for-granted social rules that govern the game, the privileged just follow their own dispositions. So where the newcomer must work for recognition, those who have been immersed in the game from youth seem to have a natural gift for it, effortlessly rising to the top by "natural" talent.[23] Hence the psychologist D. W. MacKinnon found that all his great architects came from artistic families but affected to see no significance in this, preferring his complex psychological explanations over the simpler social one.

Not only do the privileged play better, but they also better know the specific stakes that are worth playing for. They make wiser decisions on investing their symbolic and economic capitals, making better assessments of the risks involved and the likely rates of return. The aspiring hopeful from the wrong class must agonize over career decisions, and makes the safe and sensible choice. Those born to the game just seem to end up in the right job with the right firm doing the right sort of work.

Moreover, lower-class families tend to invest their social capital in a narrow range of occupations, while upper-class ones invest in a variety of fields (banking *and* medicine *and* architecture *and* politics), thus protecting themselves should one of the fields become devalued.[24]

Functions of the Field of Culture

Culture is the field over which society's symbolic battles are fought. Its general function is to reinforce the existing class system by creating covert, implicit barriers to entry into the upper classes, thereby allowing them to keep control of society's material and symbolic rewards. Specifically, the cultural field has five functions:[25]

- Legitimate the dominant culture.

- Devalue other cultures.

- Inhibit the formation of counterlegitimate cultures.

- Integrate the dominant classes.

- (Fictitiously) integrate society.

Prime among these functions is that of legitimating the dominant culture. The cultural field is responsible for valorizing those symbolic goods and practices favored by the dominant, convincing us that, in the architectural context, an architect-designed house is *culturally* superior to a project home. Lest the reader object that of course that is the case, that one does not need to be brainwashed by some sort of cultural conspiracy, because architects do design superior homes, I would ask him or her to recall the many cases where some of the most vaunted buildings by the most eminent architects of recent history are loathed by their inhabitants.[26]

The process runs both ways, between cultural producer and cultural consumer. The architect profits most by designing buildings of taste for people of taste, and displays his or her own cultivation by selecting a cultivated client as much as the client displays cultivation by selecting a cultivated architect. Alberti knew this perfectly well five hundred years ago:

There is one thing that I must not omit here, which relates personally to the architect. It is, that you should not immediately run and offer service to every man that gives out he is going to build; a fault which the inconsiderate and vain-glorious are too apt to be guilty of. . . . Why should I offer those inventions which have cost me so much study and pains, to gain perhaps no other recompense, but the confidence of a few persons of no taste or skill?

. . . I would also have you, if possible, concern yourself for none but persons of the highest rank and quality, and those too such as are truly lovers of these arts: because your work loses of its dignity by being done for mean persons.[27]

Coupled with the legitimation function is its twin, that of devaluing other cultures. I reveal my vulgarity by hanging a velveteen portrait of Elvis Presley on my wall, and my cultivation by hanging an abstraction by an up-and-coming local artist who has just had her first exhibition.

The cultural field also works to prevent the formation of countercultures. These must be distinguished from avant-garde heterodox movements *within* the field. Such movements are products of internal struggles, and do nothing to threaten the legitimacy of culture as a whole. They are discussed later in this chapter. Nascent counterlegitimacies can be seen in societies riven by deep social fissures, such as South Africa, where the subordinate non-whites have their own symbolic systems, and, after many years, a chance of legitimating them and overthrowing the formerly dominant white culture. True counterlegitimacies have a chance of formation only when the dominant class enters some sort of crisis.

Integration of the dominant classes is achieved by creating a commonality of culture. By agreeing on what symbols are important, and what are not, communication between members is facilitated. By purveying this culture as the universal property of the whole society, when it is in fact only the property of the dominant, it fictitiously unites the whole in a covenant to support the dominant. By pretending there is no division, it most effectively maintains that division—we are all middle class, are we not?

Ensuring Closure through Culture

That different classes have different tastes and lifestyles is a truism. Bourdieu's novelty consists in exploring the ways these differences between the classes operate to maintain inequality.[28] Much of Bourdieu's work has been concerned to show how taste and culture are used by groups to define and bound themselves, to prevent the intrusion of outsiders and to maximize homogeneity. All cohesive groups operate some sort of mechanism of social closure in order to protect their privileges. In modern society one of the main mechanisms is provided by the education system, which formally certifies individuals as competent to join certain occupations. But many groups, especially privileged ones, require not only this institutionalized form of cultural capital, but also other, tacit, forms of cultural capital. It is these unspoken requirements that, although absent from the formal occupational description, are nonetheless just as necessary to join the group as the diploma.[29]

Anyone who has experienced any form of discrimination—because of age, sex, or ethnic origin—is only too aware that failure is not necessarily failure to know something, but failure to be something. More subtle and more powerful is the discrimination unrecognized by all—because it is practiced by all—in which success is denied because one does not have the team spirit, the visceral sense of belonging, of fitting in, of being one of us. There is no greater barrier to success than failing to possess all the implicit requirements demanded of an occupation, a barrier all the more formidable because no one sees it. The construction worker who drinks fine wines rather than beer, attends classical concerts rather than the local rock group, and spends lunchtime reading French philosophers will find life on the building site difficult, for all the same reasons that these qualities would subtly enhance the prestige of an architect. To say one is an architect is not only to say that one has a certain sort of degree, or that one can design buildings, it is to say that one has a certain set of attitudes, tastes and dispositions, all the forms of cultural capital that distinguish an architect from a mere builder.

One therefore finds, in any privileged occupation, that its members have much more in common than what is explicitly demanded. Any academic with the experience could tell a lecture room full of engineering students from one of architecture students, and any practitioner could distinguish an engineering company's Christmas party from an architect's. Success is not simply dependent on a moderate intelligence, nor on having specific skills, nor on experience, nor on the right credentials. It depends also on having all the hidden requirements which, while never appearing on any formal job description, are the basis of the occupation's real social value. So the real purpose of a degree from Harvard or Oxford, say, is not to demonstrate that one has departed with a superior education, but that one had the social and economic capital necessary to enter those institutions.

Outline of the Structure of the Field

Behind the internal dynamics of the field of culture is a set of structural tensions. The first arises from the relation of the cultural producers to the other classes. The cultural field is the site of a double hierarchy in that its members are part of the dominant classes, possessing as they do significant amounts of cultural capital, but they are the subordinate fraction of that class, lacking as they do the massive amounts of economic capital possessed by the dominant fraction.[30] This structural ambiguity puts cultural producers in an ambivalent relationship with both the dominant and subordinate classes. As a subordinate fraction of their own class, cultural producers are engaged in a perpetual struggle with the economically dominant over the relative value of symbolic goods against economic ones, and their rates of interconvertibility.[31] Cultural production is essential to the dominant, for that is the means by which they govern so effortlessly. Culture must therefore have some significant value. But not too much value, for then it threatens the dominance of economic capital. The dominant fraction of the dominant class must therefore walk a line between over- and undervaluing the products of the field of culture, resisting the natural efforts of that field's members to overvalue symbolic goods.

As members of the dominant class, cultural producers are predestined to ensure their distinction from the subordinate by their own symbolic production. But this does not mean that they are always allied with the dominant fraction of their own class against the subordinate classes. Particularly in times of crisis they may put their power in the service of the subordinate. Such an alliance is founded on what Bourdieu calls the

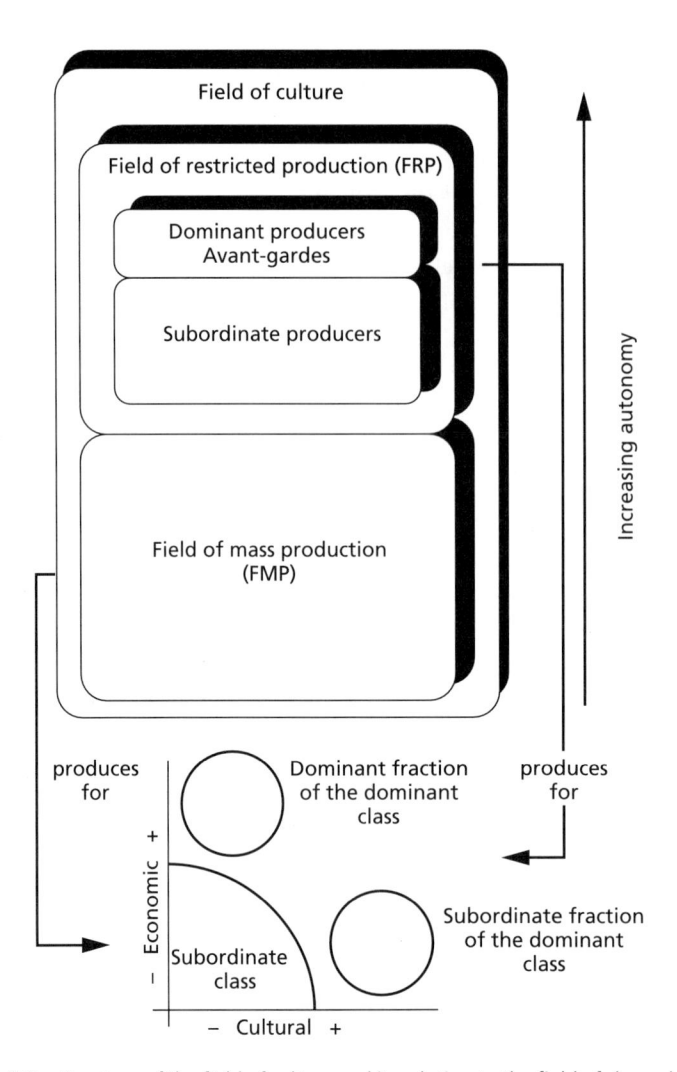

Figure 3.2 Structure of the field of culture and its relation to the field of class relations.

homology of position between the cultural producers, subordinate in their own class, and those subordinate in the field of class relations as a whole.[32]

Turning now to the internal structure of the field, the great divide is between those who produce symbolic goods for mass consumption by all classes, and those who produce for the dominant culture only (fig. 3.2). In the former, the field of mass production (FMP), culture is a commodity, purveyed through television and other media, or sold in department stores. The market is the public. In Bourdieu's terms, the dominant principle of stratification—the system by which the field measures success, by which it ranks its members—is primarily economic. In the latter field, the field of restricted production (FRP), success certainly does not mean economic success, but rather intellectual, aesthetic.

Within the field of restricted production itself, there is a second divide, that between the established members, those who dominate the field, and the newcomers, those trying to work their way to the top.[33] These two oppositions within the field are responsible for its most important dynamics. Since a description of the complicated processes that occur is best accompanied by exemplification, I will continue this description of Bourdieu's model of the cultural field, which I have so far applied elliptically to architecture, and apply it more directly to that area.

The Field of Architecture

One important consequence of looking on architecture as a field is to abolish any notion that referring to architecture as an art, science, or profession has any utility. These are all simply inadequate concepts to apply to such a complex entity. The idea of "field" sensitizes us to the fact that architects are but one part of a much wider social system. In the usual sociological descriptions, social forces are seen as acting directly on the profession. As Abbott points out, this is not so. Social forces bear upon the field as a whole, and the field as a whole mediates between those forces and its own components.[34]

Basic Structure

The basic cleavage between the two subfields, mass and restricted, is evident if one compares the mass-produced standard home to the house designed by an architect. We may start with the immediate observation that the former is called a "home" and the latter a "house" (at least in my own country, Australia). The home is intended for sale to, typically, young couples with young families. Its very name connotes that the family is buying a place to live, not simply an object, whereas the (architected) house emphasizes the objectified nature of the building, quite explicitly rejecting any connotation that people will inhabit it. The home, though it may indeed be designed by an architect, is intended for multiple replication, while the house is meant to be unique—its very appeal is in its uniqueness. A project home is successful if it is sold for the right price (from the point of view of both buyer and seller). This implies that the primary criterion of success is economic, since the standard home builder builds to satisfy market demand generated by a public of consumers. The builder who fails to satisfy client expectations goes broke. Architected houses are successful in aesthetic terms, not economic.[35]

Between the two fields we may see a whole set of structured oppositions:

- Mass-market, large-scale production versus unique objects.

- Anonymous designer versus signatured architect.

Architects Design to Please Themselves

A project home must please the client. An architected house need not, as these leaky roof stories show:

A few days after the Savoies had moved into their famous house the roof of the living room started leaking. They became very upset and immediately called Le Corbusier.

Upon arrival he was taken at once to inspect the damage and suggest a solution. He stayed for a few seconds staring at the water, then looked at the ceiling, then again down at the water. He turned to the Savoies finally and asked for a piece of paper. Mr. Savoie came back in a minute producing a clear white sheet of paper. He handed it to Le Corbusier. Corbu placed it by an adjacent table, folded it carefully and made a paper boat.

He walked to the middle of the room, bent down and placed the boat in the water, said "au revoirs" and left.

A client of Frank Lloyd once called him to tell him his living room roof was leaking: "The roof is leaking on my head right above my armchair, what should I do?" Wright replied: "Move the chair."

A. C. ANTONIADES, "Architecture from Inside Lens (sic)," *Architecture + Urbanism*, July 1979, 8, 17.

- Clients of middling means versus wealthy clients.

- Economic and functional criteria versus aesthetic and symbolic criteria.

- Production to satisfy economic demands of consumers outside the field versus aesthetic production to satisfy symbolic demands of consumers within the field.

- Explicit social function versus asocial objectification.

Architects historically have had little involvement in the mass market. Part of the reason is simply definitional: the discourse of the field is such that it has tended to avoid labeling building designers concerned with mass-market structures as architects. Call them drafters, call them developers, designers, engineers—but not architects. In this fashion the field carries out one of its prime functions, that of deciding who is a member of it. One of the ironic consequences of the increasing use of formal qualifications and licensure, which has created people who are by law entitled to the appellation "architect," is to weaken the field's right of naming and labeling. The field is nowadays obliged to honor the bureaucratic mechanisms (examinations, registration boards) that the field itself conjured into existence. These mechanisms may allow the title to some whom the field wishes to exclude, and exclude some whom it would wish to incorporate. In the anglophone nations today, Buckminster Fuller could not in law call himself an architect.

The field of architecture has also historically tended to exclude from its own discourse not only the designers of buildings produced in mass, but often buildings *for* the masses, such as transportation structures (railway stations), factories, cinemas, shopping malls, and warehouses. These usually enter the canon only when they are designed by individuals who have previously been in the field of restricted production—architects proper—or those who later come to enter it.

As the nature and values of symbolic capital within the field change, not only does the field restructure, but its boundaries change. Some of the most important struggles within fields are over their very definition, of who has a right to be counted as a member, to be heard.[36] Is it architecture, or is it building? When, for example, the modern field of architecture incorporated Buckminster Fuller as an architect, it changed its own nature, for to incorporate an individual of such unusual origins introduced a new set of capitals into the field and altered the lines of social force between all existing members.

One might therefore refer to the two components of what we could loosely call the field of the built environment as, perhaps, the field of building, concerned with mass production, and the field of architecture proper, concerned with restricted production.[37] The sociologist Robert Gutman discerned the distinction when he coined the term "the natural market" for architecture:

> Rare is the building *not* designed by an architect that represents the supreme values of a civilization. This has been true for temples, palaces, libraries, and city halls in Greece, Rome, and Europe during the Renaissance; and for museums, university structures, government buildings, and corporate headquarters more recently. The design of the great seminal monumental buildings is the unique province of architecture, its "natural market." No other profession was able to compete effectively for this market in the past, or is able to now.[38]

His point is valid, although I think he has inverted the causal link. Architects are the only people to design seminal buildings because architectural discourse defines the designers of seminal builders as architects. For ready examples one has only to cite Christopher Wren, Thomas Jefferson, and Buckminster Fuller, all of whom had many achievements in other fields, and whose built work has impressed the field so much that it cannot possibly label them merely "scientist," "politician," or "inventor." Yet Gutman has really hit the nail on the head here with his characterization of the architectural field of restricted production. To recast it in the less gentle Bourdivin conceptual schema, *the field of architecture is responsible for producing those parts of the built environment that the dominant classes use to justify their domination of the social order.* Buildings of power, buildings of state, buildings of worship, buildings to awe and impress.

Table 3.3 shows the types of buildings regarded as "architecture" against the actual composition of work of American architectural firms in 1982. For the content of the restricted field I have used an enumeration of buildings that I compiled from the *Macmillan Encyclopedia of Architects*

	Work done by *MEA* architects	Work done by U.S. firms
Institutional (government, religious, educational)	40	27
Single-family residential	32	5
Other	10	7
Commercial	9	44
Transportation	4	3
Multiple residential	3	9
Industrial	2	5

Table 3.3 Comparison of the types of buildings the field deems worthy of remembering, against the work that American architects actually do. (Source: data for the *MEA* compiled by the author; for the U.S. data, R. Gutman, *Architectural Practice: A Critical View* [Princeton: Princeton Architectural Press, 1988].)

(*MEA*).[39] The table shows that the restricted field is more concerned with single-family dwellings (built for people of taste) and institutional structures (built for centers of power) than is the wider architectural industry. Commercial buildings are especially ignored by the field.

A minor but telling exemplification of this phenomenon is provided by the professional associations in the Commonwealth nations (the old British empire, not the old Soviet one). In many of these countries, the sobriquet "Royal" can, with permission of the Queen, be used in an institutional name, as in, for example, the Royal Canadian Mounted Police. It has no function other than to imply a certain Establishmentarian solidity and genteel snobbery. In the U.K., Australia, Canada, and New Zealand, the architectural professional associations have all petitioned and received the "Royal" praenomen (such as the Royal Architectural Institute of Canada). But in each nation, none of the equivalent bodies representing the sibling occupation of civil engineering have bothered (leaving us with the Canadian Society for Civil Engineers).

The point must be emphasized that this essential function of justifying the domination of the dominant proceeds without either architects or clients being aware of it. Indeed, architecture is able to fulfill this function only if people are not aware of it, if it is misrecognized as a purely aesthetic endeavor. Architects believe—must believe—that their projects proceed in an aesthetic world, that they are indifferent to the games played in the field of power, that only artistic issues are at stake.⁴⁰ But, precisely by so doing, they most effectively produce the symbols that the dominants use to maintain their place at the top of the social order. For what are the "supreme values of a civilization" talked of by Gutman if not those aspects of culture, of the symbolic world, produced by those who dominate. Frank Lloyd Wright could best pursue his dream of a wholly American, organic architecture by designing houses for exactly the same sort of conservative, upper-class, Republican businessmen who were the erstwhile clients of those whom he most hated, those who espoused a Beaux-Arts eclecticism; and all the while he was convinced that he was engaged in the service of Architecture, not realizing that by serving his own interests best he also best served the interests *of* the "best."⁴¹

Forms of Capital

No end of trouble has been caused to the architectural occupation by confusing the two fields (restricted and mass), and assuming that they constitute a unity. Not only are they not a unified social entity, but their linkages are weak. The mass subfield has a vested interest in the existence of the restricted subfield as the producer of legitimate architectural form, but it takes its images at second hand, and must be forever ridiculed by the intelligentsia for imitating the form without understanding the meaning. In the other direction, the restricted subfield sometimes looks to its subordinate sibling, but only to aestheticize what it takes. Thus Robert Venturi's *Learning from Las Vegas* produced in the end a parodic postmodernism, densely overlain with codings that only members of the field could appreciate, rather than generate the respect for the field of mass production it was meant to.

The internal dynamics of the two fields are quite different, arising from their different structures and from the different capitals active within each. We may immediately identify two forms of capital or power (fig. 3.3). The first is professional or temporal status, in which architects compete for material or economic success and professional power. The second is intellectual prestige or status, in which architects compete to be recognized as great creators or thinkers. This symbolic status or capital is quite specific to architecture, as it is no more and no less than architec-

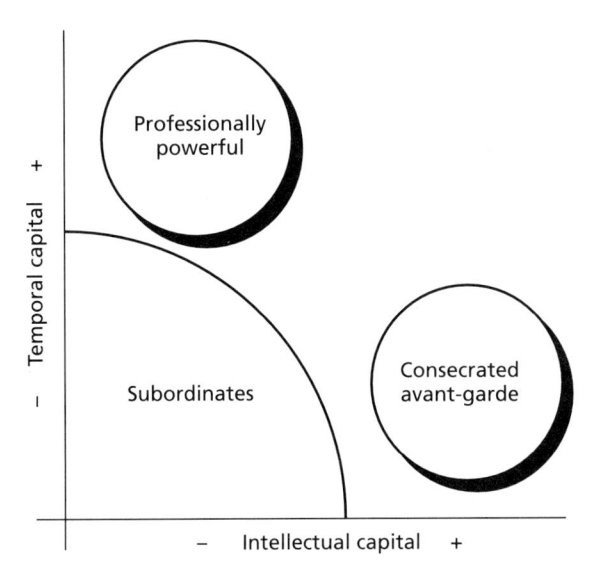

Figure 3.3 The forms of capital in the architectural field, defining its social space.

tural genius. The intellectual status that architects like Peter Eisenman or Michael Graves have within their field may be recognized outside it when, for example, they are featured in an article in the *New York Times*, but they cannot occupy the same importance in the newspaper reader's mind that they occupy in the American architects'. The point is that each field has a capital specific to it, and in so far as one accumulates that form of capital, one achieves success in that field.

Capital is not only owned by individual architects, nor even only by individuals. Critics, commentators, firms, schools, magazines, publishing houses, museums, and galleries also possess varying amounts. Each of the two forms of capital generates its own system of stratification, whereby all may be ranked by the amounts of capital they possess. Note that these two stratification systems are quite different from those usually used to classify architects and firms. A conventional sociology of architecture as a profession ranks only firms, for a start, ignoring all the other components of the field—and then only by the type of work the firm does, or by size, or income, not by any of the criteria defined here.

The two forms of capital, intellectual and temporal, are quite distinct and independent in the English-speaking architectural field. An architect can become the president of his or her national association, or sit on government boards, or found a large and wealthy firm, thereby accumulating great temporal capital, without acquiring the least intellectual capital. In her study of the process of fame-making in American architecture, Roxanne Williamson records that after 1910 those who won the American Institute of Architects' Gold Medal were never those who were important professionals. She points out that the biggest and wealthiest firms with the greatest volume of business were only rarely remembered beyond their own generation.[42] Magali Sarfati Larson makes the same point:

> Large architectural firms . . . are known, sought after, and handsomely paid for providing . . . service efficiently in very large and very costly projects. . . . From the practical professional point of view, these firms offer clients unmatched guarantees of competence, efficiency, reliability, and technical support. To employed architects, they offer the prospect of regular career advancement. Yet public fame, the aura of architecture as art, and the creator's aspirations to immortality are seldom, if ever, attached to the rationalized corporate form of professional practice.[43]

On the other side of the coin, one need only recall that Frank Lloyd Wright never desired or achieved the slightest professional position, but in his later years at least, was honored and deferred to by all those in the highest ranks of professional power. In all countries, of course, the professional associations are surrogates for the wealthiest and most powerful firms. Their relationship to those of high intellectual capital is always fraught, the Masters regarding as impertinent the pretense by which the associations purport to judge what they do not have themselves—witness Wright's ungracious acceptance of the AIA's Gold Medal. Their relationship to the subordinates in the field—the employees laboring with mouse and T-square—is also ambivalent. They must always endeavor to disguise their lack of enthusiasm for reasonable wages and decent working conditions, and their opposition to separate associations for the salaried, by claiming that these are unprofessional and against the occupation's interest.

The relative weight attached to the temporal and intellectual forms of capital depends on the structure of the field. One of the differences between the fields of mass and restricted production is that temporal (or economic) capital is the most important to producers in the former. Success in the mass field means economic success, selling products that consumers want to buy. Of course, there is a professional pride in designing a good project home, and design awards are coveted, but the motto of the field is value for the money, high quality design at an affordable price. Firms and individuals are almost entirely stratified according to the quantity of economic capital they accumulate and, by extension, their material, economic success.

Architecture's symbolic or intellectual capital is, as in other cultural fields, largely defined negatively: by the fact that it is *not* economic or temporal. This is not only a Bourdivin concept, but a notion widely believed in the field itself. It is often assumed by architects, for example, that there is in fact an opposition between the two: you can be good or you can be rich, but it is very hard to be both.[44] The sociologist Dana Cuff has reported many architects as saying that large (hence wealthy) firms cannot attain high quality design.[45] The worst insult one can make to architects is to accuse them of "selling out," of compromising their artistic integrity—which is, of course, their symbolic capital. Nothing is more vulgar than mere money, and no consideration less relevant to the aesthetic success of a building than its cost. Taste cannot be bought, and to attempt to buy it is to display precisely that one has none. *An attachment to symbolic capital implies a denial of the economic.* It is therefore no surprise that MacKinnon's great architects differed most from the average ones psychologically in their disavowal of economic values. A distaste for vulgar money goes hand in hand with aesthetic pretension.

The Quest for Autonomy
The field of mass production (building) is driven by market demands over which it has no control. In Bourdieu's terminology, it has little autonomy from other social fields, so he refers to the principle of ranking operating in the mass field (the economic or temporal principle) as the heteronomous principle of stratification. One of the main differences between social fields is in their autonomy, in the degree to which they can operate independently of demands from other social sectors.[46] A heteronomous

A Distaste for Vulgar Money

Nothing so marks those with intellectual capital than a distaste for the vulgarity of a materialist lifestyle. Here, for example is a statement by the fashionable architect Peter Eisenman, in which he simultaneously denigrates the lifestyle of the middle classes while presenting his own practices as liberating:

I'm looking for new readers. . . . I am looking for people to read my work not as a series of images but as a reading event, as texts. That is what I try to teach students: I try to open them up to what is being. That is, what is the difference between wisdom and knowledge. . . . I try to help them make architecture for themselves, and to have the capacity to satisfy themselves so they will not blow their brains out when they're 35, when they find out that the two-car garage, the station wagon, the boat, the kids, the dog, the wife are nothing. . . . I don't judge. I am, if anything, deprogramming—asking them to give up the baggage and to just dig with me in the station.

QUOTED IN D. CUFF, "Through the Looking Glass: Seven New York Architects and Their People," in *Architects' People*, ed. R. Ellis and D. Cuff (New York: Oxford University Press, 1989), 67–68.

And here a description of a young Australian architect given in a color supplement to the newspaper of record in Sydney, the *Sydney Morning Herald*:

Nonda Katsalidis is talking in his apartment, which looks like an art gallery without the art and exhibits all the visual signifiers of the modernist tradition from which he comes: raw concrete walls and ceiling, severe staircase, high glass windows, bare tables, virtually no paintings ("too bourgeois," says Nonda, who sees himself as a migrant, working-class boy and eschews self-indulgent exercises like collecting art or cars: "I don't feel I have to own things").

C. MCGREGOR, "Stretch of the imagination," *Good Weekend*, supplement to the *Sydney Morning Herald*, June 3, 1995, 26.

field, such as building, is captive to the health of the economy, the wishes of the state and the demands of consumers. The more autonomous a field is, the more it can do as it pleases, and the more its products are designed to satisfy its own requirements, not those of any exogenous market.

Bourdieu cites the pure sciences as the most autonomous fields, for they produce science for their own members, who alone have the right to judge the quality of their "product." Autonomy is measured by the ability of a field to refract external pressures into its own logic. Thus, when the pure sciences react to pressing demands on them for, say, nuclear weapons, an AIDS vaccine, a cure for cancer, better methods for finding oil deposits, these eminently practical enterprises are transmuted by the field into what it terms the quest for scientific knowledge; and if the spinoffs are indeed useful to the client—be it state or private enterprise—the most important product from the scientists' point of view is knowledge in the form of papers, articles, and books. Scientists do not measure scientific prestige by producing socially useful products, though glory it may bring, but by the results achieved in the getting there.

Autonomy in the field of the built environment is weak in the field of mass production and stronger in the field of restricted production, in architecture proper. Like other cultural fields it strives to increase its autonomy, which essentially entails increasing the autonomy of its various capitals. The dynamics of any cultural field, architecture included, arise largely from its natural tendency to want to become the sole judge of its own products. The ultimate form of autonomy develops when production is purely for producers, so that the production and consumption sides of the field are united.

The modern pure sciences come closest to this pristine state. Their achievement in this respect may be attributed to three factors: success in constructing a widely accepted ideology whereby science is held to be best judged by other scientists; an undoubted utility to the dominant fraction of the dominant class in generating economic wealth; and an implicit contract not to interfere in the social order. By claiming value-neutrality and clearly demarcating its concerns from the moral—that is, in the end, the social—it functions largely without interference.[47]

Autonomy is achieved by developing a principle of stratification entirely under the field's control, so that only producers are perceived as the legitimate judges of other producers. This implies developing capitals specific to the field whose value is assessed solely by that field. Temporal forms of capital can never fulfill this function. Temporal forms of capital, such as professional power, depend ultimately on economic capitals, and so temporal power is inevitably tied to forces operating in other fields. All architects can be ranked, if only loosely, on their employment status (salaried, owner), the size of the firm they are in, the number of professional committees they sit on, the government boards they are invited to partake in, and the consultancies they run, but these are all manifestations of temporal power, and will never propel the architect into the immortal ranks of the good and the great. Such a ranking is a heteronomous principle of stratification. In architecture, the most valued form of capital is symbolic—intellectual, aesthetic—and this provides the dominant principle of stratification, which is also an autonomous principle, as it is created by the field itself.[48]

A Semi-Autonomous Field

The fact of the drive for autonomy, whereby architects design for other architects, was brought home to me by an incident at the Faculty of Architecture at Sydney. I had been assigned to conduct tours of the school during the university's biennial open day, when Sydneysiders could come to see what they were getting for their money. The timing was excellent: the studios were filled with models for the upcoming end of semester assessments. On my first tour, I was shocked to discover that the studios had been locked, and in some cases actually barricaded to keep out the public. I later discovered that the studio masters had no interest in displaying the works of their students to the populace, but were determined to preserve them for an exhibition to members of the profession a few days later. Their excuse was that the plebs might damage the delicate displays. Perhaps, but it also showed exactly whose opinions the studio teachers valued, and whose they did not.

With incidents like this, it is understandable that many critics of the field of architecture find the quest for autonomy repugnant. When they castigate architecture as being obsessed with itself as an art, they assume that this is some sort of epiphenomenon, and with just a little reeducation the field can be persuaded to see reason and build nice, functional, humane buildings. This is not so. The criticism is misplaced and vain. A drive toward autonomy is absolutely integral to the field.

The basic dynamics of the architectural field are driven by symbolic concerns and the quest to achieve reputation through the production of great architecture, which is, of course, that which the field defines as great. Society and various groups in society place other demands on architects, though, beyond the purely symbolic. These demands greatly exceed the extrasymbolic demands placed on other artists. Clients are always interfering with what the architect wishes to do; consultants keep coming up with new problems; authorities place all sorts of requirements on buildings; and always, always: cost, cost, cost. No area of the restricted cultural field (such as sculpture, poetry, painting, music) is so bound to other social fields and hence less autonomous. The tremendous tension this creates within architecture is manifested in a varied symptomatology: architectural theory has never recovered from the loss of the certainties of Modernism; architects worry over their loss of influence in the construction industry; the educational system seems inadequate; professional associations are stricken.

It is one of the tragedies of architecture that its practitioners readily make a full-time living from it. There are a great many part-time painters, singers, musicians, printmakers and sculptors, all obliged to earn their living outside their art, and who may therefore permit themselves the luxury of indulgence without compromise. Few architects can.

Only those architects with the greatest amounts of reputational or symbolic capital—such as Wright, Le Corbusier, and Mies van der Rohe at their height—are permitted to dictate their own terms and tell clients what is good for them, for in so doing they define the client's own symbolic superiority.[49] The rest of the field is left to cope as best it may with conflicting demands. These are refracted by the field into its own logic, a logic ultimately driven by the purely aesthetic principle. Perhaps the clearest illustration of this can be found in the writings and works of the heroes of the Modern movement. While they talked a lot about developing a functional architecture, a social architecture, an architecture for people to live in, they ended up with what the logic of the field demanded of them—a style, an aesthetic. Social demands were transmuted, with mental gymnastics as heroic as their architectural daring, into aesthetic ones. As the historian Spiro Kostoff notes, none of the heroes had any intention of actually consulting the users, and if people did not fit into the new architecture, the fault was with the people.[50] So even when the field seemed most receptive to nonsymbolic demands, in the years after World War I, its logic ultimately transformed them into symbolic productions.

Architecture, unlike painting or sculpture or perhaps even cinema, has achieved only the most modest autonomy. That it has any at all may be attributed to the field's quest for autonomy through aesthetics. Not only does this create an autonomous stratification system, but it nicely removes architecture from the political arena: by refusing to consider seriously "the social good" by denying that the great architect has any such responsibility, it neutralizes itself as a political actor, and leaves the dominant fraction of the dominant classes free from criticism, at least from within the sphere of architecture.

Two examples illustrate the point. Architectural history mentions only in passing that William Morris's work in the Arts and Crafts movement was driven by his avowed socialism and his passion to overturn the social order. The dangers apparent in the Modern movement's social critique, made possible by the crisis within the dominant class that occurred after World War I, were swiftly rendered harmless, transformed into a socially innocuous aestheticism by the logic of the architectural field, with the active complicity of the movement's principal players.[51] When Bourdieu points out that the cultural field functions entirely in ignorance of its own social functions, he could perhaps find no better example of a field's navigating itself away from shoals where it may founder—by threatening to renege on the implicit contract it has with the dominant classes to serve only them—than that process whereby the contemporary field has retold the story of the social neutering of the Modern movement as the wondrous evolution of the artistic genius of its members.

What Architectural Competitions Do

The architectural competition may also suffice as an example of the field's lack of autonomy. This is one of the most enduring institutions in professional architecture, with a history several centuries long. A good quarter of the Royal Australian Institute of Architects code of ethics—a document whose ostensible aim is to mediate the relations between the profession and society, and that has, therefore, an important symbolic status—lays down basic principles for architects' conduct. Competitions have been subject to two powerful criticisms for many years. First, they force architects to work for free, to labor toward an endeavor they know may return them nothing. Second, the mechanism of the competition allows no interaction between client and architect in the most crucial part of the design process.[52] Why, then, do they persist?

Bourdieu's conceptual framework allows us to discern in the architectural competition a twofold role in the social world. First, of all the subfields of the field of cultural production, architecture has the most limited means of increasing its stock of symbolic capital. This puts it at a disadvantage compared to its competing fields within the field of cultural production. Painting, sculpture, poetry, and music may all be produced with comparatively few resources and made public in galleries, newspapers, little magazines, and recitals. Architects require huge sums of money. The competition provides a means for increasing the stock of capital of the individual architect and that of the field as a whole (as Larson has also pointed out) without the extravagant expense of actually producing buildings.[53]

Nothing reveals more the supreme importance of the symbolic aspect of architecture than the fact that drawings of buildings are at least as important as the objects they depict. An unexecuted project has virtually the same symbolic force as an actualized building, and so the drawings of those in the avant-garde are valued as much as the built products. Indeed, since drawings are more distant from the vulgar realities of the functional that buildings must be concerned with, they better approach the purely aesthetic. Competition drawings are about the only products over which the architect has complete control. No need to listen to the client beyond reading the competition brief; economic considerations can be glossed over; freedom from interacting with the many other consultants necessary on large projects; temporary respite from contemptible building regulations. None of the usual factors impinging on the architect's autonomy are present in the competition. Indeed, an honorable mention can be superior to winning a competition, for it means that the architect does not have to undergo the risk of losing symbolic capital by having his or her project tampered with, should it ever be built.

Finally, most competitions are for just those buildings of power that serve the ruling classes in some symbolic sense. Usually they are of considerable local or national importance. The competition allows the elites to remind the field that, in the end, it serves *them*. Reciprocally, the architectural competition allows the profession to make a ritual demonstration of allegiance to the elites, by showing architects to be the loyal and dutiful servants of the powerful. If the competition obliges the economically and politically dominant to aver in the most public manner their symbolic dependence on architects, the architects always reavow the covenant by affirming their material dependence on the wealthy and powerful. That most competition entries are produced with great expense, dedication, and sacrifice makes these devotional rites only the more poignant.

Priests and Prophets: Conflict within the Field
One set of relations driving the dynamics of the field of restricted production is that pertaining between itself and the field of mass production. Another is the set of relations among the various agents in the restricted field itself. It is the site of struggles within itself between artists and intellectuals, between those in the upper levels of the hierarchy and the lower levels, as to the content of the two principles of stratification and the relationship between them. It is the struggle to impose the legitimate mode of cultural production, to define who is and is not a good architect, to say who is orthodox and who heretic, to define the limits of the field and who can play the game. The struggle consists of a perpetual dialectic between architects, critics, and institutions. The quest for success here is nothing other than the quest for the right to define the contents of the autonomous principle of stratification, for the right to evaluate everyone's cultural capital in terms of one's own.

Bourdieu derives much of his model of the dynamics of the art-world from the field of religion, partly because he believes there are many analogies between their internal structures, and partly because he believes that the cultural world has largely replaced religious ideologies in justifying social domination and inequality.[54] Where medieval Christianity asserted that individuals occupied their place in the social order by virtue of

Divine fiat, modern society tends to keep people in their places by asserting the natural superiority of certain tastes and lifestyles.

The great motor driving the field is the conflict between those who have made it, the dominant fraction or established avant-garde, and those who have not, the subordinate fraction of newcomers. Bourdieu refers to the dominant fraction as the consecrated avant-garde, because their symbolic productions, their symbolic capital, are what the field has valorized or consecrated. It is crucial to realize that this authority to consecrate is vested in the field as a whole, in the network of relations between all the agents in the field. Bourdieu completely rejects the notion of an essentialist aesthetics, the idea that some buildings are inherently great. All aesthetic value is bestowed by the field, and what is valued as great or not depends on the outcome of the competition between members of the field. Of course, the field is committed to denying this very proposition. No architect who is dedicated to playing the game can possibly believe that the products of his or her unique genius are so defined merely by arbitrary judgment; that quality resides not in the singular vision but in the assessment of the collective.

Competition for success is better interpreted as competition for consecration. There are two basic strategies that can be employed: conservation or subversion. The first is employed by those who already dominate the field. They operate essentially defensive strategies designed to keep them there. These tend to be strategies of silence, not so much of defending their orthodoxy as holding it forth as self-evident.[55] All symbols are, by definition, arbitrary. But the dominant must always and everywhere deny this. *Of course* a building must be proportioned according to principles derived from the human body (Vitruvius). *Of course* a bank must have a Renaissance facade (Beaux-Arts). *Of course* Gothic is the architecture of the industrial age (Viollet-le-Duc). *Of course* we must have white walls. *Of course* there must be no decoration. *Of course* a building should express its function. Those established in the field must avoid at all costs the possibility that someone may reveal the essential arbitrariness of their aesthetic.[56]

Newcomers or those already engaged in the competition for consecration have two options before them. They can either produce buildings (or drawings or competition entries or exhibitions or treatises) that affirm the values and capital of the dominant members, and thus join them, or they can adopt the far riskier strategy of creating a new aesthetic, a new form of symbolic capital, and thus challenge the establishment. The dangers in this are greater than, say, those faced by bold members of the field of mass production when introducing a new product into the market, for while the latter respond to demands of consumers outside their field (since builders are not their own consumers), the avant-garde's endeavors precede the possible demands of their market, constituted by *themselves*.

An attempt at symbolic revolution is, therefore, best made with the knowledge that a secure redoubt lies behind one, and so the members of the field most likely to promote heresy are those with secure economic or symbolic bases. A private income is a wonderful substitute for commissions. It is true that aesthetic pretension implies a disdain for monetary acquisition, but it is so much easier to hold money in contempt if one already has it. Examples are legion in architecture, in which precocious success so often commences with designing a house for wealthy parents or relatives. One need only mention Philip Johnson, who could afford to launch the International Style at the Museum of Modern Art (MoMA) exhibition in New York in 1932 because his familial wealth was quite ample to sustain him should his revolution fail.

In some fields the products of the producers can be assessed according to criteria about which it is difficult to be in disagreement. In engineering, for example, it is universally agreed that cost is a crucial consideration, and a bridge design that is much cheaper than another has the edge, other things being equal. In the case of symbolic products, such as architecture, the criteria of aesthetic success are essentially contested. The very arbitrariness of aesthetic criteria makes competition between architects possible. As such, making one's name means achieving a recognition of difference between one's own creation and lesser works. Since to consecrate is to label as worthy, would-be avant-gardes seek labels to distinguish their products from others. To a great extent, these labels do not so much serve to mark a new avant-garde position as to create it, to produce the very difference it attempts to express. The right to name is a crucial part of the struggles between the avant-gardes. So when Jorge Glusberg, in his introduction to Geoffrey Broadbent's *Deconstruction: A Student Guide*, remarks on Philip Johnson's MoMA exhibition, titled *Deconstructivist Architecture*—

> The title was dedicated to clearing up any misconceptions, to point out that the show did not indicate the presence of a new style, movement or creed, but that it was only presenting the existence of serious similarities in the seven architects' work.[57]

—he is naive, if not positively disingenuous. The whole point of such exhibitions is to cause the audience to see resemblances, to create a school or movement where before there were but atomized individuals, thereby multiplying the symbolic capital of any single individual by allowing each one to mobilize the collective capital of the whole.[58]

The power to produce such labels, and to have them accepted as denoting a difference, is one of the greatest powers the field can bestow on an individual or institution. Hence the enormous influence that the architectural critic Charles Jencks has exerted on the field since his book *Modern Movements in Architecture* (1973) and his many articles and books since, in which, by naming such-and-such postmodern or supermodern or whatever, he *creates* the differences between new and old. This is not to deny that he has intelligence and perception: he is not spinning fantasies in the air. His initial analysis was without doubt refreshing and innovative, and as such won a wide acceptance as a lucid description of contemporary architecture. So lucid, indeed, that the field came to accept his names for movements, and to accept the groupings into schools that he had made of architects and buildings.

Bourdieu describes the established avant-gardes on the one hand and the struggling newcomers seeking to change the field on the other as *priests* and *prophets*.[59] Priests are not only the established dominants in the field, they are also embedded in the institutional apparatus of the field— in museums, in galleries, in the education system, in academies, in government, on editorial boards. They control the important consecrating institutions in the field. In particular, the education system is charged with perpetuating, transmitting and protecting the canon of the classics, the field's most valued symbolic capital, much like the Church. In the end, those in this system, those who write the histories, are those who will either raise an architect to eminence or consign him or her to oblivion.

3 Architecture as a Field

It is the authority of the priests that newcomers must decide either to affirm, and so become acolytes, or to contest, and so become heretics or prophets. To be a prophet is to have a vision that subverts the existing orthodoxy, the existing hierarchy, the existing symbolic capital of the field. It is an exceptionally risky personal strategy, one usually undertaken only by newcomers who are already members of the elite, economically and symbolically wealthy. They know that their wealth guarantees them a place in the order they oppose, and that they will always be treated indulgently.

As opponents of the dominant the prophets also oppose the whole set of the field's consecrating institutions.[60] They are committed to attacking these for their old-fashioned views, dogmatism, rigidity, stupidity, inflexibility, and failure to accommodate themselves to the new age. This passage comes from one of CIAM's declarations, in 1928:

> Modern architects having the firm intention of working according to the new principles can only regard the official academies . . . as institutions standing in the way of progress.
>
> These academies, by definition and by function, are the guardians of the past. . . . Academies vitiate the architect's vocation at its very origin. Their point of view is erroneous and its consequences erroneous.
>
> In order to guarantee the country's prosperity, therefore, States must tear the teaching of architecture out of the grip of the academies.[61]

The professional associations are the prophets' fondest targets. I have read that, for example, the "decline" of the American architect can be attributed to the AIA's 1980 decision to allow architects to submit building bids in design-build packages.[62] In so doing, the architect becomes entangled in all the economic affairs that are anathema to the field's autonomous stratification principle. From this, charge the prophets, has followed a loss of prestige and work, the collapse in American (aesthetic) building standards, a selling out for mere financial gain, and the entire betrayal of society—a veritable fall from grace. The prophets are always inclined to believe that the priests, who are closest to the powerful in other fields, are most likely to be seduced by worldly pleasures, which compensate for the priestly renunciation of True Architecture. And always, of course, the prophet's charges are *moral* indictments, with all the outrage appropriate to the censure of those who have violated the most sanctified moral boundaries. What transgression could be greater than daring to value the economic over the symbolic?

But the prophets' greatest charge is that the consecrators fail to recognize the prophet. No prophet wishes to overturn the whole system, only to overturn the stratification principles on which it is based. Those who rebel—and here you may pick your favorite architectural iconoclast—nonetheless believe, and in many cases believe more zealously than most, that the game of architecture is a serious game worth playing seriously. Their revolutions are always partial, seeking to change the rules of the game in favor of themselves, not to finish the game itself. Of course, the prophet may claim to be making the most radical attempt at reformation possible, to be questioning everything that the priests stand for. Yet what he or she does not question is the need for priests at all, and so even the most self-consciously radical attack is transmuted with the willing complicity of the prophet into an artistic act itself—as was, for example, Dada.

How the Field Works: Three Examples

From Modern Movement to International Style

The recent history of architectural thought is an excellent example of the perpetual struggle within the restricted field. In their struggles to overturn the Beaux-Arts architectural establishment, the young European avant-gardes of the years after World War I adopted a strategy that Bourdieu identifies as seeking allies with homologous interests in other fields. Since all fields divide more or less into subordinate and dominant, it is always possible for the subordinate in one field to see those in the same position in other fields as natural allies.[63] What is more natural, then, for those who would overthrow the priests of architecture, to seek in the postwar misery of the lower classes a reason and a rationale for their revolution? This is not to say that the heroes of the Modern movement were not entirely dedicated and sincere in their objectives. The field of architecture requires no hypocrisy on the part of its members for them to produce all the field's social effects.

A reading of the manifestos of the 1920s and 1930s shows the social orientation of these young heroes clearly. A strategy—an *unconscious* strategy—based on homology of position between subordinate groups provides the most powerful of rationales because it allows an architectural avant-garde to argue that the reformation, the betterment, of the whole social order can only occur if there is a reformation of the architectural field: to overturn the hierarchy of social relations as a whole requires first the overturn of the hierarchy of architects.[64] Such a grandiose objective also allows them to vent all the moral indignation that accompanies the prophetic crusade on a task of suitably epic proportions.

But, as Bourdieu has pointed out, alliances derived from homology of position are fragile.[65] The habitus of the cultural producers has more in common with that of their colleagues in the dominant fraction of the dominant class than with the lower classes. The two fractions of the upper classes are bonded together in a commonality of practices and purposes that can hardly be disturbed by additional alliances between one fraction and other classes. Moreover, any alliance of architects to those outside their field necessarily threatens their autonomy and the autonomy of the aesthetic principle of stratification. A claim to be designing for people would appear to be the most serious sort of attack on architecture's autonomy, for it would seem to impose on the field the desires of others. To a great degree the high modernists obviated any threat to their intellectual autonomy by the simple expedient of ignoring those for whom they claimed to be designing. As Spiro Kostoff puts it:

> Modernist rhetoric waxed eloquent about the needs of users. It represented architecture as the vehicle of social welfare and set public housing as the highest priority of architecture. But there was no question of consulting with the user of housing estates during the course of their design. No one bothered to explain why, since the picture was too obvious. Users were not a stable or coherent entity. And users did not know what they wanted, or more importantly, what they *should* have.[66]

The capital that an artist accumulates from a cultural practice, as Bourdieu points out, tends to decrease with the size of its audience. What credit is there to be obtained from the admiration of the untutored masses? In a way, then, it was inevitable in the heyday of modernism that the users' opinions would count for nought. Thus, when the heroes of the Modern movement moved across the Atlantic and up the hierarchy of the architectural field in the late 1930s and after the war, their advocacy of socialist housing solutions was discreetly let slide into oblivion and their social objectives disappeared. Finding themselves in the most elite areas of American academia, in the Ivy League and associated universities, their natural affinities with the economically powerful reasserted themselves. The remnants of the threat to architecture's autonomy was finally done away with by turning the Modern movement into the International *Style*, and the ancient alliance of the two fractions of the dominant classes reaffirmed by placing this style in the service of corporate America.

Attacking the Field's Autonomy
Nothing so exposes the internal workings of the field of restricted production as an attack on its most valued symbolic capitals. By implication this is also an attack on the right of the field to pronounce judgment on its own productions, on its autonomy. In fields in which it is impossible to enlist the aid of exogenous criteria (such as cost or function), all judgments depend on the authority of the judges, and these ultimately come down to their taste. Tom Wolfe's book *From Bauhaus to Our House*[67] waged a concerted attack on architectural Modernism, a movement whose principles had dominated the field from the end of the Second World War through the mid-1970s. At the time Wolfe was writing, Modernism's hegemony had clearly passed, and the various countermovements Charles Jencks was to label Postmodern were just then emerging in the works of new avant-gardes. In the racy style that had made his other books bestsellers, Wolfe recounted the history of the movement from its origins in Germany and Holland to its crossing of the Atlantic and transformation into the International Style. In four short chapters he ridiculed everyone from Walter Gropius to Louis Kahn, and in the final three he vented his spleen against the contemporary avant-garde, from Michael Graves to Robert Venturi. The book became another bestseller, much against the wishes of the American architectural establishment, many of whom would have preferred to see it and its author burnt.

Those who were not architects saw the book differently. Writing in *American Spectator*, Gavin Stamp noted that "On my last trip from London to America I soon found that the infallible method of creating a frisson of shock and disapproval at dinner was to say that, in *From Bauhaus to Our House*, Tom Wolfe had largely got it right."[68] In *The Listener*, Stephen Bayley wrote that the New York architectural establishment was "a narcissistic, superior and self-regarding crowd at the best of times. . . . Used to being treated as about second only to God in the chain of command, patrician architects did not enjoy being given the same treatment as some T-shirted freak from the boonies."[69]

Those who evaluated the book favorably found it funny, irreverent, and satirical, amusing and entertaining. The *Library Journal*'s capsule review said, "The architect and student will be thoroughly delighted with the biographical sketches. . . . Wolfe has done it again. This historical vignette on the idea behind modern architecture is always entertaining and often brilliant."[70] *Choice* called it "witty and iconoclastic." In the *National Review*, Sobran, an editor at the magazine, said, "It's a terrific book, of course. Like all his books, it will be delicious reading long after the uproar has died down and its essential rightness has been assimilated."[71]

The negative reviews, all by architectural or art critics, loathed Wolfe's style, calling it acid, vicious, malicious, and rancorous. They thought it was facile and glib, full of ad hominem attacks, a sneering little book. They pointed out that it was unoriginal and that modernism had been on the wane for some time. In the *Architectural Review*, the noted architectural historian Joseph Rykwert called it "a tissue of factual error" and an "insignificant and specious booklet." In *The Nation*, Michael Sorkin, an architect and critic, wrote that the book was "an unoriginal, if vicious, account of what Wolfe finds wanting in modern architecture and modern architects, particularly what's wanting in their clothes and complexions."

What was so bad about *From Bauhaus to Our House* (hereafter *FBOH*)? The most common complaints by the negative reviewers were that Wolfe's history was simply wrong and his style was malicious. His basic argument is that Modernist architecture is simply horrible, and that this horror was inflicted on the Americans by a group of European émigrés, who managed to install themselves in architectural academia and convince corporate America to adopt a soulless, inhuman style as its collective front.

As many reviews, both favorable and unfavorable, pointed out, his history *was* selective and inaccurate. His idea that Modernism was foisted on America is simply not true, and several reviewers noted that the tenor of Wolfe's book was quite anti-European and nationalistic. Many called him conservative or right-wing. But surely being a poor historian, or retailing racy anecdotes, was not a sufficient sin to justify the vicious counterreaction, for the book to be called "a sudden and massive regurgitation of Wolfe's psychic garbage" with "about as much distortion, falsification, general misinformation and slander as anyone could cram into the pages of a small book," as the eminent exhibition designer and architect George Nelson wrote.

Of course, one of Wolfe's failings was that he was not a consecrated member of the small and closed circle of architectural critics. A common line of defence against *FBOH* was to claim that its author did not have the architect's eye for seeing things, that he was no better than any member of the public. This is, of course, simply an assertion of the field's right to judge itself, and to be the *only* judge of itself. As David Greenspan put it in *Progressive Architecture:*

> His utter inability to *see* is what totally vitiates Wolfe's attempt to bring the Truth about Modern architecture to the American public. . . .
>
> The layman for whom Wolfe is writing may have no keener eye for architecture than he does, but that only weakens Wolfe's position: how can he criticize, with any authority, that which he cannot see?[72]

Few of the negative reviews ever mentioned the fact that modernist architecture *was* widely disliked by the public. No doubt some of the book's appeal derives from this fact. *Punch*'s reviewer Stan Davies expressed this well when he started off with:

> You may be wondering why the western world is full of glass boxes which everyone hates to live or work in, even the people who commissioned and paid for them in the first place.
>
> You may wonder, as you scuttle across the latest windswept "piazza," trying to fend off the flying grit and debris propelled into your face by the hurricane gusts generated by the fifty-story monstrosities about you, why the architects who built them should be

The Architectural Critics on Wolfe

If he is not prepared to betray his class, he is at least ready to tattle on it. Thus, when it comes time to actually defend something, it turns out to be Morris Lapidus, John Portman and Ed Stone, those architectural Liberaces. Likewise, Wolfe affirms his affection for Thai silk pillows, zebra-striped upholstery, gold leaf and a few chotchkies around the house. Such is the slippery apostasy of the bourgeoisie that it betrays, but only a little. The haut bourgeoisie affects the tastes of the petit. We go to Morey's but we drink our beer from the bottle. How very petit bourgeoisie!

Finally, Wolfe's book falls flat for the banality of its conclusions and its open contempt for its subject. Of course, any polemic hectors the facts into line. Wolfe bludgeons them and then asphyxiates what's left under an ooze of prose. Maybe because his material is so far from his sympathies, Wolfe's familiar flash turns into a whine. . . . To be sure, he delivers just about everything from his old catalogue of devices. . . . But the cleverness is only intermittent, the point hackneyed. Tom Wolfe is a great one at the snobbery of being less of a snob than thou, at playing nobody's fool. Nobody's fooled.

M. SORKIN, "Wolfe at the Door," *The Nation*, October 31, 1981, 447.

[Wolfe's argument] looks familiar, as travesties must. The dismantling of the modernist dogma has been going on for ten years or more. . . . Everyone, including Wolfe, knows something about it. But he brings nothing new to the argument except, perhaps, a kind of supercilious rancor and a free-floating hostility toward the intelligentsia.

R. HUGHES, "White Gods and Cringing Natives," *Time*, October 19, 1981, 73.

It is essential, in any good scam involving a book, that the major reviews be sharply critical, that they go into much earnest detail to show that the reviewer knows more about the subject than the author. In the case of From Bauhaus to Our House *any reviewer could pass the test. . . .*

The book, which is being passed off as a history of modern architecture, is deliberately mendacious and empty of content. The only reason for discussing it is not the book itself, but the general pollution it brings to the intellectual environment. . . .

As the fancy moves him, since no one could possibly accuse Wolfe of a concern for veracity, he calls himself a social critic or a social historian, but in reality he deals in neither history nor criticism. What it seems to be, as far as I can make out, is just gossip. Not neighborly, pass-the-time-of-day gossip, but malicious gossip. Ambiguous gossip, so that many of his victims never realize that they have been shafted by one of the world's great pros. This, for Wolfe, is one of the supreme pleasures, I would guess. . . .

The only possible good I can find in this perverse and corrupting book is that if seen for what it is, a distorting mirror of an enormously complex reality, it might do yeoman service as a text on how brains may be washed and conscience lobotomized.

G. NELSON, "Tom Wolfe's Fantasy Bauhaus," *American Institute of Architects Journal,* December 1981, 72, 74, 75.

His constituency is a new xenophobic and philistine right which (as philistine xenophobes usually do) claims a populist sanction. . . . The wives of the developers who build the nastier skyscrapers can safely have it lying about their coffee tables.

J. RYKWERT, "Camp Clown," *Architectural Review,* June 1982, 70.

the recipients of honours galore instead of being dumped into the nearest river with a couple of tons of concrete about their ankles.

You may gaze up Ludgate Hill and wonder what St Paul's looked like before it was garlanded with shards, and you may weep. You may inspect the latest Haus der Kultur put up to give a home to Shakespeare and Mozart, and as you regard its honest, simple barbarity you may ask yourself why it is that Richard Seifert and Sir Denys Lasdun cannot be simply taken out and shot. If so, this book of Tom Wolfe's will enlighten you, but it will also give you hope.[73]

The field's reactions to Wolfe's book can best be understood in terms of the description given here. In the eyes of the patrician architects Wolfe committed two great sins: he exposed the game of culture to be a game, and he attacked their taste. The hegemony of the dominant fraction of the restricted field, the consecrated avant-garde, depends on their symbolic capital being perceived as a doxa, as self-evidently valuable. As soon as it becomes possible to question it, the dominant fraction loses its best form of defense, for it then becomes an orthodoxy, and against an orthodoxy it is always possible to conceive of a heterodoxy. Writing in the *London Review of Books*, Reyner Banham saw this when he tried to account for *FBOH*'s reception in America:

> Yet this mild ventilation of the secret places can hardly account for the almost paranoid reaction. For that slightly hysterical strain I think something peculiar—very peculiar—to modern architecture in North America is to blame. Not only is it a closed sub-culture, it is also by now a very well-entrenched academic establishment. . . . In alliance with the architecture section of the Museum of Modern Art (funded by Philip Johnson's family) and the (predominantly German) art-history establishment, they effectively fixed the agenda for three if not four generations of architects, artists, critics, historians and designers. To mock all that is to threaten the intellectual and academic security of thousands who have grown up under its hegemony.[74]

Unlike the sciences, cultural areas such as art and architecture cannot point to externalities to defend their judgments.[75] It is true that all architectural theories start off with some sort of exogenous rationalization (the proportions of the human body, Platonic number theory, and so on), but these disappear within a generation as the field's natural desire for autonomy takes over. Nothing threatens more the symbolic capital of the dominant than exposing the style they defend as arbitrary, and no weapon better exposes the arbitrary than ridicule or parody. Hence the horror shown by the photography critic Janet Malcolm, writing in the *New York Review of Books*:

> Wolfe, cynically dismissing the ideology of the twentieth century modernists as a pose, writes about modern architecture as if it were something that had been put on earth simply to irk him, with no social and cultural history. His theory of the art compound—which reduces the modernist revolution in art, literature, music, design and architecture to the status of a junior high school afternoon program taken over by cliques of exhibitionistic bohemians—isn't merely preposterous, it's worrisome.[76]

Most cultural fields require a sizable investment to enter. One cannot simply buy one's way in, one must become cultivated, learning all the myriad practices and tastes that mark one as worthy to pronounce on those very practices and tastes. The naturality of good taste springs from the habitus, and habitus must be inculcated from earliest youth. An ambition to become a respected architecture critic or a great architect requires much more than obtaining formal education or knowledge, it requires the slow acquisition of all the modes and manners of the upper class. Thus the investment required to enter the field and aspire to its uppermost reaches is not a mere few years in university, it is one's whole lifetime.[77] Since an attack on the field is also an attack on its members, Wolfe threatened the devaluation of this considerable investment.

Another term for this investment is "taste." The opposite of good taste is vulgarity. And if the dominant members of the field of restricted production—the artistic priests—are those who, by definition, have the very best of tastes, the very worst tastes are those held by those whom the former must oppose, those who are economically wealthy but poor in cultural capital, those in the dominant fraction of the dominant class—the businessmen, the entrepreneurs. George Nelson best expresses the contempt that the field has for those without taste, for social inferiors, and he exposes without realizing it the essential aristocratism that is the very essence of architecture:

> I was a Wolfe fan for years and found his excursions into the world of hippies, custom car buffs, miscellaneous small people reaching for status, both illuminating and funny. Gossip goes down well with such subjects; there is little else to do with them anyway. Their unifying quality (always allowing for some exceptions) is that they all want to be somebody. An author can make fun of them and nobody minds.
>
> Architects, artists, scientists and such people inhabit a very different region. Its occupants' unifying quality is a desire to do something, and the doing, at its best, is generally pitched at an idealistic level. . . . There is a dignity in such aspirations that people recognize and respect, and even if the efforts are Quixotic or Utopian, an author cannot safely mock such people without ultimately disgusting his readers.[78]

I always get angry when I read this passage. One does not know whether to boggle more at Nelson's complete contempt for "miscellaneous small people" or his astounding presumption of the natural superiority of his own class. I leave the last word to Arthur Drexler, director of architecture and design at the Museum of Modern Art, writing in the *AIA Journal*:

> I read George Nelson's review of Tom Wolfe's nasty little book with an emotion best described as joy. . . . No literate person took that production seriously, but Nelson's review is distinguished from the others by addressing the real point: The fault in Mr. Wolfe's book is not its tendentious misinformation, however irritating it may be, but its unrelenting, stupefying, soul-destroying *vulgarity*.[79]

Decon Comes to Town

By 1980 the indignant Modernist prophets and their successors had assumed the priestly robes, and were once again allied with the bourgeois, leaving them open for a new wave of prophets to denounce them as traitors to architectural purity. All the positions occupied by the Modern movement's avant-gardes had been vacated upon their deaths. The basic principle of evaluation of the field's symbolic capital (the autonomous principle of stratification), the degree to which it conformed to the tenets of the movement, was less inclined to be accepted by the dominant fraction. A substantial increase in architecture graduates in the United States after World War II generated a pressure for new niches in the field. What new ideological weapon could newcomers use to wield against the dominant fraction of their field? Again, and quite unconsciously, the new avant-gardes employed the principle of argument from homology of position and imported an ideology that had proven most effective in restructuring the field of literary production, and propelling *its* avant-garde into positions of power: Derridean deconstruction.

Intellectual developments depend for their success or failure on the degree to which their adherents can gain social support for their promulgation. Deconstruction was used by literature academics at Yale, Cornell, and Johns Hopkins in the 1970s to advance both their own careers and the status of their disciplines, as well as the properties of deconstruction that facilitated these strategies.[80] In 1988 deconstruction entered the architectural field explosively. If one were writing a purely internalist history of architectural theory, it would be difficult to explain how what is essentially a theory of literature came to have anything to do with architecture. Even its creator, Jacques Derrida, is somewhat mystified about its applicability to the field. But other theories of architecture have sprung from flimsier premises, and if sociology teaches anything, it is that the *content* of such theories plays only a modest part in determining their historical success or failure. More important is the extent to which they can be used as instruments in the struggles that preoccupy the elite members of the field.

Deconstruction (or Deconstructivism or just plain Decon) had several properties that made it attractive to a group of architects and critics wishing to establish themselves as powers in the field:

- The theory had already proved effective in overthrowing an established avant-garde in another field.

- There was an established market of cultural consumers.

- It had the potential to enhance the field's autonomy.

- Decon originated in a field with a social structure homologous to architecture.

- Decon requires a substantial amount of symbolic capital to implement.

The effectiveness of deconstruction in clearing out an old academic establishment had been demonstrated by its success in American literature departments. These strategies had only to be emulated, rather than devised afresh. Moreover, deconstruction had established itself in the most eminent portions of the American establishment, the Ivy League schools. A theoretical revolution conducted anywhere but in the dominant institutions of the architectural field is only a peasant's revolt. Deconstruction was, therefore, a symbolic capital of considerable worth before it ever entered architecture. Most of the work of valorizing it was already done—the architectural avant-garde merely had to import it. Before deconstruction, literature departments had been on the defensive, pressured by universities to match the research output of the sciences. Decon had propelled them to positions of importance within their universities, to the very center of contemporary intellectual debate.[81] Might not the same happen to architecture, which had given the world the term "postmodern"?

One of the perennial problems of avant-garde producers is that they produce ahead of the market's demand for their products. Deconstruction short-circuited this unfortunate effect by presenting the architects with an existing market of literary consumers. The cultural elites were already primed for an architectural deconstructivism. It only needed someone to produce it.

Deconstruction had great potential for increasing the field's autonomy: it is sublimely formal, ascetic, and intellectual; and formalism, by definition, is a retreat to a hermetic purity, one that can only be appreciated and judged by those with the right instruments for decoding it. When viewed in a Bourdivin light, nothing could be more natural than the formulation of asocial and apolitical architectures, for these do not threaten the relations between the cultural producers and the dominant fraction of the dominant class, and they work to maintain architecture's autonomy. The retreat into formalism is the strategy par excellence for this, for it ensures that only those trained in the field can pronounce judgment.

Bourdieu has pointed out that cultural goods are not like money; they cannot simply be consumed. Avant-garde art, especially, can only be consumed by those who have the right mental apparatus, the right schemes of appreciation, the right codes to decipher it. An individual may have access to or even ownership of a cultural good, but can only consume it by means of the right schemes of appropriation. This works to maintain the rarity of cultural capital: although it may be readily available in museums, as buildings, or in the media, it can only be consumed by those who have the dispositions (habitus) and have taken the time to acquire the instruments of appropriation. The dominant culture may be everywhere, but it can only be consumed by the dominant fractions. The more complex the instruments needed for the decipherment, and the more that art tends to be replete with codings, double-codings, and histories, then the more its rarity is preserved, and hence appreciated (in the economic sense).

Deconstruction is a particularly dense theoretical structure, requiring a great deal of effort to understand. Wrestling with this typical product of the Gallic intellectual field, Geoffrey Broadbent laments:

> Furthermore, it is clear that Derrida and his interpreters actually intend it to be difficult. It's meant to make us feel inadequate on the grounds that it will make them seem cleverer than we. . . . [Attempts] to criticise it have been rebutted, superciliously, violently, even on the grounds that such approaches violate the very nature of "Deconstruction". . . . Enthusiasts, even, have been under fire for trying to explain "Deconstruction" to make it intelligible to ordinary mortals. . . . Clearly it threatens the "Deconstructionists" when anyone tries to open up their esoteric cult.[82]

Deconstructivist architectural theory is equally opaque—even Bourdieu's work is crystalline by comparison, and that's saying something. By rendering the theory difficult to appropriate, those who advance it may also prevent its devaluation by restricting its use to a more or less closed circle of avant-gardists. Provided one can valorize deconstructivist architecture as *the* symbolic capital of worth in the field of architecture, the theory contains within it an effective means of guarding its own worth. The vulgar outsider is prevented from acquiring the capital by the most elementary means.

This bears on the fourth property that made deconstruction appealing to the architectural avant-garde, that its internal dynamic was structured homologously to the dynamic of thought in architectural academe. In his interesting and amusing comparisons, the sociologist Johan Galtung points out that the basic ethos of the Anglo-American intellectual world owes much to the old empiricist and positivist traditions. Whether it be in philosophy or physics, data is privileged over theory, and the intellectual worker is happy in his or her daily toil to add another small piece to the grand puzzle:

> They are certainly not known for sweeping theories, for grand perspectives, for having projected the type of light that makes vast areas look bright but at the expense of all nuances, the shadows in the crevices and the canyons of doubt and so on. One could even surmise that an average saxon researcher would fall prey to vertigo if a theoretical pyramid rose five centimeters above the ground.[83]

A key criterion of scholarship is to have thoroughly scrutinized the sources, to have assessed all the data. Intellectual communities tend to look on themselves as communities of craftsmen, endowed with different skills and intellects to be sure, but with quite enough in common to communicate effectively and meaningfully with each other. In Germany and France each community consists of many separate kingdoms. The British philosopher R. M. Hare used to tell a story about a relative of his who studied philosophy under Edmund Husserl in Freiburg. Husserl's approach consisted of producing six bound volumes and saying, "Here are my books; come back in a year's time."[84] Exactly the same attitude is apparent in this story about Mies van der Rohe:

> I once asked Mies, when I was a student of his, "If the great architecture is to be a continuation of your rectilinear forms, why should there be another architect? Will our future consist only of copies of your work?" Mies's reply was, "Well . . . doesn't that satisfy?"[85]

France and Germany both tend to privilege theory over data, the reality that theory talks about seeming to be "a more real reality," as Galtung puts it, a reality free from the noise and impurities of what Anglo-Saxons doggedly take to be the real world. Writing of the tremendous influence that Gaston Bachelard, both a philosopher of science and a poet, has had in France, two sociologists of science remark:

> He confirms the French notion of revolution; you are not a scientist if you do not engender a radical revolution that totally subverts the state of science (this idea is deep in all young French scientists). He confirms the importance of theories. He confirms the

esoteric nature of science, which is always in rupture with what is known. . . . Science is never pure enough—it should always be further removed from common sense, further refined of empirical traces. . . . Purity, ever more purity, is the Bachelardian dictum.[86]

The architectural intelligentsia has always resembled more the French or German than the Anglo-American in its structure, and has preferred the European predelection for theory (some general homologies are summarized in table 3.4). In the high places that are the abodes of the architectural avant-gardes, there has never been any empathy with the Anglo-American fondness for empirically oriented, small-scale intellectual work. It is all grand theories, grandiloquent manifestos. Moreover,

The European Ways of Being an Intellectual

[In France there is] admiration for the power of conviction, the verbal display, clear light emanating from the luminaries. But there will never be full communication, if for no other reason than that each master has his own language. An effort by somebody else to communicate back that he has received the message will be firmly rejected as an infringement on the personal integrity of the master: "You have not understood me correctly, I did not say . . .". Efforts to demonstrate reproducibility will be put down as attempts at plagiarism, as lack of originality on both sides.

In Germany the structure seems by and large to be very pyramidal. There was a tremendous respect for the Professor, *the respect was not pretended but real, and his relationship to the lesser fry of assistants and students was that of master to disciple. . . . In Germany people may be proud of being disciples, they may be referred to and refer to themselves as followers of* Meister *so-and-so. . . . [The] disciples arrive at understanding the master and in so doing accept his theory without fundamentally challenging it. . . . I have almost never heard this in France: there, it sounds rather as if everybody conceives of himself as a master, or a master* in status nascendi. *One might be working in somebody's department or laboratory, but that is a temporary and necessary insult to the human mind and dignity, soon to be overcome. After that the final synthesis of Marx and Freud will be written.*

J. GALTUNG, "Structure, Culture, and Intellectual Style: An Essay Comparing Saxonic, Teutonic, Gallic and Nipponic Approaches," *Social Science Information* 20, no. 6 (1981): 836, 835.

Anglo-American intellectual field	Architectural field	French intellectual field
Natural sciences dominant	Theory and history dominant subfields	Philosophy and literature dominant
Literary style emphasizes clarity and simplicity	Ultimate aim is to develop a strong personal style	Style is valued as end in itself
Intellectuals little known outside their fields	Major architects well known in the field, and pronounce on many matters	Intellectuals are major public figures, expected to participate in public life
Few charismatic figures	Major figures are charismatic, developing schools of followers	Major figures are charismatic, developing schools of followers
Sociology well developed	Little theoretical interest in social issues	Sociology ill developed as a discipline
Empiricism and mild positivism major orientations	Hermeneutic orientation	Anti-empirical orientation
Intellectuals sometimes regarded as cultivated, sometimes as donnish	Architects regarded as cultivated individuals	Intellectuals define cultivation

Table 3.4 A comparison of some properties of three intellectual fields.

these theories in the end come down to the personal vision of the prophet-architect. They may start with some sort of perception of a real-world problem, but actual, hard data, as Spiro Kostoff notes in the quotation above, has precious little to do with it. The basic Anglo-American notion of testing theories against the evidence is irrelevant. Once the Master has devised a theory of architecture, that is that. There is no more testing of the initial propositions than there is in a religious cult, only the personal development of the great architect's vision. Architectural Truth is never obtained by achieving a correspondence between the mundane and the theoretical, but by creating a great edifice. The architectural eye has ever been elevated to the transcendental. When asked the characteristic Anglo-Saxon question of whether Palladio's theories are "valid" or "true," any architectural historian would raise his eyebrows in disbelief at the sheer irrelevance of the question. When told that his buildings hardly ever correspond to any of his own theoretical works, the historian would shrug.[87] These facts have not prevented both his writings and his buildings from being some of the most influential in all history. Palladio is a master, consecrated by the field as a genius, *and that is enough.*

No doubt this explains the curious role of Anglo-American architectural theories in the history of Western architecture. It may be suggested that the Anglo-American architectural communities live in a constant state of tension between being true to the intellectual modus operandi of their lands of origin and a yearning for the more noble cultures of France or Germany. At no time has any architectural movement indigenous to Britain or the United States come to dominate Western architectural thought. Schools such as the Arts and Crafts movement, so British in its love of the earthen, seem footling compared to the crash and thunder of the Teutonic Moderns.

So: the intellectual climate in which Derridean deconstruction flourished in its native France was similar to that prevailing in Anglo-American architecture. The structure of the academic field in which deconstruction is embedded is directly transferable to architecture's. But deconstruction could not have succeeded as it has without the aid of critics and publishers, all struggling—in the most genteel way possible, of course—for success in the field.[88] By the late 1980s Charles Jencks had established himself as a critic and historian to be listened to. Jencks joined the battle early, knowing that even though he may have disliked Deconstructivist architecture, his position as a recognized critic would endure not only so long as the field recognized him, but so long as he recognized *it*. Andreas Papadakis, owner of Academy Editions, the first publisher of Jencks's *Language of Postmodern Architecture*, had promoted Zaha Hadid and Bernard Tschumi a few years earlier. Papadakis had developed a successful marketing technique consisting of bringing some up-and-coming or controversial speakers from the U.S.A. or Japan to a symposium, inviting forty or fifty other guests for an afternoon discussion, then publishing the lot first in the journal *AD (Architectural Design)*, all lavishly illustrated, of course, then as a book. Jencks prompted the idea of a Deconstruction symposium, and so it eventuated in 1988 at the prestigious Tate Gallery in London. Philip Johnson held a similar exhibition the same year in New York at the Museum of Modern Art.

The point is that deconstruction did not succeed because of some essential aesthetic superiority, but because certain important individuals and institutions in the field were mobilized to support it.

L'Affaire Eisenman

Of all the values architecture cherishes most, originality ranks highest. Yet few disciplines expropriate so much from others. As an example I cite the altercation between the architectural academic Diane Ghirardo and the architect Peter Eisenman. In an article in *Progressive Architecture* Ghirardo charged that Eisenman had succeeded in transforming what was a scanty and mediocre oeuvre into a major movement:

More than almost any of his peers, Eisenman's prominence rests on his extraordinary ability not only to advance his own cause with unparalleled skill, but also to convince others to thrust him into prominence. . . .

The concept that best describes Eisenman's enterprise in general is that of a game, a game with the double objectives of winning and never ending. With a canny talent for showmanship more akin to P. T. Barnum than to Walt Disney, Eisenman in the early 1970s managed to parlay a miniscule design portfolio and a wide range of acquaintances into the New-York-based Institute for Architecture and Urban Studies. In a decade when he designed approximately one small house per year, Eisenman propelled his own name to the forefront of the architectural community through periodic articles in the Institute's journal, Oppositions, *its monthly magazine* Skyline, *and a regular series of events at the Institute.*

D. GHIRARDO, "Eisenman's Bogus Avant-Garde," *Progressive Architecture*, November 1994, 72.

I happen to think that Ghirardo takes the wrong tack here. Such tactics were not invented by Eisenman. Self-promotion is everywhere among the architectural avant-gardes. Illustrated lectures, articles in both the professional and popular presses, group exhibitions, and one-man shows have all been routinely used to promote individuals' ideas for at least the past century. Before that, of course, one wrote treatises. Ruthless self-promotion and the mobilization of social capital—friends in the right places—are of the very essence of all attempts by those in subordinate positions in the field to propel themselves to the top. Many of the heroes of the Modern movement did exactly the same thing. Ghirardo, in fact, deftly illustrates Bourdieu's point that avant-garde revolutions are only partial, seeking only to overturn the hierarchy within the field, not to destroy the field itself. She observes:

Eisenman represents a desire to embrace an avant-garde aesthetic, to stake out the margins of culture in a defiant expression of independence, while simultaneously enjoying all the benefits of being a centrist cultural icon.

GHIRARDO, "Eisenman's Bogus Avant-Garde," 72.

But this is not the point I wish to make. It is Eisenman's reaction to this article that I want to discuss. Eisenman adopts exactly the same tactics employed by his mentor, Jacques Derrida, in the latter's skirmish with Thomas Sheehan over Sheehan's review of a book on the Heidegger controversy. (Sheehan's review was published in the *New York Review of Books,* January 14, 1993, p. 30. An exchange of letters took place in the following five issues [all 1993]: February 11, p. 44; March 4, p. 57; March 25, p. 65; April 8, p. 49; April 22, p. 68.) Sheehan claimed that the book in question was suppressed following legal threats by Derrida over remarks critical of Derrida in the book's preface. Over several months of name-calling and vituperation, the mudslinging concluded with a petition by twenty-five scholars supporting Derrida. Sheehan's final comments on this were:

The issue in l'affaire Derrida *is one thing only: not translation rights or the rendering of French datives but Derrida's ego and the power he can muster to serve it, including the power to commandeer—by a network of faxes and phone calls (and a good deal of arm-twisting, by all reports)—the two letters printed above.*

How ironic that Derrida, who provides a language for criticizing power and for deconstructing the imperialisms of authorship, now parades himself, to the cheers of his acolytes, as the very psychopomp of power, who threatens to resort to the oldest and crudest of weapons, the police.

T. SHEEHAN, Letter to the *New York Review of Books,* April 22, 1993, 69.

I cannot comment on the validity of Sheehan's initial claim, but I agree with him that Derrida's general reaction to the Heidegger book, and to Sheehan's review, was bullying. In an identical and breathtakingly derivative move, Eisenman could only muster seventeen friends to wreak vengeance on Ghirardo in an equally browbeating overkill of a reaction (P. Eisenman et al., "Eisenman Responds," *Progressive Architecture,* February 1995, 88–91). In four densely printed pages they were allowed to present a critique of Ghirardo some ten times the length of her own article (although with about one-tenth the intelligibility).

The Field through Time

A Threefold Social Space

So far I have outlined the field's synchronic structure, that existing at any given moment. In this chapter I want to discuss its changing structure through time.[1] I begin this analysis by noting that the architects in the field cannot be regarded as a homogeneous whole, but must be treated according to their location in the field's social space, a space that is structured by the amount and type of material and symbolic capital possessed by architects, and by the relations between them. Extending the concept beyond Bourdieu's use of the term, the social space of architects can be viewed as an environment, rather like a biological environment, in which architects compete for resources. The history of the architectural community—its size, growth, expansion or contraction—depends on the absolute size of that environment, and on the quantity and nature of the resources supplied by it. Just as Bourdieu conceives of social space as one in which both symbolic and economic capitals operate, so I conceive of the architectural environment as one that provides both symbolic and economic resources. Just as architects can be differentiated by the amount of economic and symbolic capital they possess, they can also be differentiated by their environments: some live in contexts dominated by the economic, others in habitats dominated by the symbolic.

Although it is a continuum, the social space of the architect can be approximated by a threefold division based on the nature of the dominant resources involved: these can be labeled the economic, intermediate, and symbolic sectors. Since each group of architects lives in a different environment, the historical dynamics of each vary. But despite the variations, the processes operating in all environments are similar in that individuals are engaged in competition for finite resources, and this competition puts limits on the size of the community and its rate and type of growth.

At one end of the spectrum of environments is the vast body of workaday practitioners, living in a world dominated by the economic. In this subfield (which I also refer to as the subordinate sector) the essential reward is money and satisfaction from a task well done. Individuals compete on the basis of their marketable skills and the basic resource for which they compete is the job. Doing well means getting a good job with a good practice. The number of practitioners is ultimately limited by factors such as the amount of building work done and the market opportunities available to architects. The world can afford to have only so many architects, because there is only so much work for them to do. The history of the profession is in part the history of its attempts to expand its environment and the resources available in that environment so as to be able to support more architects: fending off the rapacities of other occupations, seeking protection from predators via licensing, obtaining more clients (resources) by providing more services, and so on. This sector has no control over the economic forces that dominate it, and must feel the full effects of the cycles of the national economy.

Consider now the characteristics of the smallest and most prestigious subfield, located at the other end of the continuum. The most eminent architects have the greatest amounts of symbolic capital. They exist in a space dominated by the symbolic and by symbolic resources. In this sector the reward sought is reputation for the highest creativity, reputation to be passed down to posterity. Competition is based on convincing the field to accept one's own ideas about what architecture is and how it should be done, and to realize these ideas in built form. The resource at stake is not a material one, but intellectual or symbolic shares of the intellectual field. Doing well means carving out a niche in the discourse of architecture, being a topic of conversation among others, and acquiring enduring fame.

Just as the size of the subfield of the economically dominated is limited by the resources available to it, so too is the size of the subfield of the greats. There is only so much money to go around, and so also is there only so much reputation, fame, kudos, call it what you will, to "sustain" the great. Randall Collins has developed this principle in his work on philosophers:

> I would suggest there is structurally room for only a limited number of creative intellectuals of high eminence in a field at one time (I have referred to this elsewhere as "the law of small numbers"). Hence the "market opportunities" are constrained by one's rivals in the competitive field. What counts as creative by being socially validated in the intellectual network, is determined not merely by individual background traits . . . but also by the unfolding of the structure of opportunities for everyone else in the field at that time.[2]

Collins's theory of the social dynamics of intellectuals can be usefully deployed to flesh out the model presented here. With a clarity unusual for a sociologist, he argues that the essential engine of intellectual history is conflict between individuals, competition to appropriate and elaborate existing intellectual capital.[3] This is a very similar formulation to Bourdieu's idea of a field as a battlefield. Two sorts of processes are at work. One operates across space, synchronically, as individuals compete for eminence. The behaviors observed depend on the structure of the field: how many individuals there are, where they are in their creative life cycle, the number of newcomers compared to established practitioners, and the linkages between them. The second process operates across time, as architects transmit symbolic capitals to each other through networks of personal relations.

Not every architect can dominate the field, for to dominate is to dominate others. Leaders must have followers, for otherwise they lead no one but themselves. Collins's argument is that intellectuals operate in a particular sort of social space that defines the limits of the possible. These limits are set not only by the nature of the field in which they operate in their lifetimes, but also by the subsequent history of the field. To say that there is room for only so many of the highest eminence is also to say that succeeding generations will look back and make their own judgments as to genius, raising some and lowering others, allowing only so many to be truly eminent.

At any particular time the intellectual field has room for only so many geniuses. If the symbolic space is already crowded with eminence then newcomers will experience difficulty in obtaining recognition, having to remain in the shadows of the great until the great have become shades. As the great leave the field they open up opportunities for others: perhaps epigones, successors, and heirs apparent, those who continue the work of their predecessors; perhaps rebels and heretics and new avant-gardes.

A Study of Architectural History

No architect enters the pantheon of the great and the good by aiming for purely economic success. Those who pass their reputations down to posterity, those whose goals are the symbolic rewards of acclamation for genius, live—virtually by definition—in a symbolic environment. The first problem to consider is just who these eminent architects are. There can be no question of making the selection of individuals or buildings oneself. That would be an act of the grossest presumption, leaving a professional historian open to charges of arbitrariness and subjectivity.

If a single individual, even a historian, cannot provide the fundamental data, then perhaps allowing many individuals to generate the selection is the answer. That was the solution I have adopted here, by deriving all the data from the massive *Macmillan Encyclopedia of Architects* (*MEA*). This huge work of four volumes and 2,400 pages is, as its editor-in-chief has said, "the most comprehensive assemblage of architectural biography ever attempted."[4] It contains some 2,600 biographies, varying in length from brief mentions to major essays. One historian has referred to it as "one of the indispensable publications of recent years."[5] Reviewing it for the *Journal of the Society of Architectural Historians*, the eminent historian James O'Gorman writes:

> This, then, is the flower of our generation's erudition. . . . It is a welcome addition to the reference shelf. . . . For this is a major monument of synthetic scholarship of our generation and a not-so-minor miracle of modern publishing.[6]

Is the *MEA* Biased?

It is clear that efforts were made to ensure that the architects included in the *MEA* represented some sort of consensus from the community of historians as to who has been important and who has not:

No wonder the encyclopedia's editorial board faced countless dilemmas as to whom to include and whom to leave out. Wherever possible we came down in favor of inclusion; the vernacular builder, the modest but masterly craftsman, the fantastic maverick, the accomplished amateur, and most importantly, the woman architect whose contribution has frequently been suppressed or concealed.

A. PLACZEK, "Foreword," in *Macmillan Encyclopedia of Architects*, ed. A. Placzek (New York: Macmillan, 1982), xii.

The editors of the Macmillan Encyclopedia of Architects had to balance their own preferences, knowledge of the material, and judgement concerning the relative importance of each architect with the realities of time and space as well as strong suggestions offered by regional advisors and local architectural historians for inclusive representation of their own areas. . . . [The] board enlarged the scope of the encyclopedia to include engineers, bridge builders, landscape architects, town planners, a few patrons, and a handful of writers, if their contributions were so influential as to have changed the face of the human environment. At the request of the editors, specialized advisors throughout the world reviewed the new table of contents, suggesting additions and deletions.

B. A. CHERNOW, "Introduction," in *Macmillan Encyclopedia of Architects*, ed. A. Placzek (New York: Macmillan, 1982), xv–xvi.

With an authorship of more than 600 individuals, it might be expected that it would be immune to criticisms of bias or subjectivity. Not so. The historian James O'Gorman spends most of his review censuring the encyclopedia on precisely these grounds:

Still, who got in and who did not seems capricious. . . . Edwin A. Abbey is in because he did some murals at the Boston Public Library. So did Puvis de Chavannes and John Singer Sargent, both of whom are (rightly) absent from the Encyclopedia. John Frazee is in because he carved some marble fireplace frames, but Daniel Chester French, whose sculptural contribution to the Lincoln Memorial had major architectural consequences, is not. Giacomo Balla is included in this encyclopedia even though his entry says specifically that he was "not an architect". . . . Among patrons, William Beckford is here; why not the Medici family, Louis XIV, Nelson Rockefeller, or you-fill-in-the-blank? Some 20th-century historians are in, some are not. . . . The same imbalance marks the selection of engineers and builders. . . . One Clarence Schmidt, who

seems to have knocked together a big shack in Woodstock, New York, opens volume four, but T. C. Hine of Nottingham, a major Midlands Victorian architect, and Howard Van Doren Shaw of Chicago, who housed a generation of mid-westerners in alternatives to the Prairie School, are not. Here as elsewhere the selection smacks of an unfortunate trendiness. . . . In general, to end this litany, there are many names listed that would never be sought in a dictionary of architects, and there are many expected names that fail to appear.
J. F. O'GORMAN, "Review of the Macmillan Encyclopedia of Architects," *Journal of the Society of Architectural Historians* 43, no. 1 (1984): 78–79.

Is an analysis of architectural history using a database derived from the *MEA* really an analysis of the realities of history, or is it an exploration of the prejudices of the editors and contributors? It is certainly not for me, as a sociologist of architecture, to offer my own judgments in the face of those of over six hundred historians. It seems to me that the proper attitude to take is to recall that *a field is self-defining*. The only criterion for membership in a field is being able to exert some effect in it. The *MEA* serves quite well to define the canon of the field as the field saw itself in the late 1970s. Questions as to whether so-and-so should be allotted more or less space, or be included or not, are examples of the moderate level of dissension that exists in any field. In a sense, the question of bias has no meaning. It assumes that there is some objective historical reality against which bias could be assessed. (See A. Tucker, "Contemporary Philosophy of Historiography," *Philosophy of the Social Sciences* 27, no. 1 [1997]: 102–129, for a discussion.)

Its pedigree is impressive: more than six hundred contributors from twenty-six countries, representing, according to its senior editor, "almost the entire community of scholars from the most widely recognized to the emerging generation of researchers."[7] Here, clearly, is a work that draws on the scholarship of a substantial proportion of the global community of architectural historians. I have used it to construct a database of noted architects.[8]

A breakdown of the architects of the *MEA* is given in table 4.1. This includes every individual with his or her own entry, together with all those mentioned in the articles on architectural firms and architectural families (mainly medieval masons): a total of 2,654 individuals. The editors of the *MEA* tried to keep the coverage broad by including many individuals, not strictly architects. Even so, 81 percent (2,144) of the total were architects (or masons) their whole working lives, and a further 11 percent (297) devoted themselves to architecture for a major part of their lives.[9] Only 8 percent (213) could not in any way be described as architects, masons, or building designers.

The *MEA*'s editor-in-chief and the senior editor explicitly stated that entry length was directly dependent on each architect's assessed importance. By counting column inches, some have used this for their own purposes as an indicator of architectural importance.[10] I used a simpler but more robust measure, dividing the architects into four categories: first-, second-, third- and fourth-order (table 4.2). To reside in the first-order category an individual had to have an entry of several pages. Those with entries about a page long were assigned to the second-order category. Those with entries about one column long (half a page) were designated as third-order, and all the rest, with entries of a fraction of a column, were grouped as fourth-order.

The *MEA* provides a selective list of works for each individual. I made a random selection of 38 percent (996 architects) for whom to obtain buildings data, and checked to ensure that each period, importance, and nationality were proportionately represented. The result was a total of 9,999 works (a purely fortuitous total), for each of which was noted its place, date, and type. The location was identifiable for every building, but the type could not be readily identified for 1 percent (122), nor the dates for about 1 percent (79).

The Vasari Database

In tribute to the Renaissance biographer of the arts, I named the database derived from the *MEA* the Vasari database. For each person with a biography in the *MEA* the following information was recorded:

• Birth and death dates were available for 91 percent (2,403). I was concerned with when architects entered and left the field, so the chronology of interest was not their birth or death per se, but the period of their creative lives. In general I used the standard method of taking an individual's creative period (known as the *floruit*) as extending from the age of forty to death. When birth or death dates were unavailable, I used the dates of their first and last buildings to determine this for a further 7 percent (177). Dates were therefore assignable to 2,580 individuals (97 percent).

• Nationality was unexpectedly easy to determine, given that the *MEA* covers architects from Imhotep forward. The intent was to capture the mentalities created by virtue of being born in a certain place in a certain time rather than formal citizenship. In only a very few cases—mainly medieval—was nationality problematic, and then I used ethnicity as the guide rather than formal national boundaries. In the case of migrants, I took nationality as that of their birthland if they emigrated after the teen years or so, and the country of settlement if they emigrated before. Thus Marcel Breuer was classified as Hungarian, not as American.

• The individual's place of education was the institution at which he or she obtained his or her first formal qualification, regardless of whether it was architectural. Less than 32 percent (837) received a formal education.

• Original occupation recorded individuals' intended career, as evinced by their initial training or job. So Josef Albers was classed as an elementary school teacher because he spent the first years of his working life in that occupation.

• If someone's life's work included anything other than designing buildings, I noted this as a major activity. Minor interests, hobbies, and pure dilettantism were ignored. Albers's lifetime of teaching design subsequent to his stint as a school teacher was thus recorded as such an activity. A total of 2,266 activities were recorded. If an individual started in a field other than architecture, and later turned to building design, architecture was then listed as a major activity. There were 297 such individuals.

• Finally, I noted connections or links between architects. I noted four types of connection: master, pupil, colleague, or rival. If an architect was mentioned as working in another's office, as having worked under him or her, or being taught by him or her, I registered a master-pupil relationship. Architects who worked together, or who were recorded as being close friends, or in a circle of acquaintanceship, I noted as colleagues. Sometimes a biography specifically mentioned architects as opponents, which I registered as rivalry. There are a total of 2,293 connections between architects.

4

The Field through Time

	Number	Percent
Main occupation of architect or mason	2,144	81
Of the rest, those with architect or mason as a major activity	297	11
Total architects	*2,441*	*92*
Visual artists	39	>1
Engineers	35	>1
Landscape designers	22	<1
Architectural theorists and historians	17	<1
Town planners	10	<1
All others	90	3
Total non-architects	*213*	*8*
Grand total	2,654	100

Table 4.1 Composition of the individuals of the *MEA*.

A Portrait of the Architect

Let us start with the overall characteristics of the encyclopedia's architects to gain a first impression of the field. What pursuits apart from building design can architects typically number among their accomplishments? I assigned to each individual a list of activities as described in his or her bibliography. The end result was a compendium of forty-five pursuits that architects have also followed, including such oddities as embalmer and postal worker.

Only seven activities counted as pursuits among five percent or more of the architects: architectural theory, architectural education, civil service, visual arts, teaching, engineering, and urban planning. Those listed as theorists (11 percent or 281 individuals) made some major theoretical contribution to the field—by writing books or articles, engaging in public activity, conducting speaking tours or some such—above and beyond the influence their designs alone had. Those in architectural education (8 percent, 218) held a position in an architecture school or institution. Personal master-apprentice relationships, being so ubiquitous, did not count for this category. Architects in the civil service (7 percent, 190) held some

Importance	Number	Percent
First	114	4
Second	278	10
Third	475	18
Fourth	1,787	67
Total	2,654	100

Table 4.2 Composition of the *MEA*, by importance of architect.

sort of government or state position, not necessarily as an architect. Award of a state commission to design one or more buildings did not qualify an architect as a civil servant. Visual arts (7 percent, 174) include all those who also made some sort of contribution in painting, fresco work, sculpture, and so on. Excluded from this category were those who would be considered interior designers, specializing in the internal decoration of buildings by whatever means (3 percent of the whole). Teaching (6 percent, 146) includes only those who taught at the high school level or below. It specifically excludes the teaching of architecture and allied occupations, and teaching at the tertiary level or above. Those included in engineering (5 percent, 126) produced works such as bridges, fortifications and other works designed today in the Anglo-American world by civil, military, and other engineers. The activity of urban planning (5 percent, 124) was used to represent all those who designed on a grander scale than the single building or complex, whether in modern America or baroque France, and not simply those labeled as planners.

The seven most common activity types total 1,258 instances, thereby accounting for 55 percent of the 2,266 in the database, with the other thirty-eight pursuits making up the remaining 45 percent. For some individuals "architecture" itself was listed as a major activity. These were people who started in a different occupation and later moved into building design. If we remove this category from the total, we have 1,925 activities in all.

Some questions of interest are answered by the data. Is architecture the sort of creative endeavor that draws in people from other occupations? Do the individuals entering it bring with them skills developed in other areas? Are architects polymaths, turning their attentions to creative adventures beyond their chosen occupation? There is certainly a vague general conception within the profession that architects have historically been individuals of many talents. If this is so, the evidence here does not support it.

I was generous in allocating activities to architects, but even so every ten architects could count among them only about seven (7.3) non-design pursuits that otherwise engaged their time. For almost three of the ten no major life interest could be discerned apart from building design itself. If we peruse the data for evidence of the broad interests and talents of architects we must be disappointed. If we merge the categories of architectural theory and architectural education into one category of "architecture," then every ten architects could number between them only 5.4 pursuits beyond those associated with their occupation. To put it another way, if one were to pull an individual at random from the *MEA* there would be just over a fifty-fifty chance of discovering any evidence at all that architects can see past what is often referred to as the "calling."

When exemplars of prodigiously talented polymaths—typically Wren, Jefferson, and Michelangelo—are brought out to demonstrate the versatility of the architect, one must suspect that these so often come to mind precisely because they are exceptions, not the rule.

Two other features should be noted. First, there seems to be little relationship between skill in the other visual arts and in architecture. Only 7 percent of all individuals included this as a pursuit. The proportion is greatest before 1700, when 16 percent of all architects pursued an art outside of architecture. Second, architects are not career-changers. Overall, fully 88 percent of all architects begin their lives in architecture (and stay there). Individuals are not recruited into architecture from other occupations, nor do they enter architecture late in life. Only before 1800 was there a significant presence of individuals who commenced careers in occupations other than architecture, turning to building design at some later point, as some 24 percent (before 1700) to 22 percent (during the 1700s) of them did. In our own century the social closure of the profession has ensured that a very high 94 percent of eminent architects have made this their only life's venture.

The Architects' Nationalities

Fifty-two regions or nations gave birth to the *MEA*'s architects. Of these, thirty-five produced less than one percent of the total. The remaining nations, and the proportions of architects they produced, are listed in table 4.3. Five regions clearly dominate: England, Italy, the United States, France, and Germany. Together they account for over two-thirds of all the architects the field has chosen to remember. Adding the next quartet of the Low Countries, Spain, Scotland, and Austria brings the total to some 80 percent of the whole.

That there is such a concentration is unsurprising. One does not have to posit parochiality to account for the overrepresentation of a few nations. The social world is not an egalitarian place in which each contributes or produces proportionately. Global assets, for example, are grossly unequally distributed, with about 9 percent of the world's population (in the U.S., Japan, and Germany) enjoying 50 percent of its wealth. A similar distribution applies to popular music, where 3 percent of all the artists making the U.S. Top Forty account for over half of the songs ever reaching that measure of popularity.[11] Of the thousands of classical composers, just three (Mozart, Beethoven, and Bach) have authored roughly 20 percent of the classical music that major orchestras regularly perform.[12] In the *MEA* itself, the most important four percent of architects account for about a third of its pages. These are examples of what is sometimes colloquially called the 80/20 rule, which says that the most productive 20 percent of sources account for 80 percent of the product. The precise numbers vary, of course. In the case of the *MEA*'s architects, the most productive 20 percent of architects account for about 50 percent of all the buildings listed.[13]

The Architects' Buildings

Table 4.4 shows the types of building designed by the random sample of architects I selected from the *MEA*.[14] The preponderance of single-family private residential work and religious buildings is quite striking. This illustrates the two prime social functions of the field. Private residences show their residents' taste and superiority over the lower orders. Religious buildings are structures of power. In Bourdivin terms, the former are illustrative of how architecture functions to maintain the dominance of

Age and Achievement

It is generally felt that architects are something like painters, living long and producing well into their old age. Placzek celebrated their longevity in the *MEA*'s introduction thus:

Unlike so many of the great poets and musicians, great architects are a peculiarly long-lived lot. They are tough. Dealing with material, structure, and society's demands, they have always had to be. Among the encyclopedia's twenty most outstanding architects, only two—Raphael and H. H. Richardson—died before they were fifty, and several did their finest work after they were seventy.

A. Placzek, "Foreword," in *Macmillan Encyclopedia of Architects*, ed. A. Placzek, 4 vols. (New York: Macmillan, 1982), xii.

This impression is more or less borne out by the encyclopedia. Of the deceased architects for whom lifespans were calculable (2,091), a full 24 percent (510) reached their eightieth year. Whether this is an unusual achievement is another question. In order to be remembered by posterity, individuals must have lived long enough to produce something of note, which implies that they lived to be at least 30 (only mathematics and poetry seem to be full of precocious achievers). Having reached that age, the expectation is for another 30 (in the seventeenth century) to 50 (in the twentieth century) years of life. While there is not necessarily any relation between the quantity of creative work in a lifetime and its quality, leaving a large oeuvre behind certainly enhances the chances of maintaining a reputation through time. The simple fact that individuals who live long and produce a lot have a natural advantage over those who die early and produce little, means that groups of distinguished creators will tend to have longer lifespans than for the rest of society, especially for periods prior to about 1850. We find from the Vasari database that the average lifespan of architects dying before 1700 is 68 years, and for those dying in our own century it is 72 years.

A further examination of the database reveals two unexpected facts. The first is the remarkable constancy in the productivity characteristics of architects through all the changes in the occupation from 1700 right through to the present: architects have usually produced their first notable work by 32 or 33 years of age and their last at 57 or 58 for a total median working life of 25 years. This seems a surprisingly premature termination to the period of architectural creativity. Second, contrary to my expectation at least, before 1700 architects designed their first building and reached the midpoint of their careers slightly later in life than those born in the following centuries.

More detail can be obtained by plotting creativity by decade of life, but for this to be meaningful some comparison with other fields is needed. Care is required in this. A straightforward tallying of works and the ages of their accomplishment is methodologically inadequate, as the data would be obfuscated by differences in lifespans. If, for example, it so happened that poets tended to die young, and architects not, then such a tallying would misleadingly show poets to be more productive when young. To remove the effects of such unfortunate accidents of longevity a longitudinal study is required, one that matches individuals of like lifespans.

The method chosen here was to plot the productivity only of those architects who survived to at least the age of 79. (Octagenarians produced about one percent of their total output after the age of 80.) This is shown in figure 4.1, which charts architectural productivity by decade and compares it to the productivity of scientists, humanists (historians, philosophers, novelists, "scholars"), and musicians obtained from a similar study conducted by Dennis (see W. Dennis, "Creative Productivity Between the Ages of 20 and 80 Years," *Journal of Gerontology* 21 [1966]: 1–8). The architects' productivity curve is similar to that of musicians, differing mainly in that architects produce rather less in their twenties and more in their seventies. Compared to the scientists and humanists, though, elderly architects are poor producers. In their sixties and seventies architects are only about half as productive as either group. Contrary to common wisdom, it would seem that architecture is a game for neither the young nor the old, but rather for the middle-aged.

Region	Number	Percent	Region	Number	Percent
England	436	16	Russia	39	1
Italy	420	16	Bohemia	38	1
U.S.A.	406	15	Canada	38	1
France	334	13	Sweden	37	1
Germany	224	8	Denmark	36	1
Low Countries	105	4	Ireland	33	1
Spain	85	3	Greece	29	1
Scotland	79	3	Japan	26	1
Austria	51	2	All 35 others	237	9

Table 4.3 Nationalities of the architects. (Percentage produced by each region contributing at least one percent.)

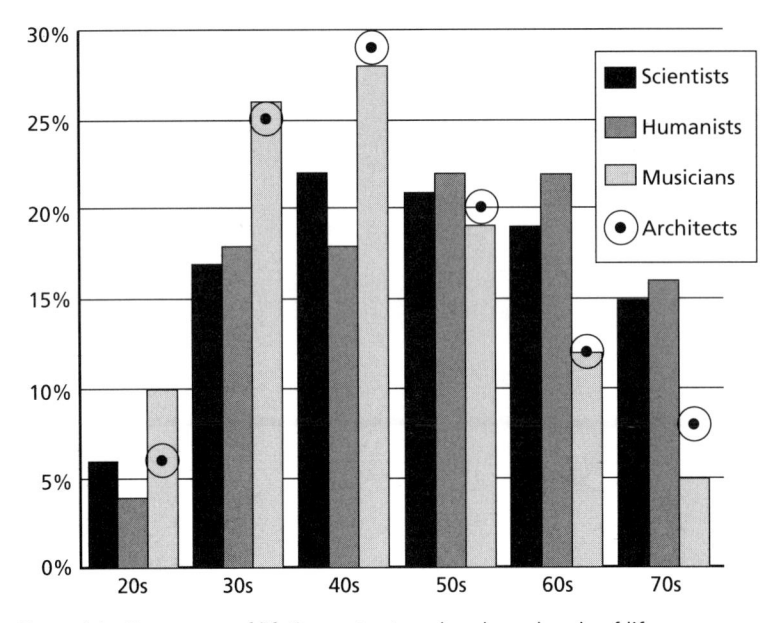

Figure 4.1 Percentage of lifetime output produced per decade of life.

Use	Number	Percent	Use	Number	Percent
Single-family residential	3,235	33	Urban	211	2
Religious	1,952	20	Medical and scientific	199	2
Commercial	856	9	Landscape	181	2
Municipal	787	8	Manufacturing	168	2
Educational	584	6	Military	126	1
State	396	4	Monument	116	1
Transport	384	4	Sports	56	< 1
Multiple residential	328	3	Theater	21	< 1
Exhibition	245	2	Unknown	122	1

Table 4.4   Buildings designed by *MEA* architects, classified by use.

individual members of the dominant classes, the latter of how it works to maintain that of the upper classes as a whole.

Historical Growth of the Architectural Community

I divided historical time into pentads[15] and calculated the number of *MEA* architects that flourished in each period. As in all analyses presented in this chapter, the raw data was subjected to a smoothing procedure. Smoothing is a process commonly used to render visible important patterns that would otherwise be lost in the random noise of the data. Figure 4.2 presents the basic growth in the numbers of eminent architects for the period from 1300 to the time of the *MEA*'s publication in 1982 (the pentad beginning 1980).

Temporal Limits
Let us be clear about the temporal boundaries of this discussion. The first is one at around 1400. Before that time the *MEA* lists hardly any individuals: only 110 flourished in the entire period before 1400, and only a handful are listed as being alive at any one time through the 1300s. The fifteenth century is therefore the first we may meaningfully bring into our

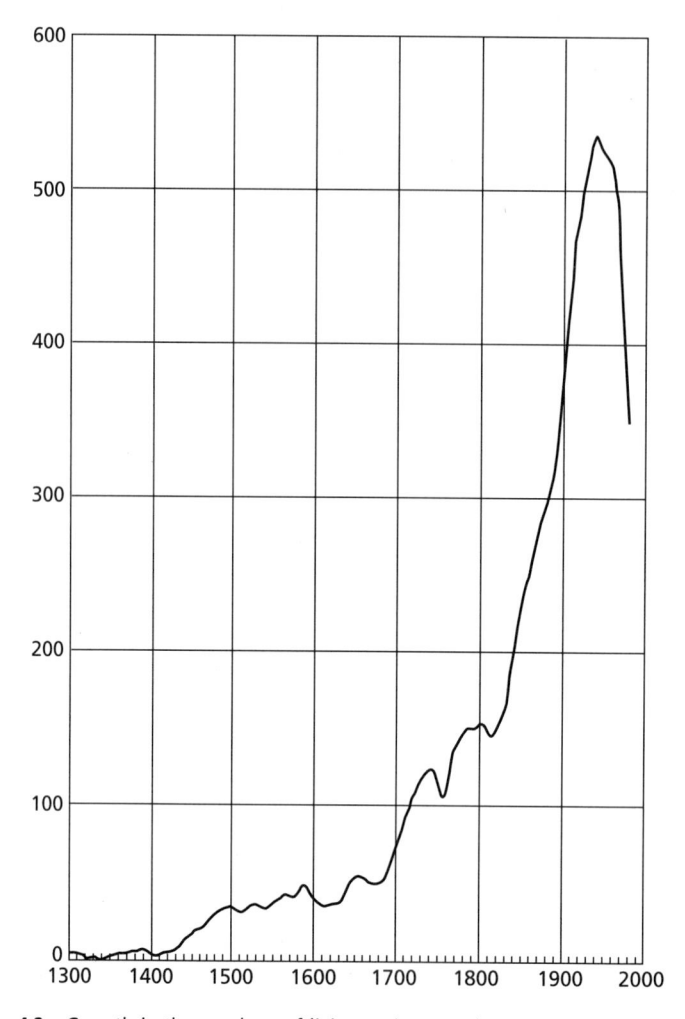

Figure 4.2 Growth in the numbers of living eminent architects. Number alive in each pentad from 1300 to 1980.

discussion. Taking the year 1400 as our starting point neatly coincides with Vasari's pronouncement that the competition in 1401 between Ghiberti and Brunelleschi, amongst others, for the second set of doors to the Florence Baptistery, marked the beginning of "modern" architecture. In general, the sparseness of data in precisely 1400 will compel us to start a few years later, in 1420 to 1450.

If this anterior parameter is easy to establish, the posterior is rather more difficult. The last possible pentad is 1980–1984, since the encyclopedia was published in 1982. Something peculiar is clearly going on after the architectural population peaks in the pentad 1940–1944 with 536 individuals. By the last pentad (1980) the population has dropped to only 351, about the same as in 1895. One cause of this must be the *MEA*'s inclusion criterion, which admitted only those born before 1931. These architects would appear in the data to be flourishing from their fortieth birthday, the pentad 1970–1974. This would then be the last pentad in which entrants could appear, and a deficit could be expected in the remaining two (1975, 1980). Yet this could have had no effect on the steep decline from 1945 on.

The most reasonable explanation is that the decline is an artifact of the processes of historical assessment: the historical community has not had the time to reach a consensus on the importance of the architects working since the Second World War. The period of population decline can then be interpreted as a strong indicator of how long consensus formation takes in the community of architectural historians. (An alternative hypothesis is that the second half of our century is deficient in notable architects. This is hardly credible, especially given the extent of the decline.) The data suggest that the period of consensus formation is some forty or so years in length, from 1940 to the *MEA*'s publication in 1982. The time taken to reach consensus is significantly longer than that of the natural sciences, in which agreement over significance is typically reached over a period of some five to ten years from publication of results.[16] This will then establish the posterior boundary for our discussion, which will hereafter be concerned only with the period from 1400 to 1940.

Per Capita Growth

What sort of growth patterns should we expect in the population of notable architects? As a first approximation we might expect to find approximately the same number of architects per capita through time.

I used the population of the Western polity based on figures supplied by McEvedy and Jones, which are probably the best available.[17] Before 1400 we have only the medieval background pattern, which we can consider the baseline datum (fig. 4.4). Within the time period under our purview, a strikingly clear set of patterns presents itself, dividing the history

Geographical Limits

Along with temporal boundaries to the analysis there are geographical ones. We have seen that the *MEA* is for all intents and purposes a catalogue of Western architects, largely a simple—if regrettable—consequence of the anonymity of building designers from other areas. We can refine this notion a little by observing that the individuals and buildings of note recorded in its volumes are drawn almost entirely from the area of the ancient Roman and Iranian polities—Europe, the southern coast of the Mediterranean, and the Near East up to the Thar Desert beyond the Indus river. This is an area bounded by the Arctic Circle, Atlantic Ocean, Sahara Desert, and the Arabian Sea, borders that have historically served to keep its inhabitants in and others out. The eastern border formed by the Urals down to the Central Asian massif and the Thar Desert is more permeable, and there have always been significant relations between the Near East, East Africa, and India. But major incursions have been few. Before our temporal limit of 1400, the Mauryas (fourth century B.C.), Yue-Chih (second century B.C.), Huns (first century), Turks (sixth century), and Mongols (thirteenth century) were the only significant incursions into the area. There have been none since 1400. On the other hand, there has been a significant excursion from the region into the Americas and a few other places, starting from the sixteenth century and lasting to the present time, amounting to perhaps 65 million people, and this must be taken into account.

We can therefore take as our geographical area of interest this Western sphere and its extension into the New World: the Western polity (fig. 4.3). The geographical space so defined includes all but a minute 34 individuals mentioned in the *MEA*.

Figure 4.3 The geographical boundaries of this study: the Western polity.

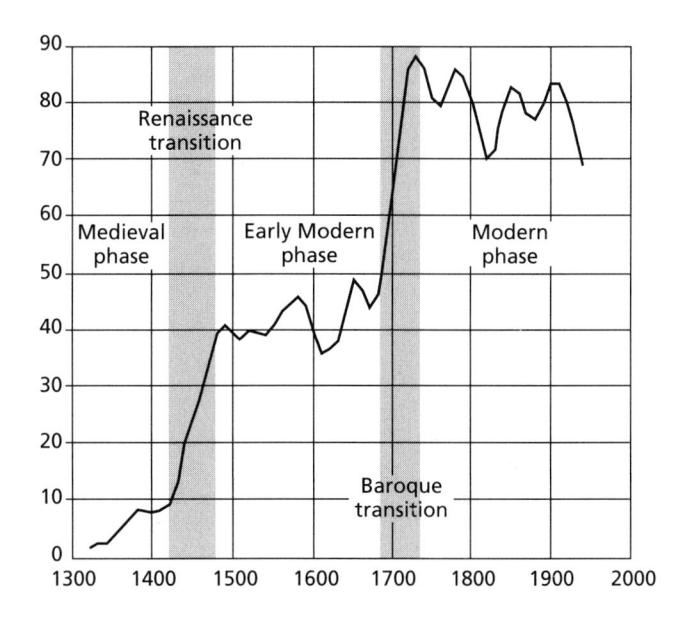

Figure 4.4 Number of architects living per 100 million people, in each decade from 1300 to 1940.

of the community into four distinct phases. The first is a rapid rise through the 1400s, obviously corresponding to the Renaissance. The curve then plateaus from about 1480 to 1680, oscillating between 35 to 50 architects per 100 million.[18] Another sharp transition follows in the years to about 1730, followed by a second plateau in which the ratio settles at 70 to 90 per 100 million.

It requires no mathematical finesse to derive these patterns, which are immediately discernible to the eye: a rapid rise, a plateau, another rapid rise, then another plateau. Uncertainties in the population figures should make us wary of searching for spurious detail, but the disjunctions among the four periods are so clear that even substantial inaccuracies in the population data would not negate the analysis. The two plateaus differ by a factor of two in the number of architects per capita.

The figure presents a surprise. The period I label Renaissance transition is entirely expected, denoting the passage from a medieval guild organization to independent artist. But the Baroque transition, a period in which the ratio of architects per capita doubles, has not been previously detected by historians. Perhaps this is because the period was not a great time of stylistic metamorphosis, but of continuity. This is the age of Wren, Hawksmoor, Vanbrugh, Fischer von Erlach, Boffrand, and Hildebrandt. The period of the transition is firmly in the middle of the Baroque period, usually held to have commenced architecturally early in the 1600s with Bernini and Bellini. The Rococo period in France does not start until the transition is well under way, in the early 1700s, and the Neoclassical not until the mid-1700s. No change in style can be mapped to either the beginning or end of the transition.

A further surprise is found if the architects are partitioned by importance. The very greatest architects, those in my first-order category, and to whom the *MEA* devotes several pages each, number only 114. This is simply a quantity too dangerously small for the sorts of analyses presented here: at any one time only a handful are alive. But if one adds to these the 278 in the second-order category, those allocated at least a page or so, then the resulting group of 392 is sufficiently large to provide a basis for robust conclusions. Let us for convenience designate them *major* architects (fig. 4.5). Those in the other two categories (third- and fourth-orders) will be designated *minor* (fig. 4.6).

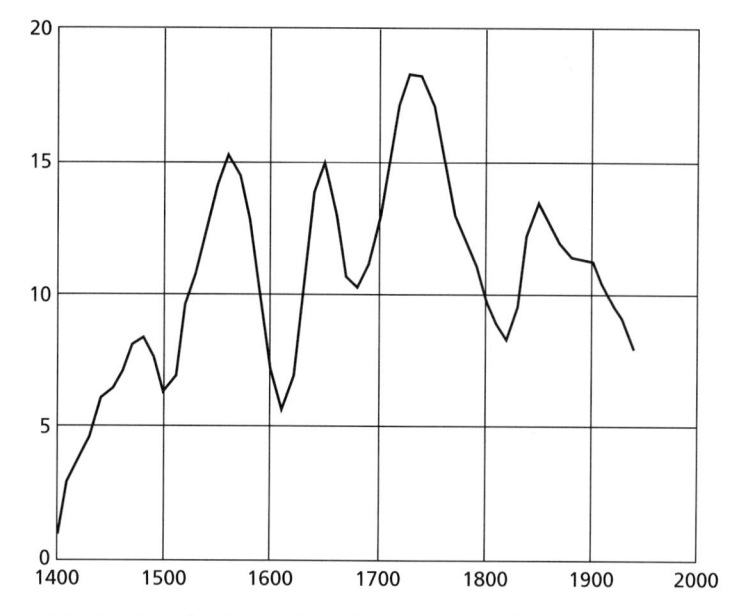

Figure 4.5 Number of major architects living per 100 million people, by decade from 1400 to 1940.

A comparison of these figures reveals that the two sectors follow strikingly different patterns of growth. The four-phase structure of the whole becomes even more pronounced for the minor community when the major architects are removed. The plateaus become a little smoother: in the first plateau, variation is now between 25 and 35 architects per 100 million per decade, and in the second between 60 and 75. On the other hand, this structure is not at all visible in the growth of the major architects. Instead there is a striking pattern of peaks and troughs.

The Two Communities of the *MEA*

We seem to have within the *MEA* two different communities, operating under different dynamics, as well as the vastly larger body of the unremembered. These three communities correspond approximately to those living in the environments of the architectural social space that I have previously denoted as dominated by symbolic resources (the major

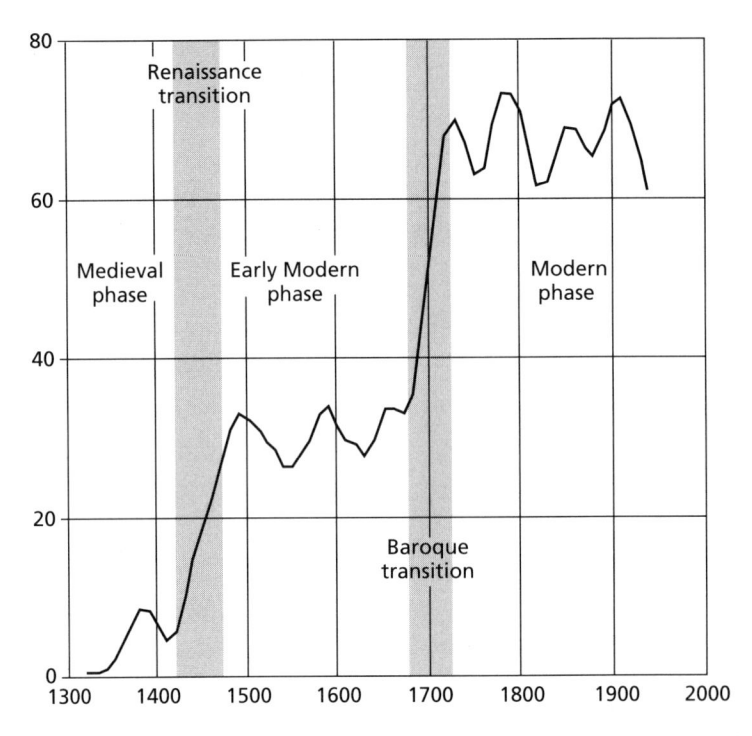

Figure 4.6 Number of minor architects living per 100 million people, by decade from 1300 to 1940.

architects); those in an intermediate environment (the minor architects); and those in an economic world (practitioners in the subordinate sector) (table 4.5). The major sector lives in a symbolic environment providing symbolic resources, and just as the body of practitioners is limited by the resources provided by its environment, so the major sector is limited by those available in its environment. Both sectors operate on ecological logics. But there are significant differences between the two. The subordinate sector lives on economic resources provided by the general socioeconomic environment, resources that it has little control over. The major sector exists within a symbolic world whose symbolic resources are produced by itself. These resources are passed down in the form of symbolic capital from architect to architect through time. Hence, the relationships between major architects—chains of masters and pupils, networks of col-

Importance in the *MEA*	Sector	Resources
First order	Major	Symbolic
Second order		
Third order	Minor	Intermediate
Fourth order		
Not listed in the *MEA*	Subordinate	Economic

Table 4.5   Summary of the sectors of the field.

leagues—help to explain the behavior of the whole. As I will show, these relationships generate the cyclic phenomena seen in the growth of the major community.

Caught between the subordinate architects and the major ones are the minor architects of the *MEA*. These live in a social space intermediate between the purely economic and the purely symbolic. They are, it will be seen, loosely connected to the networks of personal relationships connecting the major architects. They are connected sufficiently strongly to be protected from the lesser economic storms buffeting the subordinate sector, but not so strongly as to be completely unaffected.

Growth of the Major Sector

The basic pattern we should expect to find is that the size of the architectural community grows exponentially. Such growth is characteristic of living organisms, of populations (such as scientists), and of many social processes, such as economic growth.[19] The rate of growth is proportionate to the size of the population, as in any compound interest process, so that the bigger the population the greater the absolute growth.

Exponential growth can be described by a single number: by the percentage annual increase, or by the index of the exponential. These do not, however, really give much of a feel for the nature of the process described: to say that something is growing at one percent per annum rather than three percent does not convey much to the average person. More illuminating is to describe growth in terms of its doubling period, how long it will take a population to double in size. To say that something will

	Absolute numbers			Normalized to 1850 = 1		
	Profession (thousands)	Minor	Major	Profession (thousands)	Minor	Major
1850	0.6	27	15	1.0	1.0	1.0
1860	1.2	40	11	2.0	1.5	0.7
1870	2	50	18	3.3	1.9	1.2
1880	3.3	66	22	5.5	2.4	1.5
1890	8	94	27	13.3	3.5	1.8
1900	11	135	26	18.3	5.0	1.7
1910	16	153	23	26.7	5.7	1.5
1920	17	142	17	28.3	5.3	1.1
1930	23	127	17	38.3	4.7	1.1
1940	22	113	15	36.7	4.2	1.0
1950	25	109	12	41.7	4.0	0.8
1960	38	100	8	63.3	3.7	0.5
1970	57	85	8	95.0	3.1	0.5
1980	90	72	6	150.0	2.7	0.4

Table 4.6 Growth of different segments of the field in the United States. (Source: numbers for the profession are from U.S. census data.)

Producing More Architects Does Not Produce More Genius

These dynamics of the major and minor sectors are quite different from those of the body of practitioners, workaday architects. We can see this, for example, in the case of American architects, by examining the numbers of practicing architects in the United States (from U.S. census data), and the numbers of living minor and major architects (from this study) (table 4.6; the right hand shows the same data, normalized so that in each case the value for 1850 is set at 1.0).

The size of the professional population bears no relation to the number of the *MEA*'s architects living at any one time. Where the number of practitioners has increased 37-fold from 1850 to 1940 (the terminus of this study), the group of minor architects has rarely been more than fivefold its 1850 value, and the group of major architects, never more than twofold. *Producing more qualified architects simply does not have any effect on the generation of architectural genius.*

double in size in seventy years rather than twenty-four immediately conveys something that the raw annual percentage growth rates of one and three percent do not. This discussion will therefore describe growth in terms of doubling periods.

We examine the major sector first. I fitted a single exponential curve to the data, for the period 1450 to 1940. (Before 1450 the small number of architects skews the curve-fitting process.) It has a doubling time of 147 years (fig. 4.7). Figure 4.8 shows the same data when this general growth trend is removed ("residuals," in statistical terminology), showing the cycles above and beyond the expected historical growth.

Architectural creativity of the highest order is not spread evenly through time: periods of creative efflorescence are regularly followed by dearths. When architects of the first order flourish, they tend to do so in groups. In addition, this cyclic pattern is surprisingly regular. Peak follows trough at an interval of very close to fifty years on average, the peaks consistently occurring in the middle of centuries, the troughs at the turn, for a total cycle length of about a century. The pattern holds until 1870, then the expected downturn fifty years later fails to occur (table 4.7).

Growth of the Minor Sector

I also fitted exponential curves to the four phases of the minor sector revealed by the per capita data (table 4.8). The boundaries of each period were determined initially from the per capita data, then tweaked a pentad or two to provide the best exponential fit. The reader should regard the precise years as reasonable dividing points. Unfortunately, quantitative analyses such as this do require some stopping points. I am not for a moment suggesting that, for example, the Renaissance transition suddenly launched itself in the pentad commencing 1420 and ground to a halt equally suddenly in 1475.

To show the growth of the minor sector and the fitted curves, I have used a logarithmic scale on the y-axis to show the patterns more clearly (fig. 4.9). In such a scale, an exponential growth curve is depicted as a perfectly straight line. The basic pattern is that of two slow growth periods, each of about two centuries' duration, separated by two rapid-growth periods, each of about fifty years' duration. The two transition

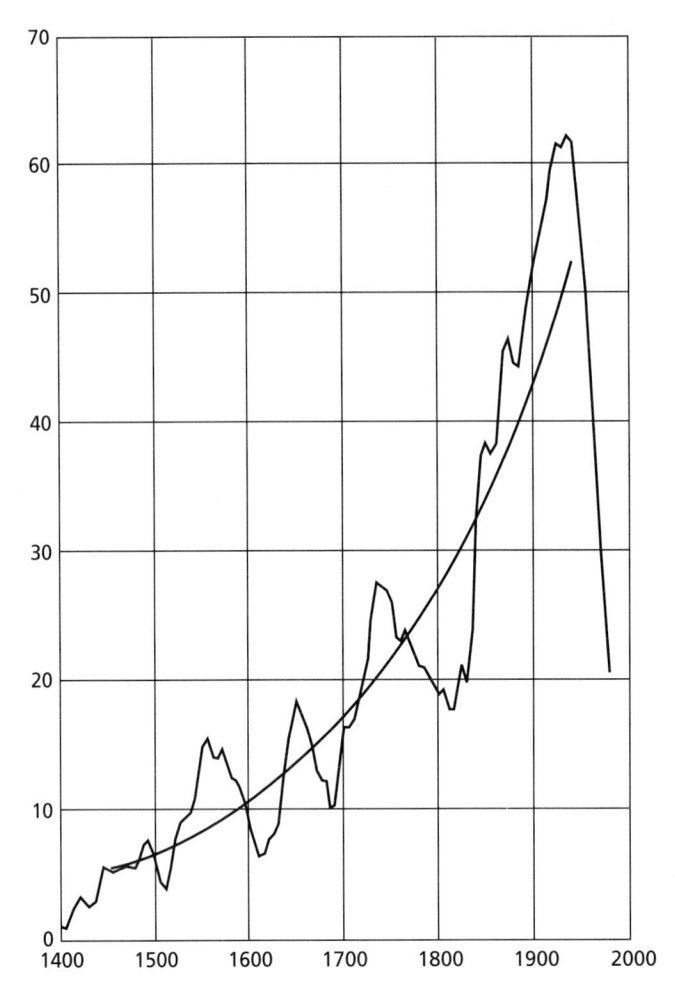

Figure 4.7 Growth of the sector of major architects, and the exponential curve plotted to fit. Numbers of architects alive in each pentad.

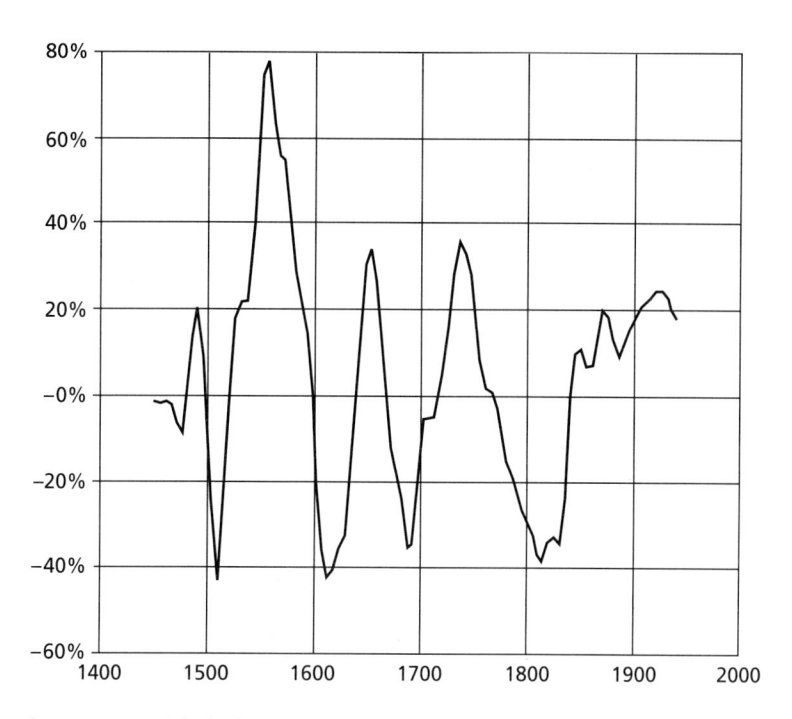

Figure 4.8 Residuals from the exponential growth trend of the sector of major architects.

Approximate center	Type	Examples for peak periods	Number of major architects alive
1480?	Peak	Alberti	8 ▲
1510	Trough	70 years between peaks	4 ▼
1550	Peak	Michelangelo, Palladio, Vignola	16 ▲
1610	Trough	100 years between peaks	7 ▼
1650	Peak	Mansart, Borromini, Bernini	19 ▲
1690	Trough	90 years between peaks	9 ▼
1740	Peak	Soufflot, Blondel, Boullée	29 ▲
1810	Trough	130 years between peaks	16 ▼
1870	Peak	Renwick, Richardson, Hunt	47 ▲

Table 4.7 Structure of the growth of major architects: summary of the peak and trough cycles.

Period	Approximate boundaries	Duration (years)	Doubling time (years)
Renaissance transition	1420–1475	55	17
Early Modern	1475–1685	210	350
Baroque transition	1685–1735	50	42
Modern	1735–1940	205	81
Overall	*1420–1940*	*520*	*97*

Table 4.8 Growth rates of the four growth phases of the minor sector architects.

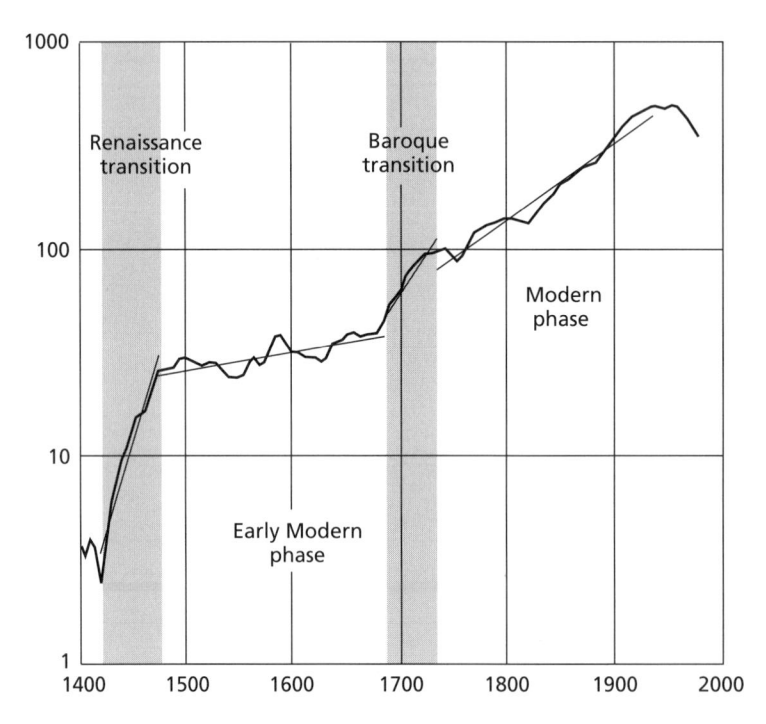

Figure 4.9 Growth of the sector of minor architects (number alive each pentad), and the exponential curves plotted to fit the four phases (logarithmic scale).

periods have fast doubling times: 17 years for the Renaissance and 42 for the Baroque. During the two plateau periods the community grew much slower: it doubled every 350 years in the Early Modern phase, and every 85 years in the Modern phase. Within the two plateau periods the growth rates are almost identical to those of the Western population.

Historical Dynamics of the Field

Let us return to viewing each population as dependent on the particular resources available to it. Each environment provides a limited amount of these resources and so can support only a limited number of individuals. The dynamics of a population are determined by the population's "natural" rate of growth—the rate of increase when there is an effectively unlimited amount of resources—and by the density of the population compared to the carrying capacity or saturation limit—the maximum number of individuals an environment can indefinitely sustain. The nearer the population is to the environment's carrying capacity, the slower it grows as individuals are obliged to compete with each other for resources.

Three broad patterns of growth are possible: exponential, logistic, and oscillating. The first occurs when the population is small compared to the carrying capacity, and growth rates are modest. The population simply continues to grow in a more or less smooth curve, unrestrained by any shortage of resources. The second, logistic, is characteristic of populations with medium growth rates in an environment with a moderate carrying capacity. At first growth is exponential, but as resources become scarcer the rate of growth slows. As the population nears and then reaches the carrying capacity growth ceases and it remains indefinitely at the saturation point. The resulting history is an S-shaped curve. The minor sector displays two such logistic curves. The third form of growth, oscillating, occurs with high growth rates and a low carrying capacity. Growth is initially exponential. Rapid growth rates increase the population before the effect of resource scarcity can be felt. The population tends to overshoot the carrying capacity. When the lack of resources becomes significant the population suffers an equally rapid fall, only to rise again as the population

The Lonely Landscape of Architectural Genius

There is one important consequence that flows from the bare fact that the architectural community has grown exponentially at a certain rate. An examination of the data shows that about one-quarter of all the notable architects who have lived are alive at any one time. For example, in 1940 there were 536 architects (major and minor) alive compared to the 2,320 who had flourished since 1400, a ratio of about 25 percent. It is a property of exponential growth that this ratio—sometimes called *immediacy*—is the same regardless of the date of the computation (for a constant growth rate), and that it depends solely on the rate of growth and the typical lifespan of individuals in the population. That is, the immediacy of a smoothly growing population would be the same regardless of whether it was measured in the year 1700 or 1900.

Compare this to the long-term growth of notable scientists, who have a doubling time of about fifty years. At this rate, the immediacy ratio is about 45 percent, so the scientists would find themselves living in an intellectual world populated by almost half the scientists who have ever lived. To these individuals, science is something being created by people who are alive now. But only one in four of all the notable architects who have ever lived are now alive (long-run immediacy of 25 percent). The intellectual world of the architect is dominated by the past. For this reason, to tell the story of science is quite different from telling the story of architecture. There is so much more history to talk about if one is an architect than if one is a scientist. No doubt this is why its own history is of so much concern to the field of architecture, in a way that it is not for any of the sciences or even for engineering. The deep sense of tradition within the architectural field arises from a simple structural property of the field, and cannot be lightly put aside.

Perhaps this phenomenon explains the lack of modesty sometimes noted in those at the very pinnacle of architectural achievement. The major sector has a doubling time even greater than that of its colleagues in the minor sector, of some 147 years. This implies an immediacy of about 17 percent. That is, at any one time, about one in six of all the very greatest architects who have ever lived are then alive. On the other hand, almost one in two of all the elite scientists who have ever lived are still working. Where the eminent scientist would see a world of eminent contemporaries, a busy and populous landscape, the great architect sees only a few other mountain peaks rising above the plains of mediocrity.

density declines. A set of cycles is the result, usually tending to diminish and converge on the saturation limit.

Dynamics of the Major Sector

An examination of various characteristics of the major sector during the turning points provides further evidence that this community behaves like a population undergoing cyclic growth. These characteristics are the average age, entry rate, exit rate, and turnover per decade of the members of the major sector. Consider first the peak periods of figure 4.8. The average age of living major architects varies over quite a wide band, from about forty to fifty years old. In general, the average age of the eminent architects just after the peak periods is in the late forties, compared to an average age of 44.5 years over all times. In the decades just after peak periods entry rates are low. Normally the community of the great is refreshed by the addition of 33 percent of its numbers to its ranks each decade. When the field is already occupied by genius this falls to about 18 percent. The years following peaks also exhibit a low turnover: fewer individuals enter, but also fewer leave.

Troughs occur when the intellectual field is sparsely populated. Major architects are, on average, some eight years younger than during the peaks, at about forty years old. Newcomers are more plentiful, with the field welcoming about four entrants for each existing ten members, and fewer of the old inhabitants survive the decade.

In an idealized version of the dynamics of the major sector (fig. 4.10), the fundamental cyclic pattern of growth is shown by the bold curve, swinging up and down every century. To summarize, when a field is crowded with eminence it is also a more stagnant one, with older architects, admitting fewer newcomers and retaining more individuals from earlier times. Those times when we see a dearth of genius are also, behind the scenes, the most dynamic: younger individuals, more entrants, fewer survivors from the old days. Taken as a whole, the picture implies some sort of validity to the ecological metaphor. The community of major architects increases until it is saturated with genius, as it were, at which point newcomers are unable to cram into the intellectual space—not necessarily through any lack of talent on their part, but because their contributions

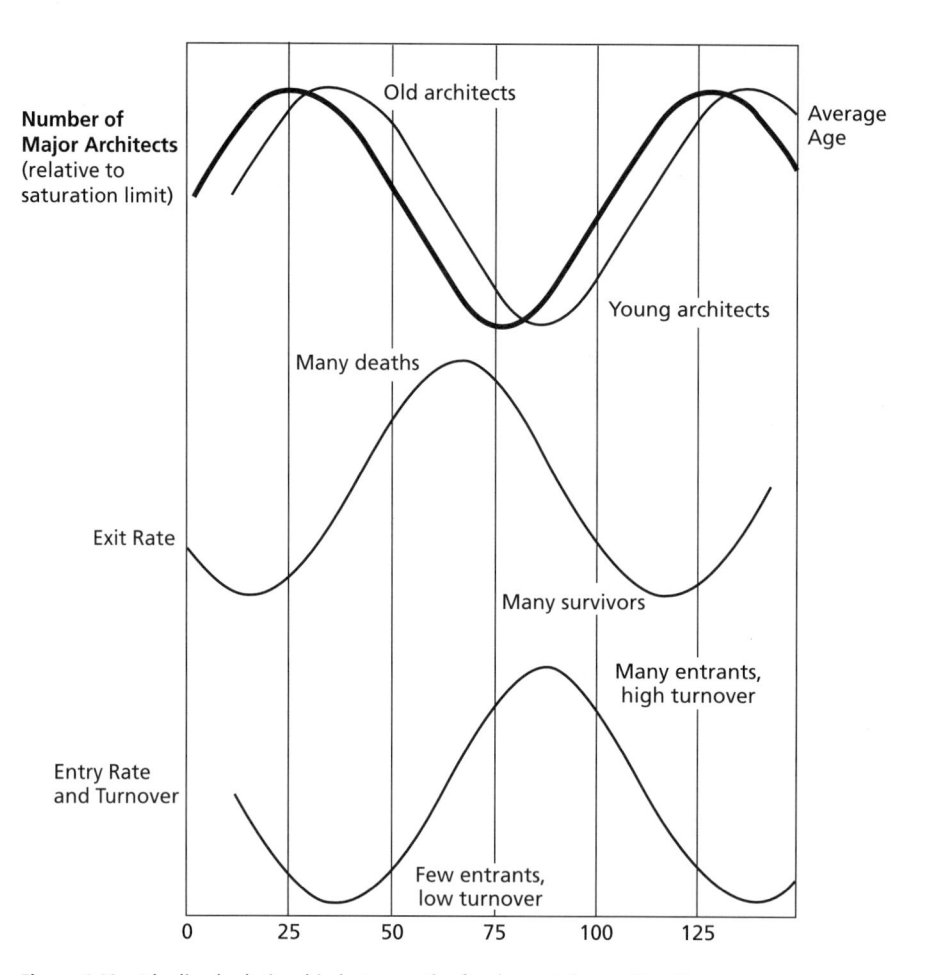

Figure 4.10 Idealized relationship between the fundamental growth pattern, average age, exit and entry rates, and turnover of the major architects. *X*-axis is time, in years. *Y*-axis is the value of the respective indicators.

are simply overshadowed by the wealth of talent already in existence. As the old die off or retire they open up opportunities for the young, creating new niches in the intellectual territory of architecture for them to explore.

How Connections between Architects Drive the Dynamics of the Major Sector
So far I have argued that the major sector is most fruitfully regarded as occupying a symbolic environment, one with finite symbolic resources,

and that the fact of this finitude puts limits on the number of the greats possible at any one time. I will now show the precise process that generates the cyclic phenomenon we have observed, and how this process also provides a mechanism linking the micro level (the individual architect) to the macro (the cycles of boom and bust).

The most fruitful path is to continue following Collins and turn to a detailed consideration of the relations between the great architects. He argues that the main social structures of an intellectual field are master-pupil chains, and that an examination of them shows that the most eminent are embedded in more chains than the lesser. In Bourdivin terms, masters pass down cultural capital to their pupils. The more eminent the master, the greater the capital that can be transmitted.[20]

Consider now the data on relations between architects. Fully one half of the major architects had a master also recorded in the *MEA*, but

Isolated Major Architects

Not every major architect belongs to a master-pupil chain, of course. Membership is not an absolutely necessary condition for eminence. Of the first-order architects in the *MEA*, those occupying several pages, only Steiner, Marchioni, Holl, Guarini, Fuga, Fathy, and Fanzago have no connections of any kind with other architects. This is seven out of 114, or six percent. Rudolf Steiner's inclusion, let alone the length of his treatment, is a minor mystery. Hasan Fathy is a "philosopher, teacher, architect, artist, poet and champion of the poor." His inclusion depends on his producing a native Egyptian architecture. Elias Holl was a mason who flourished about 1600. He was apprenticed to his father Hans, who did not make it into the *MEA*. Ferdinando Fuga (with Alessandro Galilei, mentioned below) was a pupil of Giovanni Battista Foggini, who also failed to impress the editors of the encyclopedia. Carlo Marchioni was a pupil of another absent architect, Filippo Barigioni, who had himself studied under Carlo Fontana and Mattia de Rossi, both of whom are in the *MEA*, and both of whom I classified as major. Cosimo Fanzago and Guarino Guarini seem to be genuine isolates. Apart from these, Alberti, Laugier, L'Enfant, and Galilei have collegiate connections but no masters or pupils. Thus a total of eleven (ten percent) of the greats cannot be placed in a master-pupil chain.

less than one third of the minor architects did. The disparity is greater on the output side. Again, one half of the major architects had pupils listed in the encyclopedia, but only 18 percent of the minor architects had pupils who later became eminent. About one third of the major architects (32 percent) were not in any master-pupil chain, but about six in ten (58 percent) of the minor ones were not. Again, only two in ten of the major architects had no relations (master, pupil, colleague, rival) at all with anyone else in the *MEA*, but four in ten minor architects did not.

Further information is given in figures 4.11 and 4.12.[21] These detail the number of relations for each sector, in terms of the average number of masters, pupils, or colleagues for each ten architects (to remove decimals). Every ten major architects had sixteen pupils, five of whom were also major architects, and eleven of whom were minor. They also had five major architects as masters, and four minor ones. Between them, they worked with 21 colleagues, about equally divided between major and minor. All in all they had 45 relations with others. The minor architects exist in much sparser networks, the total number of relations being only 12. The number of their pupils is strikingly smaller: every group of ten taught less than one major, and two minor architects. They also worked with substantially fewer eminent friends: about two major and three minor architects. Major architects are not only linked to many more fellow architects, but also to more eminent ones. The more eminent one is and the more eminent people one has studied under, then the more eminent one's colleagues are and the more eminent one's pupils become.

Having established the existence of master-pupil chains, we can turn to the final consideration of how these generate the particular dynamic of the hundred-year cycles found in the major sector. We return to Bourdieu and recall that one's habitus generates subjective aspirations in individuals such that they attempt what is possible given their place in the social order, a process to which he gives the rather lumbering title of the subjective expectation of objective probabilities. Habitus, being essentially the whole social order incorporated into our heads, naturally generates a more or less close fit between what one wants and what one can have. Problems arise if expectations cannot be met, if the things that a class or group believes are its due turn out to be impossible. That is, if a group's habitus is attuned to an earlier state of society it can generate

5 major architects were masters

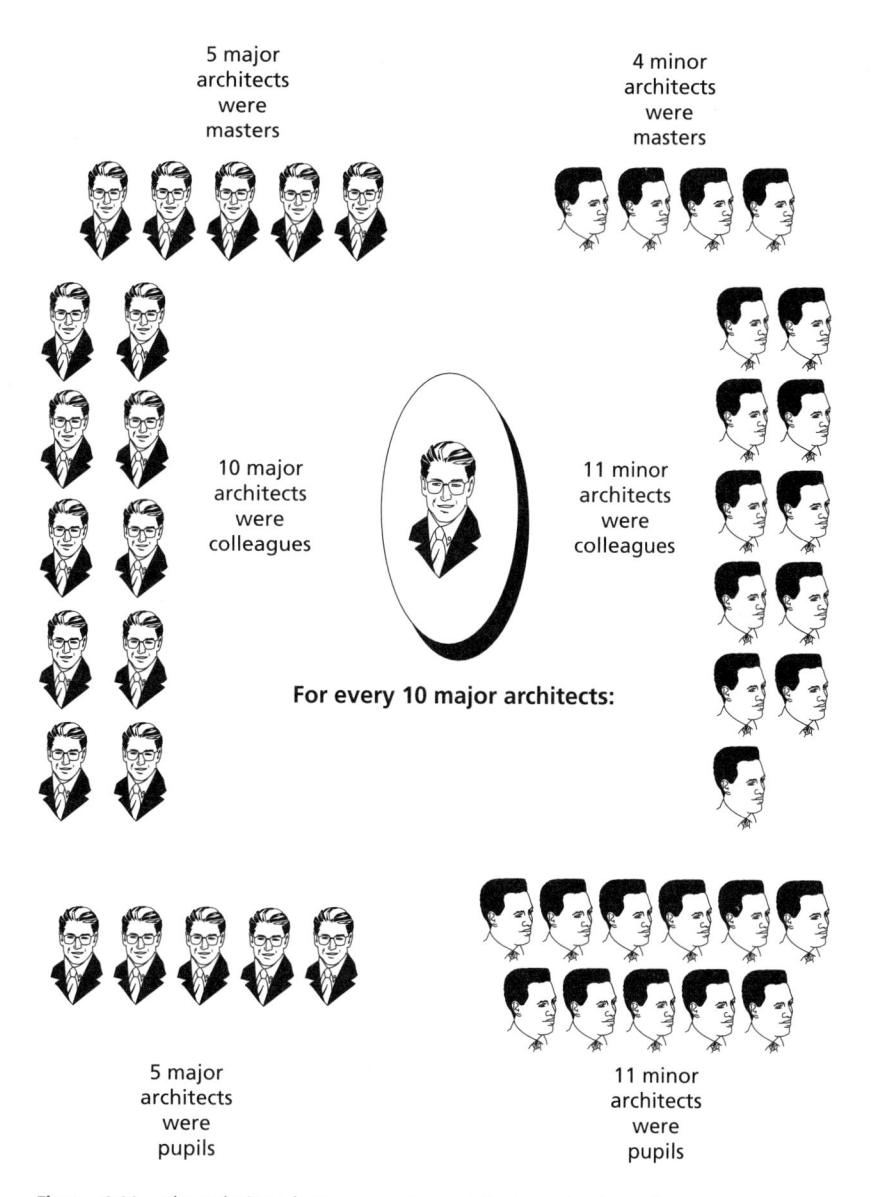

4 minor architects were masters

10 major architects were colleagues

11 minor architects were colleagues

For every 10 major architects:

5 major architects were pupils

11 minor architects were pupils

Figure 4.11 The relations between major architects and others. Numbers are for a group of ten major architects.

2 major
architects
were
masters

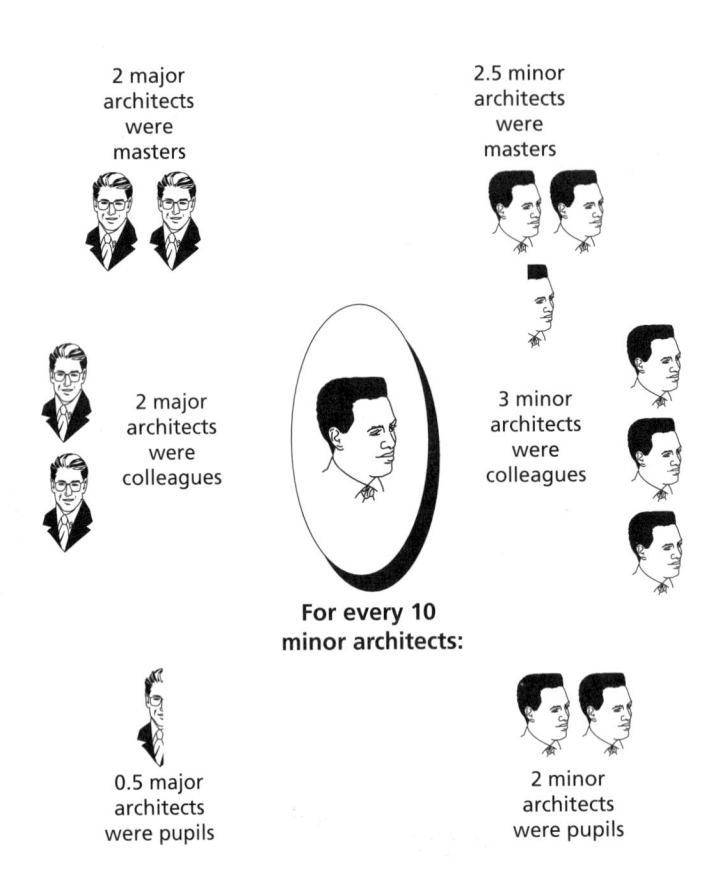

2.5 minor
architects
were
masters

2 major
architects
were
colleagues

3 minor
architects
were
colleagues

For every 10
minor architects:

0.5 major
architects
were pupils

2 minor
architects
were pupils

Figure 4.12 The relations between minor architects and others. Numbers are for a group of ten minor architects.

inappropriate dispositions and practices for the world of today (the *hysteresis effect*).²²

Personal contact with notable architects passes to the protégé, among many other things, a sense of the structure of the field, a sense of what is worth aspiring to, of the expectations that may be fulfilled, and those that may not. When the major sector is saturated with genius, individuals see fewer chances for making it to the top and aspire for less; while when creativity seems to be at a dearth they aim higher and aspire to enter into the ranks of the immortal. These aspirations and expectations are inculcated by the master-pupil chain system. The key point is that there is a lag in this system. The essential clue is that the average age difference between a master and his or her pupil is 22.1 years. In the process of inculcation undergone by the protégé, he or she will be receiving a habitus that was generated twenty years earlier, in the master's own training. The pupil's mentality, therefore, incorporates the state of the intellectual field as it was two decades before, and will contain predispositions and tastes appropriate to that time.

It is this lag that produces the cyclic phenomena we have observed. We can quantify this by using an equation from population ecology to simulate the effect of the lag in the growth of the population of major architects.²³ After substituting appropriate values for the carrying capacity and growth rate, and introducing a lag term that makes the population grow according to its size of twenty years previously, rather than its current size, cycles of hundred-year length are generated corresponding with rather surprising closeness—given the simplicity of the model—to both the temporal locations and intensities of the cycles shown in the data. By multiplying these per capita data by the actual Western population data, one returns to the architectural population size (fig. 4.13). (Note also that the data used here are figured by decade, not by pentad. The number of architects alive in a decade is necessarily higher than in a pentad, simply because the time unit is longer.)

Dynamics of the Minor Sector

The history of the minor sector falls into two distinct phases, Early Modern and Modern, in each of which the numbers of architects per capita stays

4 The Field through Time

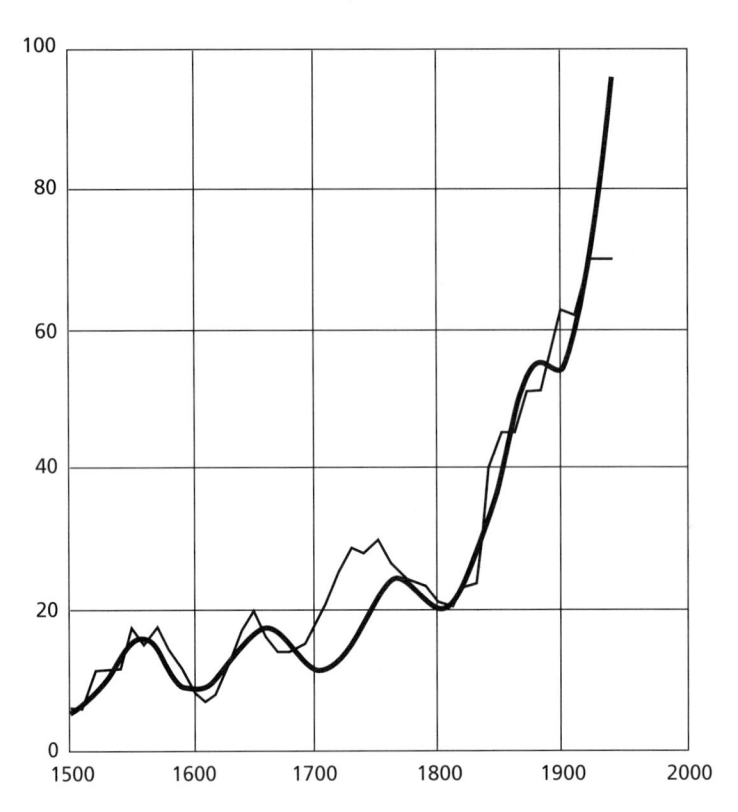

Figure 4.13 Population of the major sector in absolute numbers of living architects, by decade. Thin line is the raw data. Heavy line is the fitted growth equation.

more or less constant, separated by a transition period in the fifty or so years around 1700. The questions of interest are why the size of the field, on a per capita basis, should have remained so steady in those two periods, and why such a spectacular jump happened when it did.

The minor sector is embedded in an environment intermediate between the almost entirely symbolic world of the major sector, and the almost entirely economic world of the sector of the subordinates. Minor and major sectors are only loosely coupled. Minor architects certainly participate in the master-pupil chains that structure the major sector, but they tend to be pupils rather than pupils *and* masters, occupying terminal nodes of the network rather than being links in the chain. While half of the major architects have pupils, only 18 percent of the minor architects do. Turning to their relations with the subordinate sector, minor architects are not entirely dependent on the economic factors that regulate the demand for the subordinate sector. One can see, for example, from the American case (table 4.6) that the numbers of the minor sector are intermediate in form between the major and subordinate sectors: they do not show the explosive growth of the subordinates, but neither do they display the constancy of the majors.

The coupling between major and minor is too weak to generate the cyclic growth patterns shown for the former that would occur if the two were tightly bound. However, it is just strong enough to buffer the minor sector from the full strength of the economic forces to which the subordinates must yield. Just as the saturation limit of the major architects is determined by the size of the intellectual attention space, and that space ultimately depends on the population size, so too the minor sector has a saturation limit dependent on population size. It seems that the normal condition for the minor sector is for its population to stay near its environment's carrying capacity. This explains the stasis experienced by the minor sector in the Early Modern and Modern phases. The problem can then be rephrased as why the carrying capacity of its environment suddenly increased during the Baroque transition, almost doubling.

The basic social dynamic of the minor sector must depend on some aspect of the European socio-economic system, which was in a more or less constant state in the years prior to 1700 (Early Modern phase), underwent some type of fundamental change (Baroque transition), and then settled into some new state that has likewise remained more or less stable ever since (Modern phase). There are no obvious political causes for this change, nor are there any evident economic ones. The two transitions do, in fact, fall in what the economic historian David Fischer calls two equilibrium periods in the history of the global economy, but there are no other transitions at his other equilibria.[24] The most likely candidate, I suggest, is the European urban system, and the transformations it endured in the earlier part of the seventeenth century, transformations more important in many ways than even those of the nineteenth century. Here I rely on de Vries's comprehensive study of the urban population of Europe from medieval to modern times.[25]

Figure 4.14 The European urban system in 1600. Each circle's area is proportional to the population of the city it represents, and each area represents the same size of population on this and the next map (fig. 4.15). Each map shows the largest cities that together account for half of Europe's urban population at the time. In 1600 the largest city is Naples, with 281,000. (Derived from data in J. de Vries, *European Urbanization 1500–1800* [Cambridge, MA: Harvard University Press, 1984].)

From at least the fourteenth through to the early seventeenth centuries Europe possessed several major urban centers—in the Low Countries, the cities of northern Italy, Naples, and Paris—corresponding more or less to an industrial backbone running from Tuscany through southern Germany to Flanders (fig. 4.14). De Vries refers to this as a "polynuclear" urban system.

In all essentials the urban landscape of 1600 was still medieval, a world of closed, corporate semi-independent towns dominated by the local landed elites, the centers of regional economies. Italy and the Low Countries were by far the most urbanized regions, with about 15 percent and 22 percent of their respective populations living in towns of 10,000 persons or more in 1600, compared to 8 percent for Europe as a whole. As it had been since early medieval times, Europe's population was about evenly balanced between the Mediterranean littoral (mainly Italy and Iberia) and the northwestern areas. The "long sixteenth century" had been one of rising population and net economic expansion. Europe experienced respectable population growth during the 1400s and 1500s and an increasing level of urbanization. The effects of this were spread evenly throughout the urban system, with small towns gaining as much as larger.

Between 1600 and 1700 this urban system was fundamentally restructured. A general crisis—monetary, military, and medical—engulfed Europe in the opening decades of the seventeenth century, with every country in Europe suffering economically and demographically: after a respectable 17 percent increase in population in the fifty years before 1600, the region was capable of only a feeble 5 percent increase in the fifty years after.[26] The crisis struck first and heaviest in the Mediterranean region, from Spain through Italy. Population growth slowed considerably, the towns depopulated, the great mercantile centers of Venice and Genoa and the textile industries—the major manufacturing sector of the medieval economy—of northern Italy collapsed.[27]

While the crisis affected all Europe to some extent, the Mediterranean world proved itself less resilient than the northwest in its ability to take the shock. When the dust had settled the medieval world was gone and the framework of the modern established. Europe's industrial and demographic center had moved decidedly northward along the Tuscany-Netherlands axis. Italy and Spain were no longer industrially or commercially significant. More germane to the question under discussion here, the old polynuclear urban system was replaced by one with a single core, centered on the Low Countries, and embracing northern France and southern England, and orientated to the Atlantic and North Sea rather than the Mediterranean (fig. 4.15). With this geographical restructuring came a redistribution of population between types of city. Urban growth was highly concentrated in the largest cities, particularly the Atlantic ports and centers of administration of the new nation-states. Smaller cities, the

Industrial zone

Figure 4.15 The European urban system in 1700. The largest city is London, with 575,000.

old inland trading places, ecclesiastical centers, and towns of medieval industry, stagnated or actually declined.

The collapse in the importance of the Mediterranean is also shown clearly by the decline of the proportion of architects from Italy after 1600, and corresponding rises in France and England. Before 1600 Italy consistently produced more than half the architectural community. This declined rapidly through the 1600s until by 1700 only one quarter of European architects were Italian. A national redistribution of architects paralleled the redistribution of population and wealth, and preceded the Baroque transition.

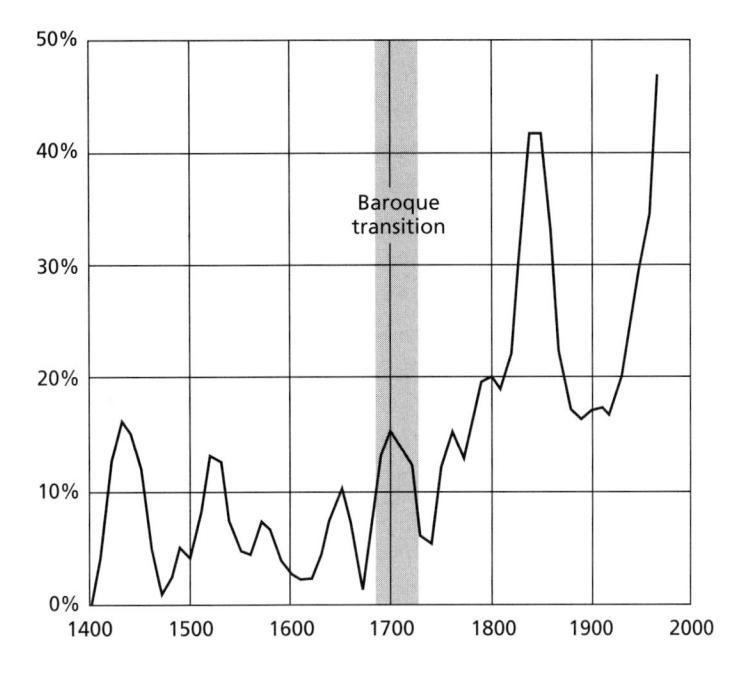

Figure 4.16 Proportion of buildings designed by an architect from outside the building's region.

By the early eighteenth century the old medieval urban system had been replaced by one essentially modern, a world whose cities were dominated by the needs of nation-states, national administrations and international markets, rather than local elites and regional markets. One can see the effect of internationalization on the architectural field from an examination of the nationalities of architects and the locations of the buildings they designed. From 1400 to the Baroque transition the proportion of buildings designed by architects from outside the building's region was rarely above 10 percent. After the transition architects became more mobile and the proportion significantly higher (fig. 4.16).

The Baroque Transition

It is clear that the urban restructuring of Europe must be a significant factor in the Baroque transition. It preceded the transition by about fifty years or two architectural generations (that is, about twice the average age

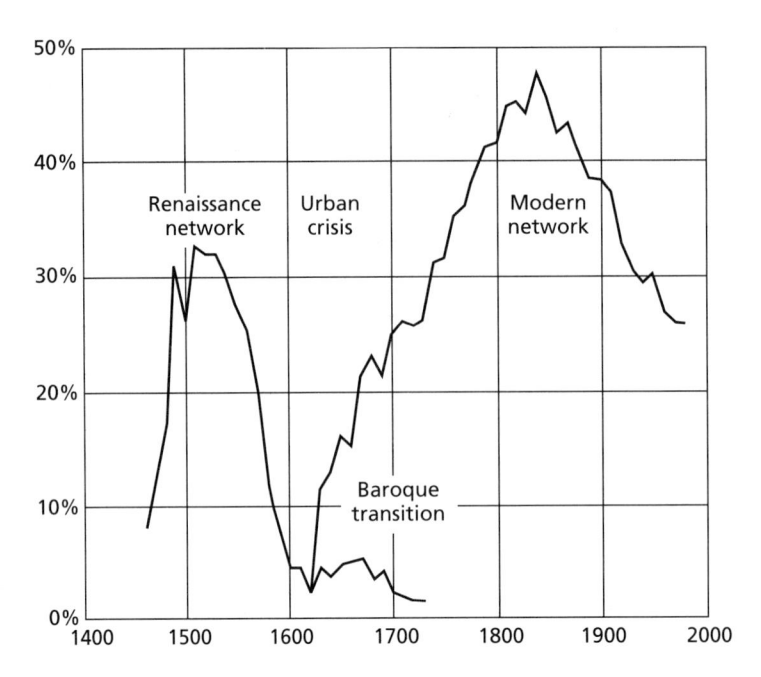

Figure 4.17 Growth and decline of the two main networks of architects. Data reflect the proportion of all architects alive in each decade who are members of the network.

separating master and pupil, 22 years), which seems a reasonable time lag. We should also note another important restructuring that was going on, this time in the master-pupil chains of the field. Some 150 separate such chains can be recorded for the entire dominant sector. Most are very short, only two, three, or four generations long, but they are cross-linked by collegiate relations. This effectively ties the whole system together in the case of the major architects. There are two particularly important chains, one from the Renaissance and one that stretches from the Baroque to the present. The length of the latter is extraordinary: it is possible to trace a direct chain of personal interaction across almost four hundred years, connecting Stanley Tigerman (among others) back to Jacques Lemercier, who flourished in the early 1600s.

These two networks are the backbone of the major sector. They are linked to other networks by collegial relations. An inspection of the rise and progress of these two key networks shows how they relate to the transition (fig. 4.17). The Renaissance network peters out during the transition, to be replaced by the main Modern network, arising at the same time as the former dies out.[28] Almost all the architects in the earlier system are Italian. When the network starts up again in the 1620s, it is in France and England.

The Baroque transition is, therefore, more than a change in the quantitative relationship between architects and the general socioeconomic environment. It marks also the destruction of the whole series of personal relations that had structured the Early Modern phase of architecture, the great net of relationships that wove the Renaissance architects into a whole. My explanation for the transition is thus twofold. Pushing the expansion of the minor sector was the urban restructuring of Europe, which created a new sort of urban environment of large cities, run by national governments, quite different in kind to the medieval system of smaller, regionally centered towns and cities. This environment was capable of sustaining twice as many minor architects per capita than that of the Early Modern phase.

Structuring the minor sector were the master-pupil chains and their collegiate cross-linkages maintained by the great architects. The great network of the Early Modern era incorporated a total of 133 architects out of 222 possibles. Some 60 percent of all architects with any link at all to another were encompassed in this. Essentially an Italian network, it collapsed with the economic decay of Italy through the 1600s.

A master-pupil network started up again in the economically more fertile soil of northwestern Europe, but when it did so the urban environment was different from that which had sustained the Italian architectural system. This environment provided greater resources for the minor architects to exist on. The engine that drove the expansion into this environment was the formation of the new master-pupil network. It was able to generate and to sustain a higher density of linkages, encompassing some 78 percent (1,169 out of 1,496). With this more effective means of transmitting symbolic capital among its members, the network could produce more minor sector architects.

The Field's New System of Reproduction

For almost the entirety of its history, the field of architecture has relied on the transmission of symbolic capital through chains of masters and pupils, webs of personal contacts, to reproduce itself. In the early nineteenth century the French state created a new method of reproduction with the formation of a school intended to train architects, the Ecole des Beaux-Arts. Through the next century and a half, the field's reproduction system gradually became embedded in national higher education systems. Figure 5.1 shows this expansion of credentialing in the architectural field. Although an indicator of the educational credentials of the most elite sector of the field, it mirrors the growth in credentialing of the whole.[1]

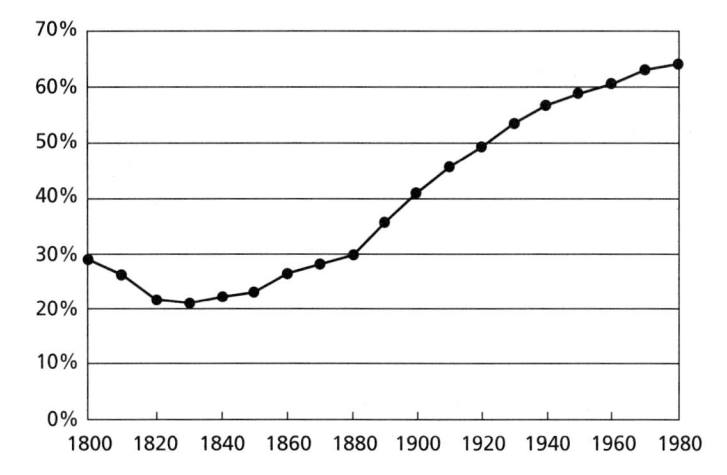

Figure 5.1 Percentage of architects listed in the *MEA* who attended an educational institution.

The consequences of this have been considerable.² The first we may note is the disruption it has caused in the traditional reproduction mechanism. In the last chapter I noted that the cyclic behavior in the changes in numbers of the great architects loses definition in the early twentieth century (see fig. 4.8). It is no coincidence that this occurs a few decades after the rise in credentialed architects that begins in the 1880s.

We can understand the full implications of the institutionalization of the field's system of reproduction by considering the history of architectural education, and reassessing the conventional wisdom about architectural schools and their relations with the occupation and their universities (fig. 5.2). The basic idea is that architecture reproduces itself through a formal system of education that is properly located in universities. The state credentials graduates in the field of architecture, formally certifying them as competent, relying on professional proxies to monitor the quality of educational programs. Apart from teaching, the academics also produce research or scholarship, which informs their teaching and increases the knowledge base of the profession.

Understanding Architectural Education

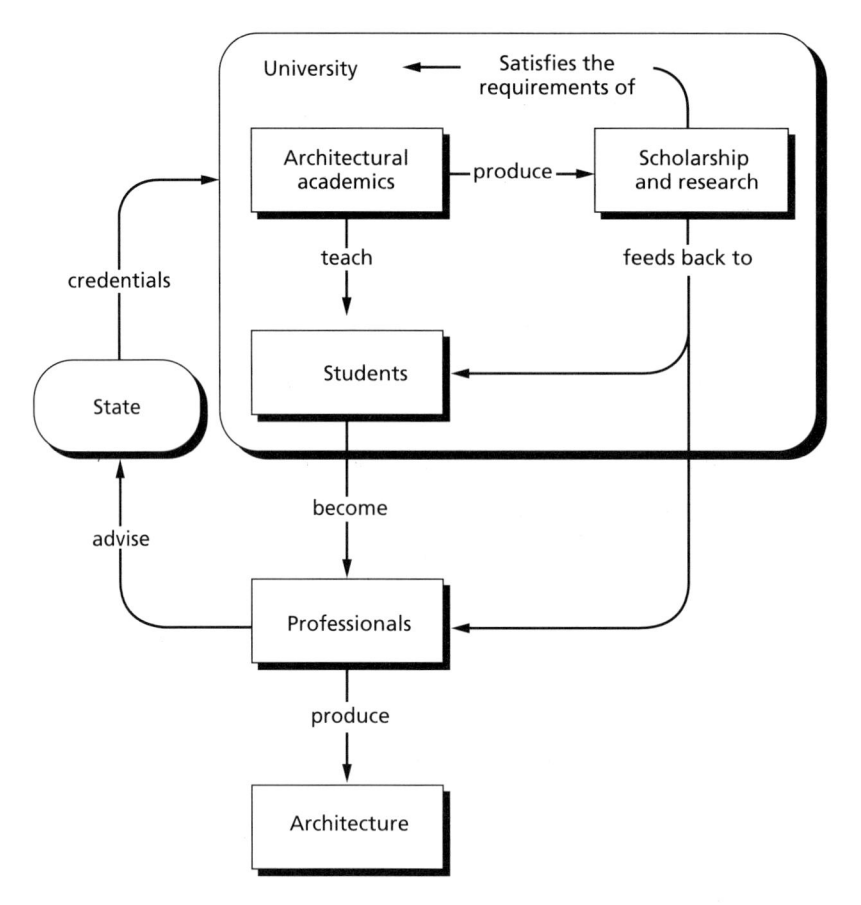

Figure 5.2 The standard model of the relationship between the universities, the schools of architecture, and the body of practitioners. Production and reproduction are united.

The Critique of Architectural Education
Straightforward though this model may be, it cannot be a correct representation of the reality, for it fails to explain why architecture schools should have such fraught relationships with both the occupation and their universities. Neither American nor British practitioners have ever been reticent about criticizing the departments, the fundamental and continuing failure of which is, from their point of view, their sheer and seemingly perverse inability to prepare students for the real world of practice.[3] The studio

Field	Doctoral production	Field	Doctoral production
Chemistry	480	Pharmacy	72
Zoology	217	History	63
Engineering	196	Literature	54
Music	140	Home economics	29
Economics	120	Journalism	15
Social work	117	Art	15
Languages	101	Architecture	11
All disciplines	*100*	Law	6
Education	79		

Table 5.1 Ratio of doctorates to lower degrees awarded in various fields, compared to the ratio for all fields (average = 100). (Source: S. E. Harris, *A Statistical Portrait of Higher Education* [New York: McGraw-Hill, 1972]. Data is for the United States, 1965–1966.)

system of education is, they say, a fantasy world in which incompetent professors who are the center of petty personality cults encourage bizarrely unrealistic expectations in students, while avoiding the teaching of anything actually to do with the hard realities of life.[4] Students learn nothing of the other activities of the construction industry.[5] They cannot draw and they know nothing of construction. The suggested remedies are usually along the lines of introducing more "pragmatic" subjects such as management and technical courses or, significantly, a partial return to apprenticeship in some form.[6]

There certainly is no problem in finding evidence that architecture is failing to perform like other academic disciplines, whose function is invariably taken to be knowledge production. Table 5.1 shows the production of doctorates compared to lower professional degrees in a variety of fields for the United States. A value of 100 indicates that the field awards doctoral degrees in the same ratio as the higher education system as a whole. If architecture were as research oriented as the average university discipline, it would graduate almost ten times as many doctoral students each year as it actually does. Even home economics, not usually regarded as the most intellectual of areas, produces more. Over the entire period 1920 to 1974 American schools graduated only 56 people with a Ph.D., a minuscule figure.[7] Perhaps one quarter of American academics in architecture schools hold a Ph.D., a degree which in other fields is mandatory for even the lowest ranks. Architectural academics do little research; neither they nor the profession find it relevant.[8] Indeed, there is often a positive hostility to the very idea of this most intellectual and academic of activities, for, of course, designing buildings—not publishing papers—increases the architectural academic's symbolic capital. As one architectural academic lamented:

> Architectural research survives as an ad hoc phenomenon which is employed when needed, remaining erratic for most subject areas and, in general, unmonitored and uninstitutionalized.[9]

Those in the occupation of architecture certainly regard research as irrelevant or redundant, but one may have expected their academic brethren to take some interest. Not so. Very few architecture departments or schools in the English-speaking world produce scholarly works on a scale considered normal for other university-based disciplines.[10] Bedford and Groak determined that fewer than half of British architectural academics were involved in research, and the proportion is probably about the same for the United States.[11] Much more study of the built environment is done outside the schools than inside, in government research centers and private industry.[12] The research that is conducted in the schools is fragmented and takes place more within particular subdisciplines (environment-behavior studies as a branch of the social sciences, lighting research as a branch of physics, engineering or physiology) than within the architectural milieu—so much so that some have wondered aloud whether there is such a thing as architectural research.[13] This is to be expected, since the actual researchers are only sometimes architects who have decided against becoming designers. Most often they are immigrants from other disciplines, with varying degrees of interest in the core activities of architecture schools. Most architects and many architectural academics would classify all this sort of work as building (not architectural) research, and quite outside their province. They are not at all sure that people without architecture degrees should be in architecture schools at all, and regard with some dismay the open warfare that exists between the supernumerary scientific (or scientistic) researchers and those who are getting on with the job of teaching future architects.[14] The only area that is unequivocally a legitimate subject for architectural cerebration is history, theory, and criticism.[15]

Quality and quantity of research output, usually manifested as academic publication, are among the primary indicators of institutional credibility for universities and for individual academics in all disciplines, save architecture.[16] Juan Pablo Bonta and others have argued that the universities should come to terms with this and accept architecture's peculiar lack of product in this regard, but the universities have tended to see things the other way around.[17] They have difficulty comprehending what the schools mean when they say that "professional service and the application of knowledge . . . together constitute much of the scholarly output of architecture," as the Boyer Report states.[18] These pursuits seem appropriate for practitioners, not academics. Over the past twenty years or so the universities have pressured the schools to come to the academic party and bring in research money, articulate faculty promotion criteria in line with other disciplines, and make an effort to accommodate academic norms and values.[19] No wonder that pressures to conform to university ideals of academe are so stressful to architecture schools.

Why should the schools find themselves derided by the profession and disdained by the universities? Why do they seem to be inadequate in their two crucial functions of *reproduction* (of the profession) and *production* (of intellectual discourse)?[20] Many of the stresses in architectural education arise from the fact that its various elements were drawn from differently structured national fields and placed into the British and American fields out of context. Our current method of giving architects their training at an institution that also conducts systematic research and scholarship in a wide variety of intellectual areas is of quite recent date, the result of synthesizing the educational systems from several countries. From France we have the notion of organized, formal architectural education; from Germany the concept that there is and should be a linkage between teaching and research, and that this occurs in universities; and the two were uneasily synthesized in the United States, where they overlaid an apprenticeship system inherited from Britain.[21]

Britain: Articled Pupilage

We must start with the "natural mode" of education for the Anglo-American system of professions, which is the self-controlling mechanism of apprenticeship or, strictly, pupilage (fig. 5.3). This was a modification of the medieval apprenticeship system. But where an apprentice exchanged his labor for instruction from a master, an articled pupil paid cash to be taught. Probably something like half of all entrants to the occupation were trained through pupilage by 1800, rising very quickly in the opening decades of the nineteenth century to displace other entry points into the occupation, such as through the building trades. Pupilage usually lasted five or six years, and often included attendance at a local arts academy, and perhaps foreign travel.[22]

    The field's reproduction function was securely vested in the body of practitioners. The United Kingdom pioneered the concept of professional association which has so structured our whole concept of profession, and these strong associations have always been the organizations primarily responsible for the reproduction of their occupations. The British system of professional education has always been dominated by practitioners, who conduct it in schools that may or may not be associated with universities. Even today such professions as law and accounting conduct most of their training outside universities. As late as 1979 it was not necessary to have a degree to be a barrister, and in the 1950s the English solicitors actually dissociated themselves from the alliance they had formed with the universities a few decades before (they returned in the 1970s).[23] British professions developed as associations of people doing similar work, not, as in Europe, as people with similar state-certified qualifications. The only universities in England in the early nineteenth century, Oxford and Cambridge, regarded the concept of vocational training as repugnant to the whole idea of a university, and were quite content to leave the new professions to educate their own, who were equally happy to develop practice-based training. The new universities evinced only marginally more interest. A few years after its foundation the University of London had two professors of architecture. They gave occasional lectures intended to supplement pupilage, not to offer any sort of substantive education in the discipline.

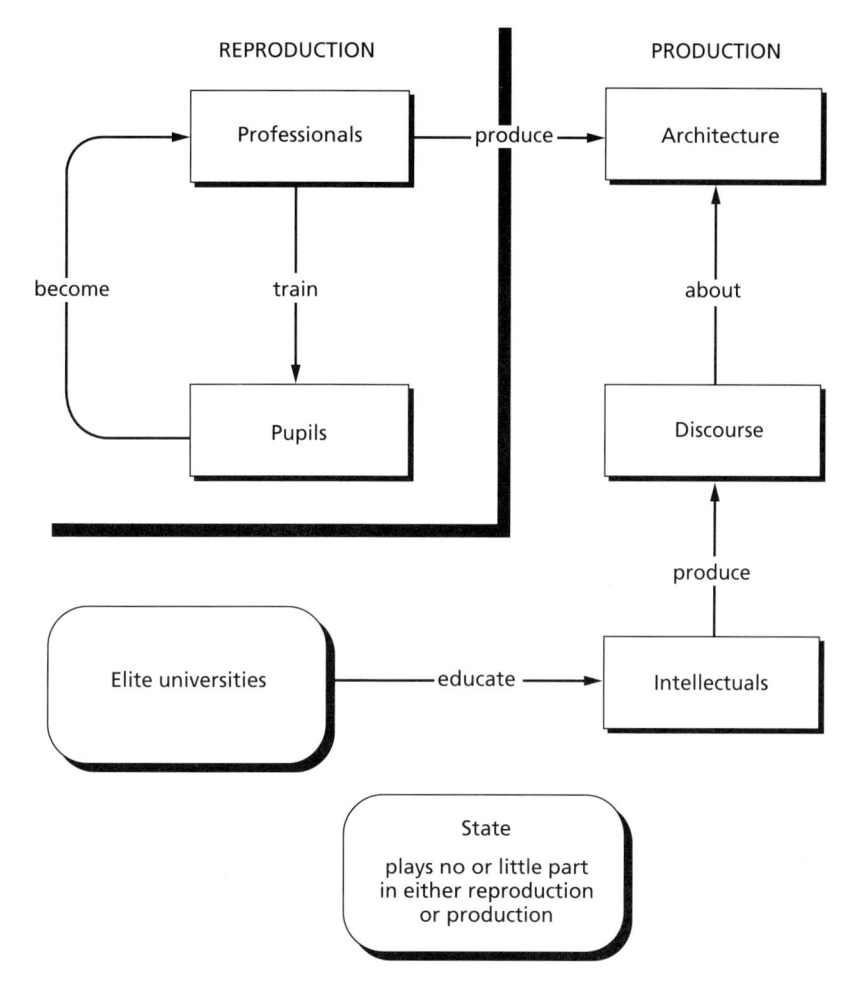

```
                REPRODUCTION                    PRODUCTION

                ┌──────────────┐               ┌──────────────┐
           ┌───→│ Professionals│──produce─────→│ Architecture │
           │    └──────┬───────┘               └──────────────┘
           │           │                              ↑
  become   │         train                          about
           │           │                              │
           │           ↓                       ┌──────────────┐
           │    ┌──────────────┐               │  Discourse   │
           └────│    Pupils    │               └──────────────┘
                └──────────────┘                      ↑
                                                    produce
                                                      │
   ┌──────────────────┐                        ┌──────────────┐
   │ Elite universities│──educate─────────────→│ Intellectuals│
   └──────────────────┘                        └──────────────┘

              ┌──────────────────────┐
              │        State         │
              │ plays no or little part│
              │  in either reproduction│
              │     or production    │
              └──────────────────────┘
```

Figure 5.3 The British pupilage model. The body of practitioners handles reproduction, and other intellectuals handle production of discourse.

The system of state certification that existed from the beginning in France and Germany was entirely absent. Certification of competence was instead provided on a de facto basis by observing the competition system of design selection. Competition was a very common means in nineteenth-century Britain for selecting designs. Winning a competition after a few years in pupilage was the rite of passage that denoted that a young architect was competent to practice by him or herself.[24]

The first school in the United Kingdom to offer a structured program of instruction was the Architectural Association (AA), founded by disgruntled architectural assistants in 1847. It was not associated with the newly established University of London and has remained unattached to universities to this day, while maintaining a reputation for excellence and innovation (and avant-garde elitism). The AA educated only a tiny proportion of practitioners through the nineteenth century, and began to offer a full-time course (of four years' duration) only in 1889. Day classes were not offered until 1901. Within a few years the first schools to be housed by universities commenced operation at King's College within the University of London and the University of Liverpool, and more schools were created after the turn of the century.

As more schools were founded the system of articled pupilage declined, until by the 1920s most architecture students were undergoing some sort of comprehensive formal training. However, few of these were in the higher reaches of academia. When, in the first important discussion on U.K. architectural education since the war (the 1958 Oxford Conference), there was a call to move education into the universities, about 63 percent of all architecture students were at polytechnics or art schools, 22 percent in universities proper, and the rest were working their way through offices.[25] Practitioners still dominated the educational system, however, through the British association of practitioners, the RIBA. Although anyone could call himself an architect prior to the 1931 Architects' Registration Act, after the RIBA instituted examinations for associate membership in the early 1880s, all schools worked toward ensuring their students would pass them. The RIBA granted partial exemption to Liverpool University a decade after its school commenced operation and slowly granted full exemption to the other new schools beginning in the 1920s. At the same time it established visiting boards to monitor the schools. With the Registration Acts the RIBA was granted de facto control over licensure of individuals and credentialing of schools, an iron grip that it holds to this day.

The advantages of apprenticeship as a means of professional reproduction are threefold. First, it allows a fine control of the supply of new practitioners. In boom times firms take on pupils and in slack times let them off. The dictates of the demand side can be responded to very quickly and supply regulated to satisfy it. In contrast, a school-based system ignores the requirements of the market and replaces them by its own quite independent logic, deriving from the schools' desire to maintain a steady flow of graduates. Second, practitioners define what is to be learnt, and have a better appreciation of the market's need for particular skills.

Third, the full weight of an individual's social capital is best exploited by apprenticeship. The importance of social capital varies, having least effect in those areas requiring formal academic certification, and most in unbureaucratized areas of social space, where the state imposes no rules and makes no tests. Of course, the social capital that can be mobilized by an individual from the upper classes is rather more than that of someone lower down in the class system. When pupilage was at its height in the late nineteenth century, it was noted at the time that English architectural apprentices came from higher strata than in Germany, where architectural education was taught at technical universities.[26]

Apprenticeship allows the well-connected to put their children into the most prestigious firms from the very beginning of their careers—indeed before their careers even begin—providing that most precocious of head starts impossible for the lower-class aspirant who, incapable of *proving* any talent, since he or she has not yet had the chance to show any, cannot and will not be given the opportunity to demonstrate sufficient worth. Apprenticeship also allows the socially privileged the possibility of success through means other than technical competence or creative flair. The history of architectural practice is littered with firms that have succeeded through combining the architectural skills of one partner with the entrepreneurial and social skills of another. One designs, the other courts the wealthy to bring in commissions.

Intellectual production was, in the British model, vested primarily in free-floating intellectuals. Until the middle to late nineteenth century in Europe and the Americas, intellectual life was something that happened outside the universities. The intelligentsia was to be found in the leisured aristocracy, in the bourgeoisie, and in the elite members of the professions.[27] Many of these were educated in the elite universities, but very few were employed by them. The continuous debate about architectural quality was conducted through the writing of articles for the

The Importance of Social Capital

The possession of social capital is and always has been of the first importance in architecture, an unlovely fact little discussed by practitioners or educators, as in this rare admission by Brendan Gill in his article on Stanford White in the *MEA*:

That McKim, Mead and White in its prime was the most fashionable firm in town is a fact that can be faced with equanimity. For architecture is an impure art, indissolubly linked to money and to the ways in which money chooses to express itself. Again and again we observe young architects beginning their careers with commissions given to them by wealthy members of their families or by wealthy friends; in some cases, the commissions are among the most substantial they will ever have. One thinks of that New York society figure, James Renwick, designing Grace Church at the age of twenty-six, and William Delano offered the commission for the Walters Art Gallery, in Baltimore, at a similar age, when he was but recently graduated from architecture school and had yet to design so much as a doghouse.

B. GILL, "Stanford White," in *Macmillan Encyclopedia of Architects*, ed. A. Placzek (New York: Macmillan, 1982), 391.

For more systematic evidence one has only to turn to Williamson's substantial study of famous American architects:

In the course of examining biographical material in the literature of architecture, I found factors that surfaced with surprising regularity. Family advantage, schools, and social connections—although not unique to architecture—are also important. In fact, it would be naive to overlook the fact that, in most careers, an avid contender for fame or financial success often gains considerable advantage from a social background providing natural contact with power brokers. For architects this means contact with wealthy potential clients and with decision makers, whether they are politically or socially based. A number of famous architects did gain access to clients because of their families' social contacts and because they attended Ivy League schools where their classmates included potential future clients. Others, like Wright, who did not attend those schools, found other ways to reach clients. Wright, for example, not only benefited from his relationship with his uncle and his uncle's congregation, but actively courted his early clients by joining their organizations and activities.

R. K. WILLIAMSON, *American Architects and the Mechanics of Fame* (Austin: University of Texas Press, 1991), 4.

cultural press, the few architectural journals, books, discussions at meetings of the AIA or RIBA, or personal communication between architects and critics.

France: The State Certification Model

If British professional education is dominated by practitioners, in France it has always been dominated by the state (fig. 5.4).[28] The Napoleonic reformation of higher education established two defining characteristics of the professions: service for the state, and state-certified academic credentials from one of the elite *grandes écoles*. Private practitioners in the same occupation, and especially those who had trained at other institutions, did not have the status or privileges (and responsibilities) that we would associate with professionals. So, for example, an architect only had to be registered to work on a government building in France: anyone could design buildings for the private sector.

As it evolved through the nineteenth century the higher education system remained, and still remains, strongly vertically stratified. In France, occupations traditionally dependent on graduates from the *grandes écoles*, who are destined for government employment (such as teaching, engineering, and public administration), enjoy much higher status than all the others whose graduates are trained in universities or other institutions. Moreover, the development of new professions through the 1800s to the present did not occur from the bottom up, with people doing similar work banding together and soliciting the state for certification, but rather from the top down, with the state creating institutions to provide specialized training for new occupations. In effect, the state defines the professions in France. The French higher education system is further complicated by the variability in the connection between research and teaching in institutions of higher education. Research is conducted either in the provincial universities, which focus on applied research and research for the various non-state professions they provide vocational training for, or in separate research institutions that are associated with neither the *grandes écoles* nor the universities.[29]

It is no surprise, then, that France invented academicized architectural education with the Ecole des Beaux-Arts. It is here that we see for

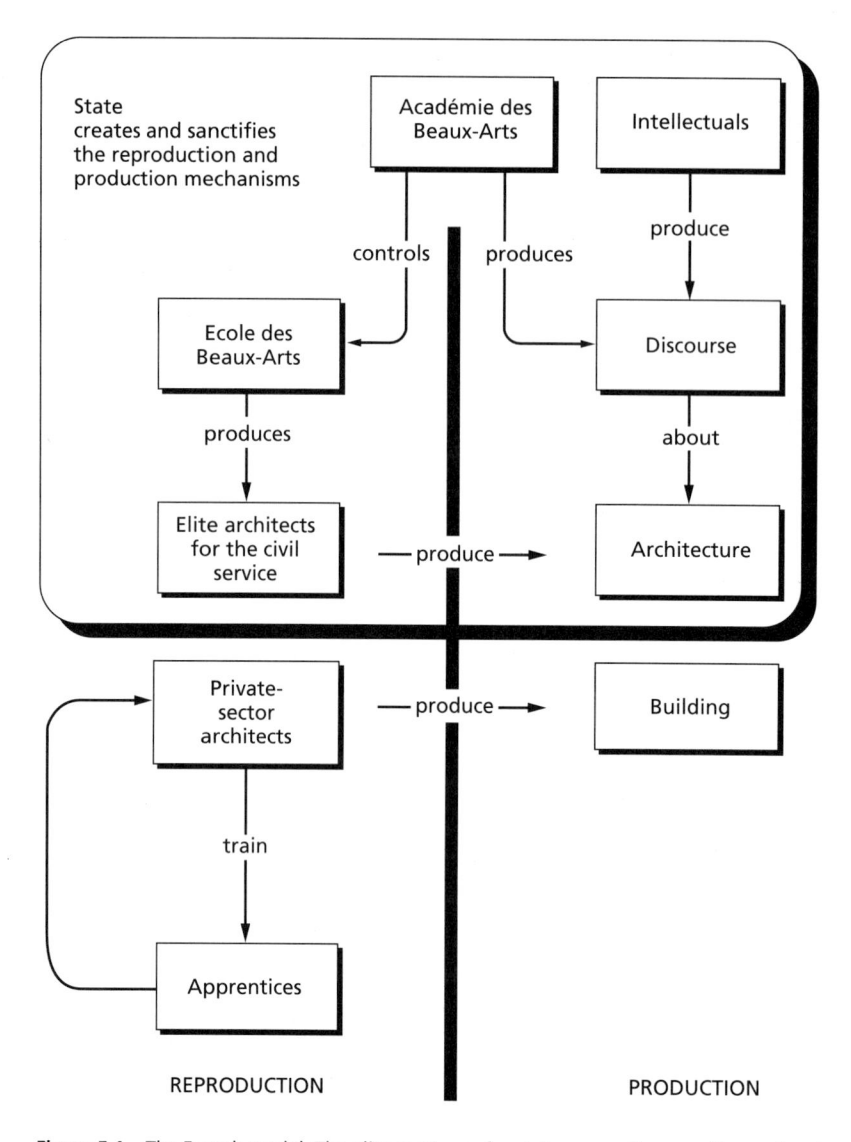

Figure 5.4 The French model. The elite sections of certain occupations are licensed and defined by the state. Other people doing similar work are not.

the first time the effect on the architectural field of an institutionalized education system. The French architectural field was structured very differently from the British, thanks to the existence of the Ecole and the Académie des Beaux-Arts. Reproduction was still partly in the hands of the profession, but many architects had some sort of tertiary education, and the elites went to the Ecole. Of the eminent nineteenth-century French architects listed in the *MEA*, about 41 percent studied at the Ecole and another 13 percent elsewhere. By comparison, only 20 percent of eminent English architects had any institutional training at all.

The intellectual production function of the field was still conducted by the urban elites, but with an additional element that was absent from the British system: the eight members of the architectural section of the Académie des Beaux-Arts. The august members of the Académie functioned as priests, in Bourdieu's terms, defining what was good architecture and who were good architects.[30] Their power was extraordinary: they set and marked all examinations, they decided who should go to the Academy in Rome, they advised the government on who to employ, they were the public and revered face of the field. The Ecole functioned much as a seminary, inducting individuals through a long period of training into its priesthood. Status increased as one moved year by year through the Ecole, entering carefully structured competitions, gaining formal awards and honors, attaining the Grand Prix, then, perhaps, the Académie itself.[31] The system of ateliers, with their intense rituals, their creation of pseudo-families of students, the instilling of the most deep-seated loyalties to patrons, taught students to love the hierarchies and to love to ascend them.

Moreover, these institutions were supported and sanctioned by the state itself. The Ecole and the Académie possessed complete power to consecrate, to pronounce some architects great and others not: outsiders such as Labrouste or Viollet-le-Duc could not penetrate the establishment.[32] They constructed a monopoly on the valorization of the field's symbolic capital. In Bourdieu's terminology, they constituted an *apparatus*, a totally dominant form of domination. No institutions with so great a weight of symbolic capital existed then or now in the English-speaking world. Hence the Anglo-Americans have always been more disposed to a tolerant sort of theoretical polytheism in architecture—the heterodox can flourish easier, as there is no centralized orthodoxy to oppose them; and yet they are less influential in the international discourse of architectural theory, precisely because there is no unified apparatus that can throw its whole weight behind one theory or another.

Like the *grandes écoles* even today, the Ecole des Beaux-Arts was not an educational organization like modern universities, in which research was a primary mission, systematically carried out by most staff and upper-level students, and expected to filter down into teaching. Prior to the foundation of the University of Berlin, research in Europe had been conceived of as a strictly private undertaking, conducted only by particularly gifted individuals with the private financial means to do so. Scholarly activities right from the Middle Ages to the Enlightenment had been only loosely tied to universities, and most scholarship was conducted outside them. At the Ecole des Beaux Arts, for example, there were only five or so full-time academic staff—the professors—responsible for the strictly optional lectures given to two or three hundred students. The dominant teachers were the patrons, leaders of the twenty or thirty ateliers into which students were organized and which represented the center of their educational lives. Patrons were invariably practicing architects, not individuals dedicated to research in any sense of the word.

Germany: Research Enters the Universities

The link between research and teaching we now accept as fundamental to the mission of universities was first forged in the early 1800s in Prussia, starting with the University of Berlin, in which professors were expected to conduct scholarly research and communicate it to various audiences (fig. 5.5). Throughout the nineteenth century the spread of the German model created a new sort of occupation, that of the researcher working also as a teacher, and the community of scholars and researchers which until then had existed outside the universities moved almost wholly into them.[33]

This research-teaching connection differed from the one prevalent today in Anglo-American higher education in structure and in content. Structurally, the German universities were organized as colleges of professors. Research was carried out in institutes organized as the private domains of the chairs. In typical Teutonic fashion, the chair was regarded as a representative of his or her entire discipline and the workers in the

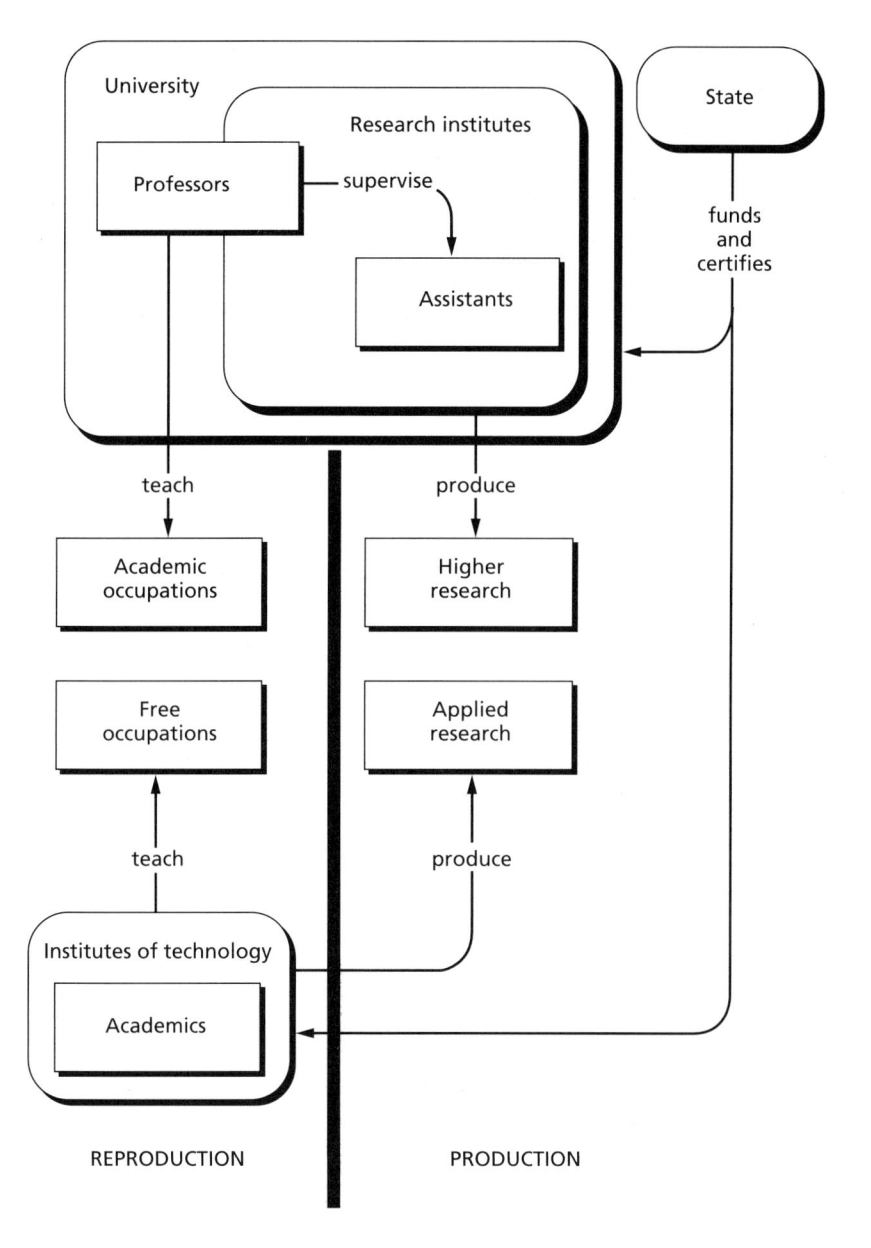

Figure 5.5 The German model of the universities.

institute were more or less assistants, helping the chair to further elaborate the world system he or she had devised.[34] One effect of this organization was that German professors tended to view themselves as academics first, constantly involved with the life and governance of the university, and members of their discipline second. With regard to content, the only sort of research conducted was that connected with the basic mission of the universities—to provide a general, cultivated education—or with the few occupations that required university training: medicine, law, theology, and high school teaching.

German professions arose with the development of powerful civil services in the late eighteenth century, and most in these privileged occupations were employed by the state until the 1850s. As late as 1880 only 42 percent of German architects were in private practice.[35] Unlike France, in which the state tightly controlled all the professions, in Germany the non-university professions (such as engineering, accounting, and dentistry) developed along lines similar to the Anglo-American ones, developing professional associations (in the 1850s, twenty years before the state professions) and later moving into polytechnics, which were transformed into technical universities and granted the right to award degrees around 1900. Architecture was one of the occupations taught in institutions—the polytechnics, or arts and crafts schools—that were not research-driven.

The United States: An Uneasy Synthesis

The United States provides a third model besides the practitioner dominated system of professional education of Britain and the state dominated system of France. We must note, first, a significant difference between otherwise similar systems of professions in the two major English-speaking nations. The major differences between the British and American systems of the professions are the much weaker historical continuity and associationalism of the latter. In Britain the archetypal professions of law and medicine have maintained an extraordinary continuity with their medieval forebears, and their powers and privileges are much as they were five hundred years ago. After the American Revolution, the American professions were deprived of state support: throughout the middle of the nineteenth century there was no licensing system for either medicine or law, and no architect needed to be licensed until Illinois introduced legislation in 1897. Their modern successors were essentially reconstructed in the decades around the turn of the century.[36] Partly because of this discontinuity, partly because of the difficulties of communication and geography, and partly because of the federal-state split of government jurisdiction, American professionals have had substantial difficulties building the sort of powerful associations characteristic among the British. Even the American Medical Association and the American Bar Association, while powerful in American eyes, are weak compared to their British counterparts.[37] In the case of architecture the difference is best seen in the proportion of registered architects who are members of their national professional body: about 66 percent belong to the RIBA and 53 percent to the AIA.

The weakness of professional associations has been critical in shaping professional education in the United States. Prior to the Civil War, American universities were in general modeled on the Oxbridge model, providing a cultivated education and some training for the clergy or teaching. Professional education started in the state land-grant universities of the postwar period, driven not by the demands of practitioners but by the universities themselves. The history of American professional education is one of these universities seizing market opportunities to provide the standardized education each atomized profession was unable to provide itself.[38] Thus, the first architecture schools of the postbellum period were housed in new universities (MIT, Cornell, Illinois), some forty years before their British counterparts. As Gutman noted, the expansion of architects in the United States has been due entirely to the considerable increase in the number of universities offering architectural programs (fig. 5.6) and, as with other professions, practitioners have been able to influence education only indirectly, usually in cooperation with elite schools and through accreditation.[39] The AIA has never exerted the control of professional education that the RIBA does: the National Architectural Accrediting Board, loosely associated with the AIA, only began its work after World War II, while the RIBA was exerting direct de facto control over university schools from their foundation. The most significant effort that the profession made to regulate education was that conducted by the Beaux Arts Institute of Design, which for two or three decades after 1910 successfully dominated education by promulgating and assessing standard design programs

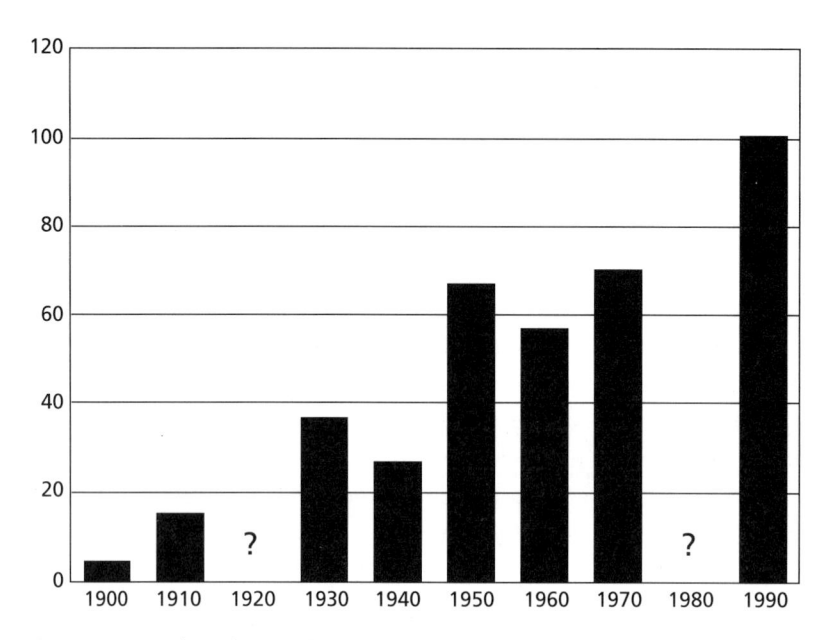

Figure 5.6 Number of U.S. architecture students per million population.

for use in the schools.⁴⁰ Even this foundered with the decline of Beaux-Arts classicism and was completely destroyed by the immigration of European modernists into the schools in the years before the war.

American professional education can therefore be characterized as university dominated, as opposed to the British practice dominated or European state dominated systems. When the American universities embraced professional education they were rather different institutions than those we have in the late twentieth century, being either of the Oxbridge type or vocationally oriented. The notion that research was a fundamental mission of a university did not appear until the importation of the German model in the latter part of the nineteenth century, with the creation of Johns Hopkins (1876), Clark (1887), and the University of Chicago (1892).⁴¹ Several important changes were made to this model as it crossed the Atlantic. First, the German chair-institute structure was dropped in favor of a departmental structure. They replaced the German autocratic polymath closely directing the researches of a group of assistants with a more egalitarian system in which the departmental chair handled administration and finance for a group of academics who more or less set their own intellectual agenda. Second, where the Germans had left applied research to industry or the lower-status polytechnics, the Americans brought it right into the universities.[42] Third, the academics at these universities tended to regard their discipline or profession as their primary milieu, not the university, the reverse of the German case. As Abbott points out, the American professions have maintained a deep ambivalence about university education, for "they were in the university but not of it."[43]

How the Schools Socialize

The mechanisms for the transmission of symbolic capital from generation to generation are today vested in the architecture schools located in universities. Much has been written about the obvious forms of this capital, the knowledge and skills, but little on the crucially important embodied capitals that are also transmitted through a much less obvious form of inculcation. The importance of the process of inculcation in the educational process depends on the relative worth of intellectual or institutionalized capital vis-à-vis embodied capital. It is of least importance in those fields within which the procedures and processes of production and acquisition of knowledge are objectified in instruments, methods and techniques, and of most importance in those areas where excellence is held to be almost entirely owing to the natural gifts of individuals, their raw talent.

It is clear that in architecture the procedures and processes of design are not at all objectified (as the dismal failure of the Design Methods movement attests)[44] and that architecture, unlike medicine or engineering or even law, requires one not only to know something as to be something: we colloquially call this quality of being "genius." Architectural education is intended to inculcate a certain form of habitus and provide a form of generalized embodied cultural capital, a "cultivated" disposition. Of course young architecture graduates must know how to draw, of course they must understand building codes, the rudiments of structural analysis, the principles of construction; but right from the moment they sit down at the drawing board of their first office to the day they retire the smoothness or difficulty of their career will be mediated by their habitus acting through their cultural capital. Habitus multiplies educational capital. Those with the right habitus and capital, those with the feel of the game, will find doors open more readily, their peers and superiors come to respect them more easily, clients look more favorably.

In earlier times educators not only readily acknowledged but positively gloried in the fact that architectural education was a cultivated education, intended to instill the appropriate habitus. Writing to parents who sent their sons to board in Paris to attend his revitalized Academy of Architecture in the late 1700s, Jacques-François Blondel reassured them that he would provide for

> fencing, music and dancing; exercises to which particular attention is paid, since they should form part of the education of all well-born persons who devote themselves to architecture, and who are destined to live in the best society.[45]

Or, as the AIA Committee on Education so clearly put it in 1906, "An architect is a man of culture, learning and refinement," and the purpose of architectural education "the breeding of gentlemen of refinement."[46] The American Academy in Rome strove to select fellows "among those only who will be recognized as gentlemen by instinct and breeding."[47] It is no longer politic to say such things; but they remain as appropriate a description now as then, as John Morris Dixon observed in the only published statements I have been able to find brave enough to discuss the class origins of architects.[48]

Objectified cultural capital in the form of educational diplomas is only marginally useful in producing cultivated individuals, who are attempting in reality to acquire an embodied form of capital. Architecture schools devalue intellectual capital compared to embodied cultural capital, for intellectual capital is simply not essential to achieve success. In their more sardonic moments some architects see this:

> Intelligence, in any absolute sense, is not a major factor in the production of distinguished architecture. Arrogance coupled with a sense of competition and a pleasure in the fashionable and exotic, are much more important.[49]

Favoring the Favored

By disguising what is actually a social process of selection that favors the privileged with one that appears to be a purely meritocratic academic one favoring nothing but native talent, the architectural education system works to preserve the existing social structure. Its success is often obscured by the fact that some individuals from the lower strata of society do make it through architecture school. Almost anyone could quote examples. Indeed, there are just enough such exceptions to make us believe that the system really is fair. Their prime function is precisely that of making the educational system appear meritocratic when it is not.

The architectural education system achieves its results in several ways:

- The disadvantaged eliminate themselves from architectural education.
- Architecture schools consecrate privilege by ignoring it.
- Schools accept the ideology of giftedness.
- Schools underestimate their inculcation function.
- The studio system favors the cultivated habitus.
- The schools favor those who favor them.

The Self-Elimination of the Disadvantaged

People try to achieve what they think is possible. Students from disadvantaged backgrounds—those with low economic and cultural capital—self-select themselves out of the system by simply saying to themselves that they have no chance of success. One may see the effect operating within the university system, as students distribute themselves among the various fields on the basis of their current economic and cultural capital, according to their perceptions of how successful they will be in increasing those capitals.

Table 5.2 shows the proportion of entrants to the various Faculties (Schools or Colleges) at my own institution, the University of Sydney, who have attended a private high school. The nature of Australian society is such that attendance at such a school is an indicator of cultural capital. It becomes clear that those areas that reproduce the cultural producers

Field	Deviation (percent)
Music	+42
Law	+35
Visual arts	+30
Architecture	+21
Arts	+18
Economics	+17
Veterinary science	+11
Medicine	+7
Social work	+1
All	0
Science	−2
Engineering	−15
Education	−22
Pharmacy	−32
Dentistry	−43
Nursing	−43

Table 5.2 Proportion of entrants to the University of Sydney who attended a private high school (expressed as a deviation from the mean for the whole university, by Faculty). (Source: author's analysis of university statistics, 1991–1992.)

(music, visual arts, architecture, other arts) attract those who already have sufficient cultural capital to obtain a good rate of return, while fields for which the possession of cultural capital is less relevant (nursing, dentistry, engineering) attract those without. Data in any form for the United States are very rare: we only have one study thirty years old, which ranked disciplines by the proportion of the senior year from the highest socio-economic class. Law, medicine, and the humanities attracted the most privileged students (about 70 percent of that year's entrants were upper-class), while the physical sciences, education, and engineering attracted the least (about 45 percent). Unfortunately, the data do not list architecture separately, although the ranking is surprisingly close to my own university, an ocean and thirty years away.[50]

Father's occupation	All University of London students	Bartlett applicants	Bartlett entrants
Management and professional	64	68	78
Clerical	9	29	20
Skilled manual	21	3	2
Unskilled	6	0	0

Table 5.3 Social class of students at the Bartlett School of Architecture, University of London (percentage of students from each social class). (Source: M. L. J. Abercrombie, S. Hunt, and P. Stringer, *Selection and Academic Performance of Students in a University School of Architecture* [London: Society for Research into Higher Education, 1969].).

Differences between classes manifest themselves most, not in differential rates of *passing* university courses, but of *entering* them. For a specific example we can cite the social origins of students at the University of London entering its Bartlett School of Architecture (table 5.3). We note, as before, the overselection of students from the upper classes into the university as a whole (column 2). Next, the self-selection of students who applied to Bartlett (column 3). Those with the least cultural capital eliminated themselves by not even applying. Finally, the bias of the selection committee in the interview process removed those with middling amounts of capital who had not the grace to remove themselves (column 4). The interview process, indeed, is the most effective mechanism for assessing cultural capital, and the only means for evaluating embodied capital. It is especially common in the more elite institutions, and in those disciplines in which such capital is most important for success.

Consecrating Privilege by Ignoring It

The higher education system as a whole has the essential function of conserving and preserving the culture of society, of passing it down from generation to generation. It is clear that it does not transmit the totality of society's culture. It transmits only those portions that those running the system consider worthy of transmission, the culture of the dominant, euphemized as "liberal education." There are continual debates, of varying vehemence, about just what should be transmitted, but these are internal struggles between intellectuals and academics, none of whom doubt that there are some things (English, architecture) that should be taught in higher education and others (automobile repair, hairdressing) that should not. No one thinks that everything is worthy of a degree.

By teaching and transmitting just one culture, that of the dominant classes, and by defining excellence and achievement in terms of that culture, the educational system of necessity favors those who have already been inculcated from birth, those for whom the dominant culture is as natural, familiar, and easy as walking. By assuming students are broadly homogeneous—for no one believes they are exactly alike—institutions of higher learning privilege the privileged, simply by ignoring their privilege. By referring generically to "students" it is possible to forget that the experience of university life affects different students differently. Entering university is markedly different for the student for whom university has always been expected as a natural career path, who has many family members with degrees, who has lived with stories of parents' college days, than for the student who has heard of college life third-hand, who hardly knows what to expect. What a gulf must have existed at the Ecole des Beaux-Arts between those from architectural families and the rest when "an architect's son [in choosing an atelier] would listen to his father's advice following the latter's personal inclination, inquiries or past loyalties."[51] And how must lower-income students in one contemporary U.S. architecture school have felt when another student, being praised for her design in a jury session, was told that she "had demonstrated an understanding of Roman urban planning, and clearly had spent time in Europe . . ."?[52]

Students can have the same practices without experiencing them as the same. To say that two students have part-time jobs as sales clerks in a store disguises the distinctions between the privileged student working for extra pocket money in the most up-market department store in town and the lower-class one at a supermarket checkout who must work to live.[53] To say that the architect's daughter and the construction worker's son are both keen photographers conceals the fact that with this same practice the former prepares herself for her chosen profession by carefully photographing interesting buildings, while the latter memorializes a personal history—birthdays, weddings, graduations, the important moments in the life of family and friends.

It is in this light that one can interpret an incident at my own school at Sydney some years ago. A new faculty member, an eminent and successful architect on the national scene, wanted to start the academic year with a celebration that would be both entertaining and instructive. The event was a daylong series of talks and exercises for the entire student body, physically and metaphorically centered around his firm's eighteen-foot skiff, which he had assembled in the architecture school's courtyard. His intention was to use the skiff as an example of excellence in design, of the highest craftsmanship, of subtlety and beauty of form, yet perfectly functional, as this sort of yacht is widely used for amateur racing.

The differential symbolic effect this had on the students was unintended. Sailing on the harbor is one of the favorite pursuits of Sydney's elites, among whom must be counted the better-off of the city's architects. Many architecture firms have their own boats, the favorite of which is the eighteen-foot skiff. For many years there has been an annual architectural racing competition, and participation in that event is a sign that one's firm has made it. Almost all the students from privileged backgrounds would have had sailing experience, and many of their families would have owned such a skiff. To them, sailing was a perfectly everyday pastime, and the professor's use of the boat as an exemplar of design was an implicit affirmation of the quality of that recreation, a comforting confirmation of the match between their cultural capital and that required for the profession. To students from lower-middle-class backgrounds the skiff was a novelty that made them uneasy. In a manner more potent and effective than mere words could have done, the cultural capital of architecture was identified with unknown experiences, and their own lack of familiarity and ease with yachting labeled them prepared, less familiar with that culture, and less acceptable as would-be entrants to the profession.

Those from the most privileged backgrounds must have been pleased to receive the syllabus quoted below, for a course in the Faculty of Architecture at the University of Sydney, which elevated their own calling and reaffirmed their superiority to others:

> With a dozen students to present class papers over a period of eight weeks, and given the necessity to allow time for producing the written version before I leave Sydney about September 24 (I am

booked to teach permaculture in Nepal), we shall have to start the student-presented seminars very soon.

. . .

I work on the assumption that Architecture students do not do things just for the marks either; that may be possible for students of Accountancy or Dentistry or even Engineering, but not for Architecture.[54]

Accepting the Ideology of Giftedness

Success, of course, depends on having some sort of talent and skill in the occupation of choice. In different degrees in different fields, success also depends on the ease with which one can acquire the culture offered by the educational system. Those with a habitus that predisposes them to play the game they have chosen to enter, and to love to play that game, will do better than those without. Students from cultured families, especially from families with heavy investments in artistic or architectural cultural capital, come to school with a habitus ready-made for reception of the peculiar education that is architecture. Such students appear to be naturally gifted, but this natural gift is—as well as being a talent—also the feel for the game that their habitus provides them, a "naturally natural naturality" that impresses all who see it as a natural ease, grace, style, and confidence. Those who say they are "born to be architects" truly are, but not in the way that the speakers intend.

The notion that one is born with natural talents completely independent of the privilege of being privileged by one's social class, is the ideology of giftedness, and in no field is this belief more strongly held than in art and architecture. No individuals confident of their own giftedness can accept the unpalatable idea that their giftedness owes as much to the unchosen determination of their own social milieu as to their own undetermined choosing, as Bourdieu puts it. If this ideology were true, then one would expect to find some sort of commonality to the psychologies of creative artists or architects and, conversely, no commonality to their social origins. Precisely the opposite is the case. The lack of a common psychology in architecture students has quite defeated the many attempts of researchers to devise selection procedures superior to the hodgepodge now operating in the world's schools, as I pointed out in chapter 1. If the analysis presented here is correct, then researchers should really be looking for students from families with high cultural capital. Perhaps such a criterion, which, it is believed, could not possibly lie behind the creative success of the young architect-to-be, would be as repugnant to the schools as its discovery was disheartening to two psychologists in their study of young artists:

> The data make clear that, to achieve success as an artist, it helps to come from a well-to-do, educated, higher status family. (This is a disillusioning thought. One would like to believe that, at least in art, money and status play no part in determining success.)[55]

Researchers have been reluctant to acknowledge the implications of their own findings, politely declining to look behind the individual to the symbolic wealth sustaining him or her. The psychologist Donald Mac-

Natural Grace

Baldassare Castiglione understood the importance of natural grace, of the "air of good breeding," when, writing five hundred years ago, he said that a courtier must be

endowed by nature not only with talent and with beauty of countenance and person, but with that certain grace which we call an "air," which shall make him at first sight pleasing and lovable to all who see him; and let this be an adornment informing and attending all his actions, giving the promise outwardly that such a one is worthy of the company and the favor of every great lord. . . . The Courtier must accompany his actions, his gestures, his habits, in short his every movement, with grace. And it strikes me that you require this in everything as that seasoning without which all the other properties and good qualities would be of little worth. And I truly believe that everyone would easily let himself be persuaded of this, because, by the very meaning of the word, it can be said that he who has grace finds grace. But since you have said that this is often a gift of nature and the heavens, and that, even if it is not quite perfect, it can be much increased by care and industry, those men who are born fortunate and as rich in such treasure as some we know have little need, it seems to me, of any teacher in this, because such benign favor from heaven lifts them, almost in spite of themselves, higher than they themselves had desired, and makes them not only pleasing but admirable to everyone.

B. CASTIGLIONE, *The Book of the Courtier*, trans. C. S. Singleton (New York: Anchor, 1959 [1528]), 30, 41.

Kinnon, mentioned in chapter 1, found that almost without exception, all his most creative architects came from families with high cultural capital, but was not interested in pursuing this most obvious of indicators.

Schools Ignore Their Inculcation Function

Educators talk about how students are socialized into "architectural culture," usually in disparaging tones, as though it were some incidental side effect, or is easily rectified by simply not teaching students certain things. The process of inculcation, I have argued, is no mere epiphenomenon, but an integral part of architectural education. This process operates at a much deeper level than is implied in the notion of a hidden curriculum. One cannot manifest cultivation by knowing, but by being. All the subtle signs of cultivation—accent, manners, deportment, bearing, dress, attitudes, tastes, dispositions—cannot be obtained second-hand. They must be slowly absorbed from those who are already cultivated. The importance of cultivation lies precisely in the fact that it cannot be picked up easily. If it were readily obtained, by simply reading a few books or attending a few lectures, it would not have the value it does. Its acquisition is essentially a matter of directly experiencing it, of soaking up all the many small things it comprises. Nor can its content be enumerated. No book can tell you that cultivation consists of x, y, or z. This sort of cultural capital exists in the tacit qualities of individuals.[56] As Alberti said:

> There is no one even slightly imbued with letters who does not in his leisure conceive the hope that he will soon become a great orator, even if he has only seen the face of eloquence at a distance. But, when he realizes that mastery of this art involves more difficulty than he drowsily thought, he strives toward this goal by reading every available book, as if we could acquire our style from books alone, rather than by our own intense efforts.[57]

A more recent statement in almost exactly the same terms can be found in this one by Paul Cret, who wrote in 1934 of his school at the University of Pennsylvania:

> All education in Fine Arts . . . has for its main object the development of the artist's personality. A consequence is that such a result can be accomplished only through personal effort and not through a perusal of textbooks.[58]

This is the crux of the matter: the cultivated habitus cannot be acquired through labored study. That is the way of the pedant, the plodder. One must have not only the right culture, but the right relationship to that culture, and that relationship depends on how the culture was acquired.[59] The dominant definition of the right way to acquire culture is by direct experience, upon actually being there. Does not every architecture student aspire one day to make the Grand Tour, the leisured journey, the pilgrimage, to actually see and experience the sacred sites of architecture? As the architectural historian Spiro Kostoff wrote on the virtues of architectural education:

> There is no substitute for the experience of travel that opens the eye and builds up a storehouse of impressions. . . . And beyond that comes life and learning. We understand the needs of others to the extent that we have insisted on a full life for ourselves; we can provide for the settings of social institutions to the extent that we have been broadly educated, broadly read, given the wherewithal to reflect on the course of human affairs and to scan the reaches of human achievement.[60]

As a means of producing a specific, cultivated habitus, architectural culture can only be inculcated in a certain way. Bourdieu distinguishes between a *scholastic* and a *charismatic* mode of inculcation.[61] The scholastic mode is what we normally recognize as pedagogy, the formal and explicit teaching of formal and explicit knowledge and skills. The charismatic mode is the informal and implicit method of inculcation which is, Bourdieu argues, the only possible means of transferring embodied cultural capital. The former is intended to produce knowing, the latter being. Hence the strong identification between work and person, so common in architectural design, which this anecdote illustrates:

> One day a professor approached for a mid-project desk crit and pointed to the model I had constructed. . . . "Is this you?" he asked. Hoping to build a casual rapport with this rather stern young teacher, I responded jokingly, pointing to myself, "No, no this is me," then to the model, "This is my model." "No!" he replied firmly, putting his hand on my model, "This is you and this is shit!" It was an incredible high when the unity between self and work brought us praise, but quite devastating when our efforts were insulted.[62]

Lecture courses play only a small part in this process, and then only some courses. Subject areas in architecture are strongly stratified, with design by far the most honored. If we were to construct a hierarchy of curricular prestige it would correspond more or less to the degree to which the course can utilize the student's cultural capital. Design, history, and theory would be at the top, and environmental science, structures, and building services at the bottom. When students protest that courses are not relevant, quite often they are simply protesting courses whose examination prevents them from displaying their cultivation. The hierarchy of curricular prestige corresponds more or less to the social hierarchy of students, those with most cultural capital doing best in the most prestigious subjects, and hence attempts to overturn the former meet with resistance from the student body.

The loudest objections to non-design-oriented courses will come from the most cultivated within the student body. They believe most strongly in the ideology of giftedness, and most strongly in their own gift, judging themselves indulgently at every point. So they will dismiss a low mark in a design project by blaming the marker's inability to perceive their gift and its manifestation in their design. Such a rationalization is possible in design studio, an area renowned for contentious assessment, but impossible in the cut-and-dried world of structures or mathematics. The privileged therefore treat with contempt those areas they consider mundane, those in which flair is irrelevant.

The design studio is the site par excellence for the operation of a charismatic mode of inculcation. It is no happy accident that the studio system has been at the very heart of architectural education throughout its entire history. The studio system is essential for socializing students with a cultivated habitus. As the architectural academic Kathryn Anthony points out, the studio provides a very peculiar form of education.[63] In conventional university education, students sit in anonymous lectures for a few hours a week, work alone, and benefit from little collaboration with other students or academics, who must be actively sought for assistance. Examinations take the form of written documents, and are conducted in private. Design students are surrounded by their peers for many hours a week, often relying on them for assistance. The studio-master will actively seek them out to provide criticism, and examination is public and by oral presentation.

The student cannot present nor the teacher assess embodied capital by the usual university means of lecture and written examination. Taste and cultivation cannot possibly be determined by multiple-choice questions. Only face-to-face contact and immediate, personal experience can do that; allowing the examiner to distinguish by all the subtle signs of body language, dress, demeanor, poise, and linguistic fluency the suitability of the examined. The point is worth reiterating: *if taste and cultivation were capable of objectification they would not have the value they do.* Difficulty in acquisition and assessment *in* person *of* the person are essential and defining characteristics. No doubt this explains the riots that broke out in the old Ecole des Beaux-Arts when the government tried to make the Ecole's own lecture courses compulsory. The government backed down soon enough, and the architecture students happily resumed their old practices of ignoring lectures for the ateliers.[64]

By saturating students with the objects of architectural culture; by presenting them with role models, living examples of embodied cultural capital (hence the insistence on the importance of having practicing architects as teachers); by displaying in all the slight ways of manner, dress, and taste that one is becoming what one wishes to be, students absorb cultural capital in the only possible way, by presenting to the studio-master's gaze their whole social being. Witness the studied manner of the studio-master, played out by the avant-garde architect Bernard Tschumi, who presented himself to at least one audience as the very embodiment of embodied capital:

> Bernard Tschumi, too, had the air of a man who'd backed the only horse in the race. He boasted a more Parisian demeanour than anyone else at the symposium, Derrida included, lecturing in the sort of scarf that forty years ago existentialists thought in, and employing the low murmur of interiority, broken by sudden implosions of assertion, that is post-structuralism's ideal mode. If I heard right, we were witnessing a "terminal crisis of the referrant." There were no boundaries; "we inhabit a fractured space made of accidents." Anything less accidental than Bernard Tschumi, the fall of his suit, the toss of his scarf, the stylised drone of his

delivery set to a slide of our starry, unpurposed universe which we viewed in a darkened auditorium, I found it difficult to imagine.[65]

The ever-present dangers of contamination are minimized by socially isolating students from peers in other disciplines and even from family:

> The prolonged, intense interaction across an academic term can result in a familial atmosphere—with the best and worse aspects of family life manifested on a day-to-day basis. The intense contact with studio-mates often makes it difficult for design students to maintain their friendships with those in other years. As many students have admitted, the more years they spend in design, the fewer nondesign students they have as friends. Cloistered into the captivity of the studio, the studio commands an increasingly greater role as the center of students' social lives, and consequently the world outside the studio becomes less important.[66]

This form of internment produces a socially and mentally homogeneous set of individuals whose homogeneity reinforces the socialization process and the closure of social capital, limiting the chances of misalliances and laying the foundations for future patterns of cooperation in later career.[67] Insisting that all their faculty have a professional degree in architecture, the schools also intellectually isolate their students. Within the schools this isolation is exacerbated by denigrating lecture courses, and failing to set reading, except for those purely architectural influences the studio-master wishes students to absorb. As Anthony reports one student saying:

> Architecture school was like boot camp: twelve hours a day seven days a week in basic design. . . . In retrospect it was the beginning of a major shift in my education—a totally anti-intellectual period in my life. I can honestly say I hardly read a book in my three years of architecture school. . . . Every minute, I was being made to feel like a first-grader. . . . My first design instructor was a bit like a drill sergeant. You're more or less being broken.[68]

The Studio System Favors the Cultivated Habitus

One can succeed more easily if one is already halfway successful. The design studio, by relying so much on the presentation of the self to those who will assess the self, favors those who come to architecture already knowing some of the strategies of the game of culture. The natural grace, the feel of the game, which those from cultured—and especially architectural—families possess, makes them far better prepared to cope with the peculiarities of the language of design. Consider these examples:

> The language of the professor has an inherent logistical [sic] problem: it is vague. The ambiguity of the professor's language renders the student unable to discern good from bad, to get a sense of value of their own or someone else's work.[69]

> There is little effective communication of ideas in juries. Tangential remarks are difficult to apply. The level of abstraction, vague language and allusions, elliptical discourse, and often denigrating commentary are barriers to drawing anything useful from the juror's response.[70]

It is obvious that talent in design is necessary for success in design. It is less obvious that talent in talking about design is also required. The studio system requires students to spend a great deal of time talking about their design, talking to other students, talking to professors at desk crits, and, of course, talking at jury presentations. Students from cultured families have already acquired the basic dispositions required to further their symbolic mastery of architectural language. They already know how to talk and manipulate culture, and most important, they already have a visceral feel for the nature of the game they are playing. This may also explain the never-ending calls for "integration," by which is generally meant moving everything into the studio, transforming performance in the most objectified areas of architecture (construction, structures, etc., where possession of symbolic capital counts least), into assessments of social being. In effect, this denies those with the wrong sort of cultural capital even the least chance of asserting their competence in some area of architecture.[71]

The Schools Favor Those Who Favor Them
All processes of enculturation must accomplish two things: first, successfully enculturate; second, remove those who will not be enculturated. The objective is to produce individuals who want to play the game of choice (whether it be architecture or law or engineering or whatever), to take pleasure in the game, to believe in the innate rightness of the game, and

to believe that hardships endured now are but necessary steps on the path to election hereafter.[72] The enculturation process is most clearly seen operating in the change of dress and manner students undergo throughout their time in school. This is no mere transition from adolescence to adulthood. As I have observed it in my own school over many years, students become more alike in dress, taste, and deportment: they become more homogeneous.

Within the educational system students are kept in a more or less tame state, varying from place to place, time to time, and discipline to discipline. In disciplines in which authority is lodged outside the individual (such as the physical sciences or engineering), where criteria of excellence have been incorporated into objects, techniques, or instruments that can, it is thought, speak for themselves, the enculturation process need no more than point to these externalities for legitimation to quiet the fractious. In those areas, such as architecture, where excellence is embodied in individuals, the system adopts other means to convince all of the worth of the game, and to make students love to play the game.

The means used in architectural education to enforce this state of docile acceptance is by keeping students in a permanent state of insecure expectation. In the old Ecole des Beaux-Arts a particularly effective means of doing so was to allow students an indefinite period to complete their studies. Whatever other virtues it may have had, this held out to all the possibility that success could come next year if not this, if only a little more work were done, if only the game were played a little better.

Financial, legal, and institutional pressures have removed this mechanism from most places, although it is still in use at non-university elite schools. Today there are three ways to ensure docility. The first is by the control of students' time.[73] Design studio may represent some 70 percent of their credit-hours, but it consumes 90 percent of their time. The number of nights without sleep becomes a currency of great symbolic worth, a currency of devotion, whereby they demonstrate to the studio-master that they are coming to love the game. The second is with the use of vague, allusive, and elusive language in the design studio, which requires students to struggle to wring meaning, to worry about whether they have understood, frantically to hope they will please:

> Anyways, we would be working in the studio, designing swimming pools (which our professor called "negative volumetric spaces"). This professor would walk around the studio as we worked, pausing before each student's drawings to say "the . . . space . . . it lacks . . . the purpose of essence . . . in its own idea of . . . limitation . . . but within the constructs of the idea of . . . space within . . . time . . . it reflects . . . conscience . . ." and he would look off into space for a while in silence and then just wander off. Behind him came the assistant professor who would whisper to us "You should make that line heavier, clean up those eraser marks, and redraw that curve there." It was a curious mix of the ephemeral with the practical.[74]
>
> Throughout the year, we had each been responsible for presenting a historical outline and drawings of landmark buildings by a handful of "master architects". . . . I generally liked the house I worked on . . . but I could not isolate what made it good, or in advance of its time. To me, many of the other examples were as confusing. When the teachers gave clear identification of what they valued about these masterworks, we took what they said as gospel and stored it in our nervous minds.[75]

The third way to instill a sense of obedient acceptance is to encourage intense competition between individuals. The notion of competition—between individuals, between schools, between firms—is one of the enduring values of architecture. At the Ecole, competition was lauded as a virtue in itself, and progress was made by success in competition. Kathryn Anthony has documented in detail the necessary rigors that competition imposes on students: sleepless nights, stress, and anxiety.[76] Competition creates a whole symbolic market whereby students can show their dedication to the game. By atomizing the student body the studio system obliges students to play a serious game seriously, to realize that they play the game against others, and to devote their energies to the playing rather than to questioning the rules. The disciplines, ordeals, and vexations of studio competition—most especially in those competitions where there can only be one winner, as in the world of practice—demand from students a specific acquiescence and in particular a special form of acceptance.[77] By constantly competing for approbation and for approval, students can display to their teachers their desire for and acceptance of the game of architecture.

Longevity of the Studio System

The singular opportunities that the studio system provides the architecture student for acquiring and displaying a habitus must explain its longevity in architectural education. It is much the same as it was almost two hundred years ago when the Ecole des Beaux-Arts was founded. Prior to the foundation of the state French engineering school, the Ecole Polytechnique, both architecture and engineering had been taught by practitioners to small groups of students. If some theoretical instruction was needed, it was provided by a professor or a senior student on an ad hoc basis. The primary teaching site was the atelier, while formal lecturing remained separate from and marginal to the main process.

In the early years of the nineteenth century the founders of the Ecole Polytechnique devised a new method of pedagogy. The Polytechnique introduced the idea of having academics teach general theoretical subjects such as mathematics and mechanics for several years before introducing students to specialist knowledge in one or another branch of engineering. The school also introduced the now standard pedagogical technique of the lecture to a large number of students. Interspersed with the lectures were laboratories taken by subgroups of the whole working under a tutor.[78]

These techniques have become standard in the world's universities for many disciplines. One of the interesting aspects of architectural education is that it retains at its heart the rather older methods that the Polytechnique abandoned, but which were preserved by the Ecole des Beaux-Arts and passed down to modern American schools. One still hears the terminology of Paris from two hundred years ago—esquisse, charrette, jury. The other anglophone nations have been less beguiled, but even so they maintain the studio system as the unquestioned heart of architectural education.

Architecture as a Discipline

Let us now consider the field's production function, that is, the way it generates intellectual discourse. This is the responsibility of the *discipline* of architecture, the object of university administrations' despair and other academics' contempt. No great labor is required to unearth an article in the academic press that excoriates architecture for its failings as a discipline. Amos Rapoport's invited piece for the jubilee issue of one of the profession's most prestigious journals, the *Journal of Architectural Education,* can be taken as typical.[79] He bases his attack on the grounds that architecture has failed in its mission, which is the creation of environments for users: "The only justification for architecture as a profession is in providing better environments for people." To succeed in this, he argues, requires the development of a discipline-based profession. He remarks that the search for well-founded reliable knowledge "is precisely what a discipline is all about," and that architecture has made no attempt to develop such knowledge. Describing his own area of environment-behavior studies he amplifies his concept of what a discipline is:

> It tries to build explanatory theory without which normative statements are impossible. It is committed to rationality and reason, to explicit goals based on knowledge, goals which can be tested and refuted if wrong; in this way it is committed to the creation of a self-correcting discipline on which the professional/practice side must be firmly based.[80]

That this task is not as simple as Rapoport would have us believe may be gleaned from the fact that even to the individuals whom one would most readily identify as being its members—academics—it is not entirely clear if there actually exists a discipline of architecture, or just what architecture is. Rapoport complains that architecture's problem is precisely that there is no discipline worth the name, but that if there were one, its function would be to help architects do their job of creating decent environments for the users of buildings. As well as specifying its proper content he determines the discipline's form: it should resemble one of the social sciences. Others feel that there is no single discipline called "architecture" but a collection of intersecting research communities whose work feeds back mainly to their parent disciplines.[81] Some have wondered aloud whether there is anything to architectural research that is not building research, noting that the latter is not of much interest to architects.[82]

Other authors have made a case for the affirmative, that there is a discipline of architecture. One academic felt he had to spend several paragraphs convincing the reader of its existence and proceeded to define its concerns as the theories of what architects do and how they explained what they did.[83] Royston Landau, a historian and critic, also decided that the articulation and study of theories of architectural action was the proper focus of the discipline, defining it as essentially a historical and philosophical enterprise à la Foucault.[84] Linda Groat's conclusion, arrived at by quite a different route, is strikingly similar in arguing for studying architecture as a cultural process.[85] Both Landau and Groat argue that the heart of the matter is architectural culture, understood as consisting of architects and their audiences, a collection of individuals and discourses about them.

The Discipline in the Field

It is important to acknowledge that the field of architecture is much larger than the discipline of the same name.[86] Nor is the discipline wholly contained within the field. Members of the discipline are also members of the field of education, which commits them to teach, and to produce scholarship or research, not to just produce buildings. That is, disciplinarians must generate some sort of intellectual product. Many members of the *field* of literature write, producing novels, stories, poems, and plays. Members of the *discipline* of literary studies need not have written a work of fiction in their lives, but they must have produced some critical work about literature. Just so in architecture, as many architectural critics have never designed a building themselves.

Further, the discipline is not at all the same as the profession, and membership of the two only partly overlaps. The profession is full of people producing architecture, while the discipline is mainly filled with people who talk about architecture. The discipline is a second-order activity, a pursuit wholly dependent on the existence of architectural producers. *The central function of the discipline of architecture is to provide the intellectual instruments by which "architecture" is valorized. Discourse about these instruments constitutes the primary symbolic capital of the discipline.*

The nature of the particular intellectual instruments so devised— that is, the *content* of the discipline—is not of interest here. We can simply note in passing that all the instruments are arbitrary in that they could be other than they are, provided they served to convince others that certain parts of the built environment are good and great, and others are not. So, for example, in the Middle Ages one simply appealed to Platonic number theory to justify built form. Vitruvius was enlisted in the Renaissance and a more refined numerological mysticism introduced. Thence to the end of the nineteenth century architects fell back on an explicit declaration that some people—that is, they—had innately better taste than others, and that was that. Eighty years ago one talked about function. The content of the justification is irrelevant, as long as one can persuade the rest of the field that it is the right justification.

Structure of the Discipline
Architecture differs in several fundamental ways from disciplines such as the sciences. For those that have become most entrenched in universities, such as physics or sociology, the schools provide three important structures: an intellectual market of symbolic capital; a system of production of "knowledge" or "scholarship"; and a system to reproduce members of the discipline. The unification of these structures is most complete in the fully institutionalized disciplines, and least so in those at the other end of the continuum. So, for example, many physicists are employed in universities or associated research centers, and the discipline is firmly centered on these academic units. Academic departments reproduce physicists, employ physicists, and produce physics. Academic scientists produce their science in their capacity as academics. A scientist who stops producing science and starts talking about science is held to have moved into another area (such as history and philosophy of science). There is a very clear disjunction between doing science and producing discourse about it.

None of these things is true of architecture. Academic departments of architecture produce only a fraction of the total discourse of architecture, unlike their colleagues in the sciences. Similarly, chemistry departments, for example, are dedicated to producing members of the *discipline* of chemistry, whereas architecture departments are not committed to producing members of the discipline. Instead, they produce members of the *occupation*, architects. Further, while science departments produce science, architecture departments rarely produce architecture, but instead talk about architecture. When architectural academics design buildings, they do so in their capacity as members of a design firm quite distinct from their university department.

Architecture is clearly not nearly as academicized as physics or chemistry or the other natural sciences. At most two percent of American architects are employed as full-time academics, and the figure is probably rather closer to one percent.[87] Between ten and fifteen percent of American scientists are so employed.[88] Whether one takes the proportional difference as five or fifteen times, it is clear that a significantly higher proportion of scientists is embedded in academe compared to architects. Not at all surprising, but it does drive home the point that this necessarily gives the discipline of architecture a different character than that of any of the sciences. Academics exercise far less power in the field compared to those in other disciplines.

Universities employ only a proportion of those who would consider themselves members of the discipline. A large number of disciplinarians work as media critics, in galleries, museums, in the private sector, historical conservation, and in various cultural organizations that contribute to the work of the area. We may take the membership of the Society of Architectural Historians as an indicator: about a third are academics, a little less than a third are practicing architects, and most of the rest are working in historic preservation.[89]

A small fraction of practitioners would also consider themselves intellectual producers, but even if this amounted to only one percent of the professionals it would constitute a body of similar size to the academics. University-employed academics carry little clout in the discipline. As a result, the universities are not consecrating institutions in the way that they are for other disciplines. In other fields an authoritative opinion is sought from an eminent academic, whereas in architecture the equivalent authority is granted to, say, the critics of the *New York Times* or *Architectural Review*.

The importance of this lies in the fact that as a consequence the discipline of architecture is rather less affected by influences from other scholastically dominated disciplines and their academics. The scholastic virtues that the corporate university attempts to enforce on all its members are brought to bear on only a fraction of the members of the architectural discipline. Perhaps architectural publishing provides the best examples.

In the sciences, most journals are edited by academics and produced by academic presses. Papers are usually unsolicited, and blind-refereed by anonymous reviewers. The aim, whether it succeeds or not, is to remove personal bias from the process. The assumption, whether it is valid or not, is that a scientist's peers have the right to pass judgment on their fellows' work, and to determine what is publishable.

Architectural journals are usually produced by practitioners, local professional associations, arts institutions, or private publishers. The late *Progressive Architecture, Architecture,* and *AIA Journal* in the United States, *Architects' Journal* and *Architectural Review* in the United Kingdom, and *Domus* and *Architecture and Urbanism* elsewhere, for example, have nothing whatever to do with universities. Editors compete to obtain the rights to the most fashionable projects and architects. They practice what is euphemistically called "access journalism," which simply means that a bankable architect allows his or her work to be published if nothing particularly critical is said of it. In the worst cases, the architects insist on bowdlerizing articles prior to publication. Some of the most widely read journals and presses are little more than vanity publishing houses, relying on their favorite architects to pay for photographs and to buy a couple hundred books or magazines for use in self-advertising.[90]

Intellectual influences tend to penetrate architecture less through specific academic channels than through the wider communication system of the field of culture—media such as the *New York Review of Books*, the *Times Literary Supplement*, Channel 4, PBS, and so on. Conventional academic communication is minimal compared to other disciplines, a fact to which the paucity of architectural academic journals attests.[91] Two points should be made here. First, the great intellectual tides of the time bear on architecture more than specific ideas originating in other disciplines, and, second, they do so not so much through their influences on academics as on the other members of the field. Deconstruction offers an instructive example. It has been noted that this particular literary theory has penetrated various other disciplines, moving from academic departments of English to others. In architecture the movement was not from academic to academic, but from the architecture profession to the schools. Deconstruction underpinned the work of certain avant-garde architects, the writings of some critics, and some exhibitions at important galleries before it became a major topic of discussion in academe.⁹² In the English-speaking world, certainly, the universities have never been the major sites of intellectual production in architecture.

The capital par excellence in the *field* has always been that associated with the design of buildings or, more properly, with images of buildings, since it need hardly be said that some of the most important architecture has never been built: the drawings of Frank Lloyd Wright, Le Corbusier, most of the deconstructionists, and Boulleé come to mind. Images are often more important than any personal experience. For example, as Juan Pablo Bonta has demonstrated, one of the most influential buildings of the first half of the century, Mies van der Rohe's Barcelona Pavilion, existed only for a few months. It only achieved its status years after its destruction, through the promulgation of photographs.⁹³

Architectural discourse circulates as a secondary capital within the *discipline*. Deconstruction could be seen as an attempt by disciplinarians to revalue their capital to a status comparable to that of architecture per se. In this it is a weapon in the perpetual conflict between academic and architect, the former relegated to the role of mere exegete to the titanic demiurges of the profession. Within the sciences, academics hold a substantial portion of the symbolic capital of the field and therefore rank highly in its stratification systems. Elite scientists are embedded in academe and control its system of reproduction, around which research is organized. This is not so in architecture. Academics are secondary figures in the production system but dominate the reproduction side. Elite architects have little direct influence on the reproduction system, and even this is exercised only in sporadic and brief royal progresses through the design studios of the more elite schools, or the occasional hortatory harangue published in the popular architectural journals.

Architecture and Related Disciplines
To say that architecture produces instruments of valorization is to say that it produces the instruments of taste, the discourse that labels some buildings and architects great, and others not. This is not to say that this discourse is devoid of "knowledge," but to emphasize the fact—invariably ignored by architectural academics—that it does more than this. It is no

wonder then that areas one might normally consider of interest to architects, such as acoustics, or psychology, or sociology, carry so little weight in the discipline, for they are relevant to its central function only when the intellectual fashions of the time require their service in the formulation of the instruments of valorization. Architectural acousticians, for example, are really acousticians who happen to be working in architecture schools. They are predestined always and forever to be members of the discipline of acoustics, not of architecture, until such time as the turn of the intellectual wheel of fate might necessitate the enlistment of their discourse, as it did for a short while the discourse of psychologists in the 1970s. The fundamental failings discerned by psychologists and environmental scientists (such as Rapoport, quoted earlier) and all the others from disciplines "allied" to architecture (namely, the utter failure of architects to listen to them, the dismal and seemingly perverse inability to integrate the fruits of their scholarly labors into the architectural process) can be seen to be no fault of the architects, but the failure of others to perceive that their work has no bearing at all on the valorization of architecture.

Prime examples of this effect were provided by my own department at the University of Sydney. When we began offering courses in neural network analysis, accounting, photorealism, and loudspeaker design, is it any wonder that the designers and historians in our sister department of architecture asked what was going on? My department's new chair, educated in engineering and computer science, felt so little empathy with the architectural habitus that he inveigled the university into changing his title from Professor of Architectural Science to Professor of Design Science. No trace of my department could be found in that most comprehensive of architectural indexes, the *Avery Periodicals Index*. One had only to look at the departmental names (Architectural and Design Science; Architecture, Planning and Allied Arts) to realize that only the university's bureaucratic craving for neat organizational charts kept all of us under the one roof.

CONTEMPORARY TRANSFORMATIONS

The Expansion of the Subordinate Sector

In his introduction to a collection of essays on modern architectural practice, the eminent architectural academic Peter Rowe described the contemporary professional scene as one of malaise: chronic underemployment; low remuneration; declining respect from other occupations; and a sense of no longer being central to decision-making about the built environment.[1] Although later in the article Rowe fudged the point, it seems to me that this malaise is no more than a symptom of the massive deformation of the field produced by the huge increase in what I have termed the subordinate sector—the mass of practitioners—since the Second World War. To return to the United States as an example: from 1890 to 1950 the ratio of architects to population remained within 130 to 190 per million (fig. 6.1). Since then it has climbed steadily to almost 500 per million. During this period, the sector of eminent architects (those who are intellectually dominant) has remained quite small in absolute numbers (refer to table 4.5).

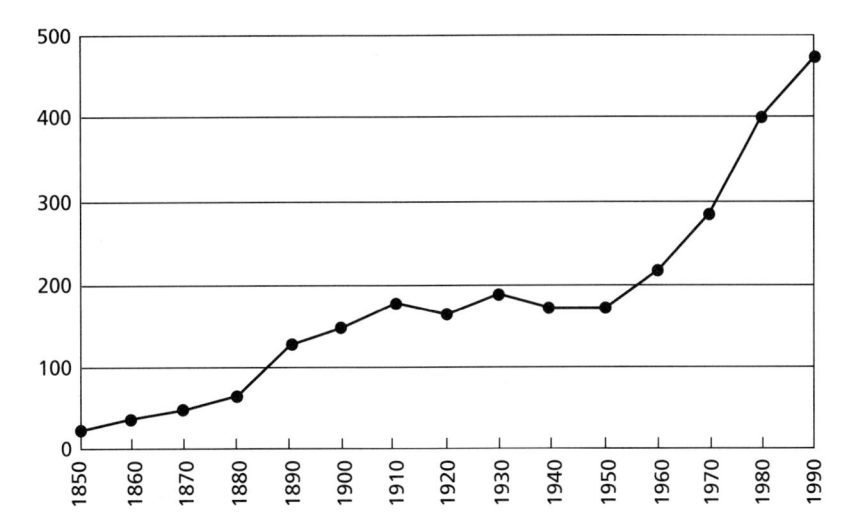

Figure 6.1 Number of architects per million population in the U.S.A. (Source: U.S. census.)

This expansion of the subordinate sector is the most significant development in the field in our century. It has changed the entire notion of "architect" by creating a huge class of people who are ideologically accustomed to take as their role models the members of the symbolically elite sector, but who can never hope to enter their ranks. We can expect to see great stresses in the occupation as a result. The ancient social function of the architect, I have argued, was to produce buildings of power and taste for people of power and taste. This is still the function of the sector of intellectually dominant architects. The networks I have described acted and still act as the primary mechanism whereby the most valued symbolic capitals are transmitted from architect to architect. But these networks have remained modest in size since the Renaissance, failing to grow anywhere near as quickly as the subordinate sector. No doubt they are constrained by the numbers of social ties that a single individual can maintain. As a result, the elite sector now stands in a different relation to the mass of practitioners than it did, say, a century or even fifty years ago.

The eminent architects are responsible for their own reproduction through what is in effect a perpetuation of the old apprenticeship system; but the subordinate sector of architects is reproduced by the university-based educational system. The institutionalized schools have arisen as a second site for the transmission of symbolic capital alongside the network of the most eminent. They have succeeded prodigiously in increasing the numbers of workaday architects, but have had no effect on the production of architects of genius. Those whose names will endure, the architects occupying a symbolic social space, must acquire their capital the old way, by participating in a master-pupil chain.

The two transmission systems intersect, but only at the most prestigious institutions. One is vastly more likely to encounter the leading architects of the day at Harvard, Yale, or the Architectural Association than in provincial colleges. Likewise, these same architects are vastly more likely to welcome as interns to their offices students they have personally encountered than others. Since only the privileged have the resources (and the habitus) to enter the most prestigious institutions, the net effect is to maintain—*with neither conscious intent nor labored effort*—a more or less closed system whereby the privileged are more likely to become eminent architects than others.

The Permanent Crisis in Architectural Education

The profession has never been reticent about criticizing those responsible for the growth in the subordinate sector, the universities. Complaints of the rupture between education and practice have been made in the U.S.A. and the U.K. since the 1930s.[2] One wonders just what it is that the regular accreditation reviews are reviewing if the state of education is as bad as painted. One's suspicions are further aroused when two characteristics of architectural academics are noted. First, architecture schools use very large numbers of outsiders, nonacademic practitioners, in the school system: approximately 22 percent of full-time equivalent academic staff are casuals in the United States. Second, schools are usually quite insistent that their academics have an architecture degree, and preferably be licensed or eligible for licensure. With such a remarkable penetration of practitioners into academe, it is at first sight extraordinary that there should be such a disjuncture between the needs of practice and the skills of graduates.

The Critique of the Intellectually Dominant

We can explain with little effort the eternal criticisms from the elite segments, the architects with high amounts of intellectual capital. As Bourdieu has pointed out, denunciation of the backwardness, mediocrity, or incompetence of the schools is almost de rigueur for the leaders of the avant-gardes, the prophets. But the educational system serves an important function precisely by being behind the times. The prophetic project, which seeks to change the structure of the field, is necessarily opposed to the endeavors of the educational system, one of whose crucial functions is to preserve the accumulated symbolic capital of the field. As a conservator of society's cultural capital, the educational system of necessity changes slowly: the American and British architecture schools took until the 1950s to abandon Beaux-Arts curricula, and some American schools have even revived them.[3]

The prophets must oppose their individual charisma to the institutional authority of the educational system. They feel cheated of recognition by those who merely interpret and elucidate, without themselves creating architecture. There is something of a class conflict in this too, since the prophets, having adopted a risky strategy to success, were usually brought up in the highest social strata; whereas the academics, having taken the more stolid and secure path of salaried employment, tend to originate from a rung or two down the social ladder.[4] But, carp as they may, the prophets need the schools to conserve the works of the great for posterity. Without the educational system to conserve their memories, they know they would pass into oblivion.

We must therefore accept that critiques (often bitter) of the schools from the avant-garde will always be with us, and understand that they arise from no particular defect in architectural training, but from the very structure of the field.

The Critique of the Professionally Dominant

In some cases the criticisms originating from the professionally dominant members seem to be little more than whining. CAD training provides a case in point. CAD systems had been used by a small number of large firms since the mid-1970s, but they only became common in the mid-1980s when falling prices made the machines and programs affordable for the small and medium-sized firms predominant enough in practice. Since those running the firms were not inclined to sit in front of the screens themselves, an acute shortage of CAD operators developed. Practices discovered that those they trained in-house often moved on to higher-paid jobs elsewhere with little trouble. This was quite a shock: the firms had been accustomed to a large supply of docile and readily replaceable workers. Unused to anything but a buyer's market for skills, they decided that CAD training was "uneconomic" to do themselves, by which they meant that the schools should bring the price of operators down by flooding the market with CAD-trained students. The eminent members of the accreditation panels began castigating the schools for failing to possess the foresight they so markedly lacked themselves, and took them to task for not responding to a demand that had not existed but five years before.

It is most unlikely that the ongoing complaints by practitioners really have much to do with the level of skills of graduates. As one who taught CAD for many years, I feel that such skills are best acquired in the office, where students can hone their skills with hours of practice: university is the worst place to do it. As the sociologist Randall Collins has discussed at length, there is a great deal of empirical evidence that academic schooling does not significantly enhance the practical effectiveness of future practitioners in any profession.[5] The content of schooling does not provide the direct practical skills that neophytes will eventually acquire in offices; there is little relationship between academic performance and performance in practice; most practical skills are learnt on the job; and there is no clear superiority in the performance of those with degrees compared to those without.[6] If this is so, why does the profession keep complaining?

Transformations of the Field

The New Market for Credentials

The most recent examination of architectural education, the Boyer Report, discusses the education-practice breach, and recommends closer ties between the two spheres.[7] What I find quite remarkable in this well-intentioned but self-satisfied and sociologically naive document is that, while the authors record the fact that the rupture has been a subject of complaint for sixty years or more in report after report, they utterly fail to see any significance in the longevity of the criticism. Any characteristic of the field that endures for generation after generation can be no mere accident of academic incompetence, but must arise from deep structural properties.

I suggest that the so-called rupture is an artifact arising from the creation of new symbolic markets. By instituting formal schooling that leads to a credential of some kind, the English-speaking architectural field created a new form of market. When occupations become credentialed a market develops for the credentials themselves, regardless of the type and quality of the skills provided.[8] Over time, the skills market tends to dissociate from the credentials market. As the supply of credentialed persons is dependent on the suppliers (the universities) and not on the demands of the market for architects, and as the universities can always fill their quotas, an oversupply tends to develop. The system can react to market demand by opening more schools, but has more difficulty reacting to a lack of demand by closing them.

A credential's worth is proportional to its rarity. When hardly anyone in a society has a high school education, a bachelor's degree is a guarantee of a good job. When almost everyone has a bachelor's, it is not. As the proportion of credentialed individuals rises, the very nature of the occupation for which they are credentialed slowly changes. To think of "architect" as simply a synonym for "designer of buildings" is to ignore all the social qualities attached to the occupation, qualities that were quite different, say, in the United States in 1900, when there were 145 per million of the population, than in 1990, when there were some 460 per million. As important as absolute changes—such as proportion of degree holders—are the relational ones, how a group stands in relation to others.

In 1800 a construction worker, for example, did not have to be able to read or write as a requirement for his job, and quite possibly was actually illiterate. This put him into a certain social relation with other illiterates in the population (fairly close) and into another with degreed individuals (very distant). Today the proportion of illiterates among laborers is substantially smaller, increasing their social distance from other illiterates, and decreasing their distance from college graduates.

An increase in the number of credentialed practitioners caused by an increase in the field's reproductive capacity therefore sets up tensions in an occupation. Qualifications are worth what their holders are worth, so opening up an occupation to those with substantially less economic or social capital than existing occupants downclasses the whole.[9] The old occupants feel threatened not only by the sheer volume of newcomers, but by their lower-status origins. The newcomers, entering an occupation with a chronic oversupply of credentialed individuals, find that the expected rewards—symbolic or material—fail to appear. So what appears to be a simple clash of old versus young is, in fact, a conflict brought about by the different generations having different relations to the educational system.[10] The result is the creation of new trajectories for an occupation's entrants, as they struggle to achieve what they feel their credentials owe them.

New Trajectories

There are various ways to prevent a downclassing of the whole occupation in the face of a sudden increase of members. One way is to institute credential inflation. In order to retain their hold on the most lucrative occupations, the dominant classes tend to redefine the criteria needed for access to those jobs, slowly and constantly upgrading the credentials needed for them. Practitioners, believing that graduates are inadequate, call for longer training leading to higher degrees: at first a bachelor's degree is all that is needed, then a master's, then perhaps some form of postgraduate diploma or continuing professional development system. The process is most obvious in the United States. The professional medical degree there is an M.D., a Doctor of Medicine, whereas other Anglophone nations have been content to award what they call a bachelor's degree (often a double bachelor's) for the same length of schooling. In the American legal system, which has been flooded by entrants in the last fifty years, a J.D. is increasingly common as a terminal degree. An identical process is happening in architecture: many schools in the United States graduate their students with a terminal master's degree, and several years ago a D.Arch. was mooted for both American and European architects.[11]

Another method is to create a dumping ground, a place where newcomers can effectively be prevented from ascending the hierarchies. They may call themselves architects, but find that they never proceed along the career paths promised by their educators, denied the material and symbolic rewards they feel their credentials entitle them to. This, I believe, is the function of computer-aided design in architecture. In a sense, CAD came along at just the right time for the architectural profession. CAD has allowed firms to park the oversupply of graduates in front of machines, and to surreptitiously deny them advancement to higher levels by devising new and covert career ladders, in which a hardening of the division of labor between CAD operators and others is relegating the former to a path that will never lead to management levels. The profession should also be grateful that the productivity gains hyped by the CAD vendors failed to materialize. We would have an even greater oversupply if they had. My own investigations (unpublished) indicate that between 1972 (when hardly any firms used CAD) and 1992 (when almost all did), the profession's productivity *declined* by 3 percent.

This is one new trajectory that has developed in the contemporary field, but one that will be taken by those with the least amount of cultural capital, students who did so well in the architectural science courses I used to teach, yet labored to understand what was required of them in the design studio. There are, fortunately, other social spaces available for them. Project, construction, and facilities management, for example, are all viable options for those who lack the symbolic capitals necessary for success as an architect. They allow these individuals to devote themselves to the economic aspects of construction, and to achieve success on an economic rather than a symbolic dimension.

Different trajectories will be found by those with more cultural capital who nonetheless choose not to join the profession. They will migrate to indeterminate new occupations where they can attempt to achieve the rewards promised by their devalued credentials, areas where charm, cultivation, and good taste can be deployed. The media, graphic design, interior design, historical conservation, fashion, and theater are possible locations. We can expect to see an increase in occupational titles with fuzzy definitions, blurred areas of social space with no particular academic requirements, where those with architecture degrees can convert their symbolic capitals.

These processes will at first be misinterpreted by commentators, who will see the new trajectories as a celebration of the versatility of the architect. But the individuals without the occupational title of "architect" will not associate themselves with other architects. They will not sit the registration exams. They will not join their professional associations. They will become part of the movement in the English-speaking world that is transforming the architecture degree into something like its Italian counterpart, a particular sort of liberal arts education.

Explaining Some Puzzles

I can now explain the tensions and misunderstandings between my own department of Architectural and Design Science (DADS) and that of Architecture (DAPAA) at the University of Sydney.

Each academic (professor), and the courses they taught, could be defined by their position in the usual twofold social space. DAPAA, and especially the design studio staff and the historians, occupied a point of high symbolic (or aesthetic) and low temporal (or economic) capital. All their endeavors centered on the valorization of architecture. DADS occupied a very different position: none of its courses had anything to do with the symbolic.

Compare, for example, the social universes of the two extremes, the computerists in DADS and the historians in DAPAA. From the computerists, one only ever heard of the size of their research grants, the frequency of their overseas travel, their constant conferences, how many emails they sent each day (or was that each hour?), how many committees they sat on, how many honorific titles they had, how many papers they wrote each month, the number of graduates they had, how fast their field was changing. Their discourse was all numbers, and everything ultimately was construed in economic terms: how do we do things better, faster, cheaper? The social philosopher Steve Fuller was quite right to define the so-called knowledge society as "what advanced capitalism looks like to intellectuals, once they have been assimilated into its mode of production."[12] Although I had been active in CAD research until the late 1980s, I found in the late 1990s that I could barely understand their research topics. I would be surprised if the average architect could. The same architect could have read the works of the historians in DAPAA without trouble. These professors were content to produce a book each decade or so, a paper every now and again. The quality of their doctoral students, and the quality of their relationships with them, was more important than their numbers. They didn't really have much use for research money, save for travel. Every quantitative indicator the bureaucratic university prized, they were indifferent to.

Architecture's hapless position in the university system was no fault of its own. The standard model we have today holds, first, that architectural education should be formal and institutionalized, and, second, that this institutionalization is best achieved in universities. From this follows the corollary that, since universities conduct both research and teaching, these two pursuits should also be linked in architecture schools.

None of these propositions has any inevitability about it. The apprenticeship system functioned effectively in the United Kingdom until the 1950s, and in the United States until the 1930s.[13] Architecture in those countries seems to have suffered little in the nineteenth century because of it. There are still several potent examples of the system's efficacy, such as the Frank Lloyd Wright Fellowship. A student's apprenticeship has simply been delayed until his or her later years, as when he or she tries to find employment in the offices of charismatic architects.

The concept that architecture should be institutionalized at all was derived from French and German education, but in those nations the schools existed outside research-centered organizations, whether in special institutions such as the Ecole or in the non-university higher education sector, as the Bauhaus was. The existence of the AA, Cooper Union, and BAC, among others, shows that even today it is perfectly possible to disengage architectural teaching from research.

At the time the American universities took on the task of professional education, they were not research-driven institutions. That transformation occurred several decades later. The professions found themselves in organizations whose entire nature had changed around them, and are still coping with the problems this has caused.[14]

Given this, surely there can be little point in castigating architectural schools for their lack of research or "know-nothing-ism." Research, as envisaged by scientists, is simply not a natural function of the architectural education system of the English-speaking world, *and never has been.* "Research" implies that a discipline produces knowledge and nothing more. Architecture also produces taste and ways of valorizing buildings. As a result, its productions bear scant resemblance to those from other areas.

In France, where the major actors in the field were institutionalized in the Ecole and the Académie, substantive theoretical work was the responsibility of those actors. In the U.K. and the U.S.A. the most important theoretical work—both in architecture and in what others would call building—has always been conducted outside the universities or by individuals only loosely affiliated with universities. The structure of the Anglo-American architectural field locates the most important positions in contexts other than academia, among the urban intelligentsia, as most disciplines did before the coming of the German type of research university late in the nineteenth century. Those positions are what have driven the field of architecture. The same is true for other disciplines, such as law. A closer look at the critics of the schools' lack of any sort of research orientation would show that they themselves invariably come from disciplines—especially psychology, sociology, and the physical sciences—in which most research is conducted in universities or in organizations attached to universities. Such individuals assume that the universities are the normal and traditional place where all intellectual work is conducted, and found their criticisms on this assumption.

When the universities complain of the inadequacies of architectural academics *qua* academics, they are not really playing fair. The profession did not ask the universities to reproduce it, the universities decided to take this on themselves. After they had done so they changed the rules of the academic game by transforming themselves into research-driven institutions. This has suited the sciences, which today organize their research around graduate training, thus completely uniting the production and reproduction functions.[15] The universities should not expect all disciplines to look like the sciences, nor try to force on them ill-suited structures of intellectual production.

As for the complaints from the architecture profession: if it really wanted better practical training from the educational system, then the best response would be to close the university-based schools and either institute part-time schools outside the universities (like the original AA) or return to the apprenticeship system, with perhaps a supplementary period of training in technical subjects such as structures and building services. I find nothing of merit in the notion that the increasing complexity of the building process necessitates degreed individuals. While it is true that buildings have become more complex, all these complexities have passed outside of architecture's domain and into that of other occupations.

But architecture is not about to leave the universities. In the European Union, bureaucracies will not only insist on a degree, but one requiring a specific duration to earn. In the United States, universities will not abandon a market as long as it is profitable. The inexorable pressures of credential inflation also militate against an abandonment of the universities.

It is a tragedy that the field as a whole maintains the fiction that the huge new segment of the field created this century is identical in nature to the older and much smaller sector inhabited by the eminent. Architects, critics, and academics alike take as feasible for all what is in fact feasible only for the few architects inhabiting the purely symbolic space of the field. The confusion is not only made possible but encouraged by the fact that all have the same occupational title of "architect" (in the English-speaking world, at least). By conflating "architect" and "building designer" the field obfuscates the fact that *why* one designs—whether through (economic) necessity or for (symbolic) renown—is more important than the fact that one designs at all, and that those at the summit of the field who design structures of power and taste for people of power and taste have little in common with those who toil at CAD workstations detailing supermarkets.

NOTES

Chapter 1 Targeting the Favored Circle

1. There is a considerable body of literature on this topic, several journals, and at least one professional organization—the Environment and Design Research Association (EDRA)—devoted to it. A good review can be found in an unexpected source: D. L. Lawrence and S. M. Low, "The Built Environment and Spatial Form," *Annual Review of Anthropology* 19 (1990): 453–505.

2. T. L. Donaldson's inaugural lectures at University College London in 1841 were "Architecture as an Art" and "Architecture as a Science."

3. J. Templer, "Architectural Research," *Journal of Architectural Education* 44, no. 1 (1990): 3.

4. D. W. MacKinnon, "The Nature and Nurture of Creative Talent," *American Psychologist* 17 (1962): 484–495; "The Personality Correlates of Creativity: A Study of American Architects," *14th International Congress of Applied Psychology* (Copenhagen, 1962), 11–39; "Creativity and Images of the Self," in *The Study of Lives,* ed. R. W. White (New York: Atherton Press, 1963), 251–278; and "Personality and the Realization of Creative Potential," *American Psychologist* 20 (1965): 273–281.

5. Corroborated by A. D. Kanner, "Femininity and Masculinity: Their Relationships to Creativity in Male Architects and Their Independence from Each Other," *Journal of Consulting and Clinical Psychology* 44, no. 5 (1976): 802–805.

6. See H. E. Schmidt, "Personality Correlates of the Creative Architecture Student," *Perceptual and Motor Skills* 36 (1973): 1030; J. M. Peterson and G. Lansky, "Left-Handedness among Architects: Partial Replication and Some New Data," *Perceptual and Motor Skills* 45 (1977): 1216–1218; J. M. Peterson and G. Lansky, "Left-Handedness among Architects: Some Facts and Speculation," *Perceptual and Motor Skills* 38 (1974): 547–550; J. M. Peterson and L. M. Lansky, "Success in Architecture: Handedness and/or Visual Thinking," *Perceptual and Motor Skills* 50 (1980): 1139–1143; and J. M. Peterson and G. Sweitzer, "Field-Independent Architecture Students," *Perceptual and Motor Skills* 36 (1973): 195–198.

7. H. E. Schmidt, "The Identification of High and Low Creativity in Architecture Students," *Psychologia Africana* 15 (1973): 39.

8. A. M. Dolke and R. S. Sharma, "General Aptitude Test Battery (GATB) as a Predictor of Academic Success in Architectural Courses," *Indian Journal of Psychology* 50, no. 2 (1975): 163–173.

9. D. E. Domer and A. E. Johnson, "Selective Admissions and Academic Success: An Admissions Model for Architecture Students," *College and University* 58 (1982): 19–30.

10. P. Stringer, "The Role of Spatial Ability in a First Year Architecture Course," *Architectural Research and Teaching* 2, no. 1 (1971): 23–33.

11. M. Karlins, C. Schuerhoff, and M. Kaplan, "Some Factors Related to Architectural Creativity in Graduating Architecture Students," *Journal of General Psychology* 81 (1969): 203–215.

12. R. Weisberg, *Creativity: Beyond the Myth of Genius* (New York: W. H. Freeman, 1993).

13. Those traits one might consider undesirable are simply not talked about. Little is said, for example, that on the Minnesota Multiphasic Personality Inventory, MacKinnon's talented group scored moderately highly on the scales for psychopathic deviation, paranoia, and schizophrenia.

14 S. Ahrentzen and L. N. Groat, "Rethinking Architectural Education: Patriarchal Conventions and Alternative Visions from the Perspectives of Women Faculty," *Journal of Architectural and Planning Research* 9, no. 2 (1992): 100.

15 R. Gutman, "Architects and Power: The Natural Market for Architecture," *Progressive Architecture,* December 1992, 39–41.

16 R. Gutman, "Human Nature in Architectural Theory: The Example of Louis Kahn," in *Architects' People,* ed. R. Ellis and D. Cuff (New York: Oxford University Press, 1989), 107.

17 H. J. Gans, "Toward a Human Architecture: A Sociologist's View of the Profession," *Journal of Architectural Education* 31, no. 2 (1978): 27.

18 D. Cuff, "Through the Looking Glass: Seven New York Architects and Their People," in *Architects' People,* ed. Ellis and Cuff, 64–102.

19 B. Hillier, "Quite Unlike the Pleasures of Scratching: Theory and Meaning in Architectural Form," *9H* 7 (1985): 66–71.

20 S. Kostoff, "Foreword," in *Architects' People,* ed. Ellis and Cuff, xiii.

21 Really, nothing could be further from the truth than that "the nobility of architecture has always rested on the idea that it is a social art," as the Boyer report into architectural education described it (E. L. Boyer and L. D. Mitgang, *Building Community* [Princeton, NJ: Carnegie Foundation for the Advancement of Teaching, 1996], 3). This profound asociality, curiously, extends into the associated field of computer-aided architectural design. Many of the most eminent theoretical works in this area are strikingly formalist and unpeopled, such as W. J. Mitchell, *The Logic of Architecture* (Cambridge: MIT Press, 1990). For further discussion, see A. Ward, "The Suppression of the Social in Design," in *Reconstructing Architecture,* ed. T. A. Dutton and L. H. Mann (Minneapolis: University of Minnesota Press, 1996), 27–70.

22 Three examples will suffice: G. Rose, "Architecture and Philosophy: The Postmodern Complicity," *Theory, Culture and Society* 5 (1988): 357–371; J. Knesl and K. Frampton, "Cultural Resistance in the Postmodern Condition," *Precis* 6 (1987): 113–117; and S. Zukin, "The Postmodern Debate over Urban Form," *Theory, Culture and Society* 5 (1988): 431–446.

23 R. Collins, "Sociology: Proscience or Antiscience?" *American Sociological Review* 54 (1989): 124–139, and R. Collins, "Cumulation and Anticumulation in Sociology," *American Sociological Review* 55 (1990): 462–463.

24 T. J. Diffey, "The Sociological Challenge to Aesthetics," *British Journal of Aesthetics* 24, no. 2 (1984): 168–171.

25 S. Woolgar and D. Pawluch, "Ontological Gerrymandering: The Anatomy of Social Problems Explanations," *Social Problems* 32, no. 3 (1985): 214–227.

26 A fourth area could be called the consultative, in which the sociologist tries to explain to the architect what benefits sociology could bring to his or her work, such as in Gans, "Toward a Human Architecture"; R. Gutman, "Architecture and Sociology," *American Sociologist* 10 (1975): 219–228; and J. Blau, "The Context and Content of Collaboration: Architecture and Sociology," *Journal of Architectural Education* 45, no. 1 (1991): 36–40.

27 J. Balfe, "Moving toward a New Paradigm on Social Sciences and on Social Sciences and the Arts," in *Social Science and the Arts, 1984: A State-of-the-Arts Review from the Tenth Annual Conference on Social Theory, Politics, and the Arts,* ed. J. P. Robinson (Lanham, MD: University Press of America, 1985), 5–16.

28 V. L. Zolberg, *Constructing a Sociology of the Arts* (New York: Cambridge University Press, 1990).

29. See, for example, T. Adorno, *Introduction to the Study of Music* (New York: Seabury Press, 1976 [1962]); A. Hauser, *The Sociology of Art* (Chicago: University of Chicago Press, 1982); and J. Wolff, *The Social Production of Art* (London: Macmillan, 1981).
30. A review of the sociology of art can be found in J. R. Blau, "Study of the Arts: A Reappraisal," *Annual Review of Sociology* 14 (1988): 269–292.
31. R. Gutman, *Architectural Practice: A Critical View* (Princeton: Princeton Architectural Press, 1988).
32. The illegal underpayment, or even nonpayment, of young architects is attacked in T. Fisher, "The Intern Trap: How the Profession Exploits Its Young," *Progressive Architecture,* July 1994, 69–73.
33. Almost ten years after Gutman's observation, the AIA was still being savaged as expensive, irrelevant, ineffective, and incompetent. See M. J. Crosbie, "AIA: Worth the Price of Admission?" *Progressive Architecture,* April 1994, 61–100.
34. Discussion of whether low morale is the fault of the educational system or practice can be found in P. Carolin, "Expectation versus Reality in Architectural Education," in *Strategic Study of the Profession,* ed. F. Duffy (London: Royal Institute of British Architects, 1992), 171–182.
35. D. Cuff, *Architecture: The Story of Practice* (Cambridge: MIT Press, 1991).
36. J. Blau, "Where Architects Work: A Change Analysis, 1970–1980," in *The Design Professions and the Built Environment,* ed. P. Knox (Beckenham, U.K.: Croom Helm, 1988), 127–146; J. R. Blau and K. L. Lieben, "Growth, Decline, and Death: A Panel Study of Architectural Firms," in *Professionals and Urban Form,* ed. J. R. Blau, M. La Gory, and J. S. Pipkin (Albany: State University of New York Press, 1983), 224–250; and J. Blau, *Architects and Firms* (Cambridge: MIT Press, 1984).
37. M. S. Larson, G. Leon, and J. Bolick, "The Professional Supply of Design: A Descriptive Study of Architectural Firms," in *Professionals and Urban Form,* ed. Blau, La Gory, and Pipkin, 251–279.
38. M. S. Larson, "Emblem and Exception: The Historical Definition of the Architect's Professional Role," in *Professionals and Urban Form,* ed. Blau, La Gory, and Pipkin, 49–85.
39. D. Brain, "Practical Knowledge and Occupational Control: The Professionalization of Architecture in the United States," *Sociological Forum* 6, no. 2 (1991): 239–268.
40. D. Brain, "Discipline and Style: The Ecole des Beaux Arts and the Social Production of an American Architecture," *Theory and Society* 18 (1989): 807–868.
41. M. S. Larson, "In the Matter of Experts and Professionals, or How Impossible It Is to Leave Nothing Unsaid," in *The Formation of Professions: Knowledge, State and Strategy,* ed. R. Torstendahl and M. Burrage (London: Sage, 1990), 24–50.
42. M. S. Larson, *Behind the Postmodern Facade* (Berkeley: University of California Press, 1993).
43. M. S. Larson, "Architectural Competitions as Discursive Events," *Theory and Society* 23 (1994): 469–504.
44. R. Filson, "Can Schools Span the Gap to Practice?" *Architectural Record,* November 1985, 59.
45. Blau, "Context and Content of Collaboration."
46. R. Ferris, "Introduction," in *Reflections on Architectural Practices in the Nineties,* ed. W. S. Saunders (New York: Princeton Architectural Press, 1996), 8–9.

　　For more detail, the reader anxious to confirm that architecture is a "true profession" might refer to Cullen's discussion of the degree to which architecture meets five selected criteria of professionalism. Cullen's criteria were the complexity of relationships to people, the strength of occupational associations, length of training, legal requirement for licensure, and prestige. He concluded that architecture was not as professionalized as medicine or law, but was most certainly a "true profession." J. Cullen, "Structural Aspects of the Architectural Profession," *Journal of Architectural Education* 31, no. 2 (1978): 18–25.

47 T. Fisher, "Can This Profession Be Saved?" *Progressive Architecture,* February 1994, 45–49, 84.

48 A. Abbott, *The System of Professions: An Essay on the Division of Expert Labor* (Chicago: University of Chicago Press, 1988).

49 E. Freidson, "The Theory of the Professions: State of the Art," in *The Sociology of the Professions,* ed. R. Dingwall and P. Lewis (London: Macmillan, 1983), 19–37.

50 M. S. Larson, *The Rise of Professionalism: A Sociological Analysis* (Berkeley: University of California Press, 1977).

51 J. Kocka, "'Bürgertum' and Professions in the Nineteenth Century: Two Alternative Approaches," in *Professions in Theory and History: Rethinking the Study of the Professions,* ed. M. Burrage and R. Torstendahl (London: Sage, 1990), 62–74.

52 R. Torstendahl, "Knowledge and Power," in *University and Society,* ed. M. Trow and T. Nybom (London: Jessica Kingsley, 1991), 35–46.

53 R. Collins, "Changing Conceptions in the Sociology of Professions," in *The Formation of Professions,* ed. Torstendahl and Burrage, 11–23.

54 Z. B. Jaszczolt, "Introduction," in *Architectural Practice in Europe 4: Benelux,* ed. K. Hall (London: RIBA Publications, 1975), 5–9.

55 V. Clark, "A Struggle for Existence: The Professionalization of German Architects," in *German Professions 1800–1950,* ed. G. Cocks and K. H. Jarausch (Oxford: Oxford University Press, 1990), 143–160.

56 B. Allies, H. Anderson, and L. Hellman, "Students of Europe 1," *Architects' Journal,* 20 April 1988, 35–49.

57 H. B. Ellwood, "Introduction," in *Architectural Practice in Europe 3: Italy,* ed. K. Hall (London: RIBA Publications, 1974), 5–9.

58 J. M. Dixon, "P/A Reader Poll: Fees and Encroachment," *Progressive Architecture,* November 1988, 15–17.

59 Source is the Union Internationale des Architectes, quoted in L. Rogers and J. Welsh, "World Cup," *RIBA Journal,* June 1995, 10–13. Counting architects (or architecture students) is not the simple task it might appear. Do we count people with architecture degrees, those who are registered (licensed), or those who call themselves architects at census time? I know quite a number of architects who have never bothered to sit the registration exam, and some who have neither a degree nor registration. The matter is even more confusing in those countries that have regional rather than national registration, such as the U.S.A., Australia, and Italy.

60 Larson, "In the Matter of Experts and Professionals."

61 E. Freidson, "The Changing Nature of Professional Control," *Annual Review of Sociology* 10 (1984): 1–20.

62 Abbott, *The System of Professions.*

63 Brain, "Discipline and Style."

64. Best estimates are that architects are involved in the construction of between 30 to 50 percent of the contract value of buildings produced in the developed world. See R. Verges-Escuin, "Present and Future Missions for the Architect," *Fifteenth World Congress of the International Union of Architects* (Cairo, 1985).

Chapter 2 The Sociological Toolkit of Pierre Bourdieu

1. D. Brain, "Cultural Production as 'Society in the Making,'" in *The Sociology of Culture,* ed. D. Crane (Oxford: Blackwell, 1994), 191–220.
2. S. Lash, "Pierre Bourdieu: Cultural Economy and Social Change," in *Bourdieu: Critical Perspectives,* ed. C. Calhoun, E. LiPuma, and M. Postone (Cambridge, U.K.: Polity Press, 1993), 193.
3. "Le Palmarès," *L'Evénement du Jeudi,* 2–8 February 1989, 66.
4. P. Bourdieu, *Distinction: A Social Critique of Taste,* trans. R. Nice (Cambridge: Harvard University Press, 1984).
5. R. Jenkins, *Pierre Bourdieu* (London: Routledge, 1992), 11.
6. D. Swartz, *Culture and Power: The Sociology of Pierre Bourdieu* (Chicago: University of Chicago Press, 1997); D. Robbins, *The Work of Pierre Bourdieu: Recognizing Society* (Milton Keynes, U.K.: Open University Press, 1991); B. Fowler, *Pierre Bourdieu and Cultural Theory* (London: Sage, 1997); *An Introduction to the Work of Pierre Bourdieu: The Practice of Theory,* ed. R. Harker, C. Mahar, and C. Wilkes (London: Macmillan, 1990); *Bourdieu: Critical Perspectives,* ed. Calhoun, LiPuma, and Postone; and Jenkins, *Pierre Bourdieu.* I recommend Swartz and Robbins; Jenkins is easier to read, but unremittingly hostile to his subject. Fowler is quite dense, and strictly for other sociologists. An on-line and well-maintained (at the time of this writing) bibliography can be found at http://www.massey.ac.nz/~NZSRDA/bourdieu/home.htm.
7. Evidence is provided by the Institute for Scientific Information's Citation Indexes. Citations of Bourdieu in the *Arts and Humanities* and *Social Sciences* indexes combined have outnumbered those of Jacques Derrida since 1994. Citations of Foucault are about twice as numerous as those of either of his comrades.
8. D. Crane, "Introduction: The Challenge of the Sociology of Culture to Sociology as a Discipline," in *The Sociology of Culture,* ed. Crane, 1–20.
9. P. Bourdieu and L. J. D. Wacquant, *An Invitation to Reflexive Sociology* (Chicago: University of Chicago Press, 1992).
10. J. Galtung, "Structure, Culture, and Intellectual Style: An Essay Comparing Saxonic, Teutonic, Gallic and Nipponic Approaches," *Social Science Information* 20, no. 6 (1981): 830.
11. C. C. Lemert, "Literary Politics and the *Champ* of French Sociology," *Theory and Society* 10 (1981): 645.
12. Bourdieu, *Distinction,* 23.
13. R. Collins, "Cultural Capitalism and Symbolic Violence," in *Sociology Since Midcentury: Essays in Theory Cumulation,* ed. R. Collins (New York: Academic Press, 1981), 173.
14. I. Craib, *Modern Social Theory* (London: Wheatsheaf, 1984).
15. P. Bourdieu, *Sociology in Question,* trans. R. Nice (London: Sage, 1993).

16 L. J. D. Wacquant, "On the Tracks of Symbolic Power: Prefatory Notes to Bourdieu's 'State Nobility,'" *Theory, Culture and Society* 10 (1993): 1–17; L. J. D. Wacquant, "From Ruling Class to Field of Power: An Interview with Pierre Bourdieu on La Noblesse d'État," *Theory, Culture and Society* 10 (1993): 19–44; and R. Johnson, "Pierre Bourdieu on Art, Literature and Culture," in P. Bourdieu, *The Field of Cultural Production: Essays on Art and Literature,* ed. R. Johnson (Cambridge, U.K.: Polity Press, 1993), 1–25.

17 D. Gartman, "Culture as Class Symbolization or Mass Reification? A Critique of Bourdieu's Distinction," *American Journal of Sociology* 97, no. 2 (1991): 421–447.

18 See M. Sabour, "Bourdieu's Renewed Critical Evaluation of Cultural Capital, Symbolic Violence and Vocation of Sociology," *International Journal of Contemporary Sociology* 28 (1991): 129–139; and E. Wilson, "Picasso and Paté de Foie Gras: Pierre Bourdieu's Sociology of Culture," *Diacritics* 18 (1988): 47–60.

19 P. Bourdieu, "Back to History: An Interview," in *The Heidegger Controversy: A Critical Reader,* ed. R. Wolin (New York: Columbia University Press, 1991), 274–281.

20 D. Ghirardo, "Eisenman's Bogus Avant-Garde," *Progressive Architecture,* November 1994, 70–73.

21 Lemert, "Literary Politics and the *Champ* of French Sociology," 647.

22 An extended discussion with Bourdieu is in L. J. D. Wacquant, "Towards a Reflexive Sociology: A Workshop with Pierre Bourdieu," *Sociological Theory* 7 (1989): 48.

23 P. Bourdieu, "The Historical Genesis of a Pure Aesthetic," in *Analytic Aesthetics,* ed. R. Shusterman (Oxford, U.K.: Blackwell, 1989), 147.

24 See, for example, Ward, "The Suppression of the Social in Design," in *Reconstructing Architecture,* ed. T. A. Dutton and L. H. Mann (Minneapolis: University of Minnesota Press, 1996), 27–70.

25 J. R. Snyder, "Building, Thinking, and Politics: Mies, Heidegger, and the Nazis," *Journal of Architectural Education* 46, no. 4 (1993): 260–265.

26 M. S. Larson, "Architectural Competitions as Discursive Events," *Theory and Society* 23 (1994): 469–504; M. S. Larson, *Behind the Postmodern Facade* (Berkeley: University of California Press, 1993); and Brain, "Cultural Production as 'Society in the Making.'"

27 S. Lash, *Sociology of the Postmodern* (London: Routledge, 1990).

28 Wacquant, "Towards a Reflexive Sociology"; and L. J. D. Wacquant and P. Bourdieu, "For a Socio-Analysis of Intellectuals: On Homo Academicus," *Berkeley Journal of Sociology* 34 (1989): 1–29.

29 R. Collins, "For a Sociological Philosophy," *Theory and Society* 17 (1988): 669–702.

30 For those who want to tackle Bourdieu directly, I suggest starting with his book *Distinction,* and two collections of his essays: *The Field of Cultural Production* (cited above) and *The Rules of Art* (Stanford: Stanford University Press, 1996).

31 This is one of Jenkins's few concessions to Bourdieu, in Jenkins, *Pierre Bourdieu.*

32 Wacquant, "On the Tracks of Symbolic Power."

33 See L. J. D. Wacquant, "Bourdieu in America: Notes on the Transatlantic Importation of Social Theory," in *Bourdieu: Critical Perspectives,* ed. Calhoun, LiPuma, and Postone, 235–262.

34 See R. Brubaker, "Rethinking Classical Theory: The Sociological Vision of Pierre Bourdieu," *Theory and Society* 14 (1985): 745–775.

35 See D. McCleary, "Extended Review of Bourdieu's *Choses dites,*" *Sociological Review* 37 (1989): 373–383.

36 See P. Bourdieu, *Logic of Practice* (Cambridge: Polity Press, 1990), and an assessment of his work in G. Hage, "Pierre Bourdieu in the Nineties: Between the Church and the Atelier," *Theory and Society* 23 (1994): 419–440.

37 See Hage, "Pierre Bourdieu in the Nineties."

38 Craib, *Modern Social Theory.*

39 J. B. Thompson, "Introduction," in P. Bourdieu, *Language and Symbolic Power,* ed. J. B. Thompson (Cambridge, U.K.: Polity Press, 1991), 1–23. Craib, *Modern Social Theory,* has an excellent summary.

40 This breakdown is modeled after Brubaker, "Rethinking Classical Theory."

41 M. Waters, *Modern Sociological Theory* (London: Sage, 1994), and Craib, *Modern Social Theory.*

42 P. Bourdieu, "Social Space and Symbolic Power," in P. Bourdieu, *In Other Words: Essays Towards a Reflexive Sociology,* trans. M. Adamson (Stanford: Stanford University Press, 1990), 125–139.

43 J. Kelley and M. D. R. Evans, "Class and Class Conflict in Six Western Nations," *American Sociological Review* 60 (1995): 157–178.

44 Wacquant, "Towards a Reflexive Sociology." The same view is held by many other leftist sociologists; see, for example, S. G. McNall and J. C. M. Johnson, "The New Conservatives: Ethnomethodologists, Phenomenologists, and Symbolic Interactionists," *Insurgent Sociologist* 4 (1975): 49–65 (what a title for a journal!).

45 B. Hillier, "Quite Unlike the Pleasures of Scratching: Theory and Meaning in Architectural Form," *9H* 7 (1985): 66–71.

46 D. Schön, "Reflections in Action," *RIBA Transactions* 2 (1982): 65–72.

47 Further information on Bourdieu's epistemology and methodology can be found particularly in Bourdieu and Wacquant, *An Invitation to Reflexive Sociology,* and Bourdieu, *Sociology in Question.*

48 In his usual caustic dismissal Bourdieu holds the old mainstream of American sociology to have been inept and harmful, and its doyens, Robert Merton and Talcot Parsons, as having "school-level views." See Sabour, "Bourdieu's Renewed Critical Evaluation."

49 Recent reviews are B. Barnes, "How Not to Do the Sociology of Knowledge," *Annals of Scholarship* 8, nos. 3–4 (1991): 321–335; and R. Hagendijk, "Structuration Theory, Constructivism, and Scientific Change," in *Theories of Science in Society,* ed. S. E. Cozzens and T. F. Gieryn (Bloomington: Indiana University Press, 1990), 43–66.

50 K. Knorr-Cetina, "Primitive Classification and Postmodernity: Towards a Sociological Notion of Fiction," *Theory, Culture, and Society* 11 (1994): 1–22.

51 S. Ward, "The Revenge of the Humanities," *Sociological Perspectives* 38, no. 2 (1995): 109–128.

52 A good discussion appears in Johnson, "Pierre Bourdieu on Art, Literature and Culture".

53 See J. Elster, *Sour Grapes: Studies in the Subversion of Rationality* (Cambridge: Cambridge University Press, 1983).

54 See N. Garnham and R. Williams, "Pierre Bourdieu and the Sociology of Culture: An Introduction," in *Media, Culture and Society: A Critical Reader,* ed. R. Collins et al. (London: Sage,

1986), 116–130; and T. Moi, "Appropriating Bourdieu: Feminist Theory and Pierre Bourdieu's Sociology of Culture," *New Literary History* 22 (1991): 1017–1049.

55 P. Bourdieu, "On the Family as a Realized Category," *Theory, Culture and Society* 13 (1996): 19–26.

56 The metaphor "game" is defective, since Bourdieu uses it without connoting that anyone can say what the rules of the game are, or that there are explicit rules at all.

57 P. Lamaison, "From Rules to Strategies: An Interview with Pierre Bourdieu," *Cultural Anthropology* 1, no. 1 (1986): 110–120.

58 P. Bourdieu, "A Reply to Some Objections," in Bourdieu, *In Other Words: Essays Towards a Reflexive Sociology*, 106–119, and P. Bourdieu, "On Symbolic Power," in Bourdieu, *Language and Symbolic Power*, 163–170.

59 See P. Bourdieu and J.-C. Passeron, *Reproduction in Education, Society and Culture*, trans. R. Nice (London: Sage, 1990).

60 M. Lamont and R. Wuthnow, "Betwixt and Between: Recent Cultural Sociology in Europe and the United States," in *Frontiers of Social Theory: The New Syntheses*, ed. G. Ritzer (New York: Columbia University Press, 1990).

61 P. Bourdieu, "The Forms of Capital," in *Handbook of Theory and Research for the Sociology of Education*, ed. J. G. Richardson (New York: Greenwood Press, 1986), 241–258; and M. Lamont and A. Lareau, "Cultural Capital: Allusions, Gaps and Glissandos in Recent Theoretical Developments," *Sociological Theory* 6 (1988): 153–168.

62 See M. Granovetter, "The Strength of Weak Ties: A Network Theory Revisited," in *Sociological Theory 1983*, ed. R. Collins (San Francisco: Jossey-Bass, 1983), 201–233.

63 See R. L. Zweigenhaft, "Prep School and Public School Graduates of Harvard," *Journal of Higher Education* 64 (1993): 211–224.

64 Moi, "Appropriating Bourdieu."

65 P. R. Baker, *Richard Morris Hunt* (Cambridge: MIT Press, 1980); L. M. Roth, *McKim, Mead and White Architects* (New York: Harper and Row, 1983).

66 P. Bourdieu, "Price Formation and the Anticipation of Profits," in Bourdieu, *Language and Symbolic Power*, 66–102.

67 P. Bourdieu, "What Makes a Social Class? On Theoretical and Practical Existence of Groups," *Berkeley Journal of Sociology* 32 (1987): 1–16.

68 See Bourdieu, *Distinction*.

Chapter 3 Architecture as a Field

1 An excellent review of the literature on class is in R. Crompton, *Class and Stratification: An Introduction to Current Debates* (Cambridge, U.K.: Polity Press, 1993).

2 B. Rigby, *Popular Culture in Modern France* (London: Routledge and Kegan Paul, 1991).

3 Jenkins, *Pierre Bourdieu* (London: Routledge, 1992).

4 P. Bourdieu, "On Symbolic Power," in P. Bourdieu, *Language and Symbolic Power*, ed. J. B. Thompson (Cambridge, U.K.: Polity Press, 1991), 163–170.

5 D. Gartman, "Culture as Class Symbolization or Mass Reification? A Critique of Bourdieu's *Distinction*," *American Journal of Sociology* 97, no. 2 (1991): 421–447.

6   See Rigby, *Popular Culture in Modern France*.
7   J. R. Blau, "Study of the Arts: A Reappraisal," *Annual Review of Sociology* 14 (1988): 269–292.
8   M. Lamont, *Money, Morals and Manners* (Chicago: University of Chicago Press, 1992).
9   In Bourdieu's France, the upper classes may still be snobs rather than omnivores. See B. Bryson, "'Anything but Heavy Metal': Symbolic Exclusion and Musical Dislikes," *American Sociological Review* 61 (1996): 884–889; R. A. Peterson and R. M. Kern, "Changing Highbrow Taste: From Snob to Omnivore," *American Sociological Review* 61 (1996): 900–907; P. DiMaggio and M. Useem, "Cultural Democracy in a Period of Cultural Expansion: The Social Composition of Arts Audiences in the United States," in *Art and Society: Readings in the Sociology of the Arts,* ed. A. W. Foster and J. Blau (Albany: State University of New York Press, 1989), 141–171; and P. DiMaggio, "Are Art-Museum Visitors Different from Other People?" *Poetics* 24 (1996): 161–180.
10 Lamont, *Money, Morals and Manners*.
11 P. Bourdieu, *Distinction: A Social Critique of Taste,* trans. R. Nice (Cambridge: Harvard University Press, 1984).
12 N. Garnham, "Bourdieu, the Cultural Arbitrary, and Television," in *Bourdieu: Critical Perspectives,* ed. C. Calhoun, E. LiPuma, and M. Postone (Cambridge, U.K.: Polity Press, 1993), 178-192.
13 See Bourdieu, *Distinction*.
14 L. J. D. Wacquant, "On the Tracks of Symbolic Power: Prefatory Notes to Bourdieu's 'State Nobility,'" *Theory, Culture and Society* 10 (1993): 1–17.
15 R. Landau, "Enquiring into the Architectural Agenda," *Journal of Architectural Education* 40, no. 2 (1987): 41.
16 Quoted in H. Lipstadt, "The Building and the Book in César Daly's *Revue Générale de L'Architecture,*" in *Architectureproduction,* ed. J. Ockman and B. Colomina (New York: Princeton Architectural Press, 1988), 50.
17 A good discussion is in D. Robbins, *The Work of Pierre Bourdieu: Recognizing Society* (Milton Keynes, U.K.: Open University Press, 1991).
18 P. Bourdieu, "Field of Power, Literary Field and Habitus," in P. Bourdieu, *The Field of Cultural Production,* ed. R. Johnson (Cambridge, U.K.: Polity Press, 1993), 161–175.
19 D. Brain, "Discipline and Style: The Ecole des Beaux Arts and the Social Production of an American Architecture," *Theory and Society* 18 (1989): 807–868.
20 P. Bourdieu, "The Field of Cultural Production, or: The Economic World Reversed," *Poetics* 12 (1983): 311–356; P. Bourdieu, *Sociology in Question,* trans. R. Nice (London: Sage, 1993); and L. J. D. Wacquant, "Towards a Reflexive Sociology: A Workshop with Pierre Bourdieu," *Sociological Theory* 7 (1989): 26–63.
21 A good discussion of the accumulation of capital is in Thompson's introduction to Bourdieu, *Language and Symbolic Power,* 1–23.
22 R. Harker, C. Mahar, and C. Wilkes, eds., *An Introduction to the Work of Pierre Bourdieu: The Practice of Theory* (London: Macmillan, 1990).
23 P. Bourdieu, "A Reply to Some Objections," in P. Bourdieu, *In Other Words: Essays Towards a Reflexive Sociology,* trans. M. Adamson (Stanford: Stanford University Press, 1990), 106–119.
24 The "family values" that so often appear in political rhetoric could be seen as another way in which the upper classes coopt the lower into helping the former maintain their domina-

25. Adapted from P. Bourdieu, "The Market of Symbolic Goods," *Poetics* 14 (1985): 13–44, and Bourdieu, *Language and Symbolic Power.*

26. Examples can be found throughout *Architects' People,* ed. R. Ellis and D. Cuff (New York: Oxford University Press, 1989).

27. L. B. Alberti, *Ten Books on Architecture* (London: Alec Tiranti, 1955), 207.

28. J. Frow, "Accounting for Tastes: Some Problems in Bourdieu's Sociology of Culture," *Cultural Studies* 1, no. 1 (1987): 59–73.

29. See Bourdieu, *Distinction.*

30. P. Bourdieu, "Thinking about Limits," *Theory, Culture and Society* 9, no. 1 (1992): 37–49.

31. See N. Garnham and R. Williams, "Pierre Bourdieu and the Sociology of Culture: An Introduction," in *Media, Culture and Society: A Critical Reader,* ed. R. Collins et al. (London: Sage, 1986), 116–130.

32. P. Bourdieu, "The Intellectual Field: A World Apart," in Bourdieu, *In Other Words,* 123–139.

33. Empirical confirmation for this description of the structure of a cultural field comes, for example, from literature. See H. K. Anheier and J. Gerhards, "Literary Myths and Social Structure," *Social Forces* 69, no. 3 (1991): 811–830; H. K. Anheier and J. Gerhards, "The Acknowledgment of Literary Influence: A Structural Analysis of a German Literary Network," *Sociological Forum* 6, no. 1 (1991): 137–156; H. K. Anheier, J. Gerhards, and F. P. Romo, "Forms of Capital and Social Structure in Cultural Fields," *American Journal of Sociology* 100, no. 4 (1995): 859–903; and J. Gerhards and H. K. Anheier, "The Literary Field: An Empirical Investigation of Bourdieu's Sociology of Art," *International Sociology* 4, no. 2 (1989): 131–146.

34. A point also made in A. Abbott, *The System of Professions: An Essay on the Division of Expert Labor* (Chicago: University of Chicago Press, 1988). We must question those analyses that posit a direct connection between building and social structure, relating the production of architectural works directly to the social origins of their creators, or even their clients. See also R. Johnson, "Pierre Bourdieu on Art, Literature and Culture," in Bourdieu, *The Field of Cultural Production,* 1–25.

35. Another example of the dichotomy: two friends of mine have identical qualifications, and (at the moment) do identical work, namely tenancy coordination. One works for a large builder, the other for a large architecture firm. One is paid almost exactly twice as much as the other. Guess which?

36. See Bourdieu, "The Field of Cultural Production."

37. R. Gutman, "Architects in the Home-Building Industry," in *Professionals and Urban Form,* ed. J. S. Blau, M. La Gory, and J. S. Pipkin (Albany: State University of New York Press, 1983), 208–223.

38. R. Gutman, "Architects and Power: The Natural Market for Architecture," *Progressive Architecture,* December 1992, 40.

39. A. Placzek, ed., *Macmillan Encyclopedia of Architects,* 4 vols. (New York: Macmillan, 1982).

40. P. Bourdieu, "Outline of a Sociological Theory of Art Perception," *International Social Science Journal* 20 (1968): 589–612.

41. See L. K. Eaton, *Two Chicago Architects and Their Clients* (Cambridge: MIT Press, 1969).

42 R. K. Williamson, *American Architects and the Mechanics of Fame* (Austin: University of Texas Press, 1991), 13.

43 M. S. Larson, *Behind the Postmodern Facade* (Berkeley: University of California Press, 1993), 8.

44 M. S. Larson, "Architectural Competitions as Discursive Events," *Theory and Society* 23 (1994): 469–504.

45 D. Cuff, *Architecture: The Story of Practice* (Cambridge: MIT Press, 1991).

46 Bourdieu is not entirely consistent on just what the autonomy of a field makes it autonomous from, giving two possible answers: either from the specific demands of the dominant class, or from operations in the whole social field. See S. Lash, "Pierre Bourdieu: Cultural Economy and Social Change," in *Bourdieu: Critical Perspectives,* ed. Calhoun, LiPuma, and Postone, 193–211.

47 J. Ben-David, *The Scientist's Role in Society: A Comparative Study* (Englewood Cliffs, NJ: Prentice-Hall, 1971).

48 Bourdieu's notion of stratification is congruent with the finding by Abbott that professionals give highest status to those colleagues involved in the purest work, that is, in work most closely approximating the ideal professional problem, purified of extraneous considerations (like people or money). See A. Abbott, "Status and Strain in the Professions," *American Journal of Sociology* 86 (1981): 819–834.

49 See A. Saint, "The Architect and the Architectural Historian," *RIBA Transactions* 2, no. 2 (1983): 5–17, and especially A. Saint, *The Image of the Architect* (New Haven: Yale University Press, 1983).

50 S. Kostoff, "Foreword," in *Architects' People,* ed. Ellis and Cuff, ix–xix.

51 D. Brain, "Cultural Production as 'Society in the Making': Architecture as an Exemplar of the Social Construction of Social Artifacts," in *The Sociology of Culture,* ed. D. Crane (Oxford: Blackwell, 1994), 191–220.

52 There is a moderate amount of literature available on architectural competitions. See H. Lipstadt, "The Experimental Tradition," in *The Experimental Tradition,* ed. H. Lipstadt (New York: Princeton Architectural Press, 1989), 9–19; B. Bergdoll, "Competing in the Academy and the Marketplace: European Architecture Competitions 1401–1927," in *The Experimental Tradition,* ed. Lipstadt, 20–51; and J. Bassin, *Architectural Competitions in Nineteenth-Century England* (Ann Arbor: UMI Research Press, 1984).

53 See Larson, "Architectural Competitions as Discursive Events."

54 B. Fowler, "The Hegemonic Work of Art in the Age of Electronic Reproduction: The Case of Pierre Bourdieu," *Theory, Culture and Society* 11 (1994): 129–154.

55 P. Bourdieu, "The Production of Belief: Contribution to an Economy of Symbolic Goods," in *Media, Culture and Society: A Critical Reader,* ed. Collins et al., 131–163.

56 Hence the establishment's disdain for parody, which, if taken too far, reveals through ridicule the arbitrary nature of the establishment's symbolic products.

57 J. Glusberg, "Foreword," *Journal of Architectural Theory and Criticism* 1, no. 2 (1991): 9. This publication is remarkable on several grounds. First, although it purports to be a journal, it is really a monograph, a well-written introduction to Deconstructivist architecture by the admirable British architectural academic Geoffrey Broadbent. Its purported sponsor is the International Union of Architects (UIA), an organization supposedly regarded as the United Nations of architects, and is about as effective and efficient. Second, the author's name is absent from the cover, replaced by that of the publisher.

58 P. Bourdieu, "Intellectual Field and Creative Project," *Social Science Information* 8, no. 2 (1969): 89–119.

59 P. Bourdieu, "Genesis and Structure of the Religious Field," *Comparative Social Research* 13 (1991): 1–44.

60 Bourdieu's most complete exposition is P. Bourdieu, *The Rules of Art* (Stanford: Stanford University Press, 1996).

61 Quoted in *Programs and Manifestoes on 20th-century Architecture,* ed. U. Conrads (Cambridge: MIT Press, 1970), 112.

62 D. Bucsescu and A. Cheng, "Factors Other Than Price," http://www.ounce.com/301a/factors.html, 1996. (I am loathe to cite Web sources since they are susceptible to what Bill Mitchell in his book *City of Bits* [Cambridge: MIT Press, 1995] calls "link rot," but I do not have a written reference. Good luck finding it.)

63 P. Bourdieu, "Social Space and Symbolic Power," in Bourdieu, *In Other Words,* 125–139.

64 This strategy is possible on an individual as well as a group level. For example, in their early years, both Le Corbusier and Frank Lloyd Wright worked mainly for clients occupying similar positions in their social spaces as those architects did in theirs. See L. Soth, "Le Corbusier's Clients and Their Parisian Houses of the 1920s," *Art History* 6, no. 2 (1983): 188–198. It is worth noting that the Modern movement is the only successful example of a revolution by an architectural avant-garde to have used the principle of coopting allies by structural homology. Previous partial attempts, such as the Arts and Crafts movement, proved abortive.

65 Bourdieu, "The Intellectual Field."

66 Kostoff, "Foreword," in *Architects' People,* ed. Ellis and Cuff, xiii.

67 T. Wolfe, *From Bauhaus to Our House* (New York: Farrar Straus Giroux, 1981).

68 G. Stamp, "Review of *From Bauhaus to Our House,*" *American Spectator,* April 1982, 32.

69 S. Bayley, "Snapping Wolfe," *The Listener,* April 15, 1982, 21.

70 E. Nilsson, *Library Journal,* November 1, 1981, 2130.

71 J. Sobran, "Case Closed," *National Review,* November 27, 1981, 1426.

72 D. Greenspan, "Right Again?" *Progressive Architecture,* December 1981, 108, 110.

73 S. Davies, "Crying Wolfe," *Punch,* March 24, 1982, 497.

74 R. Banham, "The Scandalous Story of Architecture in America," *London Review of Books* 4, no. 7 (1982): 8.

75 Whether one accepts these externalities as sufficient justification is another question entirely. One of the successes of the modern sociology of science has been to show how much science relies on a socially constructed reality. The point is that—at present at least—architecture explicitly relies on the authority granted by charismatic geniuses.

76 J. Malcolm, "Wolfe in Wolfe's Clothing," *New York Review of Books* 28, no. 14 (1981): 15–16.

77 See Bourdieu, *Sociology in Question.*

78 G. Nelson, "Tom Wolfe's Fantasy Bauhaus," *American Institute of Architects Journal,* December 1981, 79.

79 A. Drexler, Letter to the *American Institute of Architects Journal,* February 1982, 8.

80 M. Lamont, "How to Become a Famous French Philosopher: The Case of Jacques Derrida," *American Journal of Sociology* 93, no. 3 (1987): 584–622.

81 B. Robbins, "Poaching off the Disciplines," *Raritan* 6, no. 4 (1987): 81–96.

82 G. Broadbent, "Deconstruction: A Student Guide," *Journal of Architectural Theory and Criticism* 1, no. 2 (1991): 11, 35.

83 J. Galtung, "Structure, Culture, and Intellectual Style: An Essay Comparing Saxonic, Teutonic, Gallic and Nipponic Approaches," *Social Science Information* 20, no. 6 (1981): 828. Galtung's theories are supported in other areas by, for example, G. Bowker and B. Latour, "A Booming Discipline Short of Discipline: (Social) Studies of Science in France," *Social Studies of Science* 17 (1987): 715–748; and G. Freudenthal, "Science Studies in France: A Sociological View," *Social Studies of Science* 20 (1990): 353–369.

84 R. M. Hare, "A School for Philosophers," *Ratio* 2 (1960): 107–120.

85 Quoted in N. L. Prak, *Architects: The Noted and the Ignored* (Chichester, U.K.: Wiley, 1984), 97.

86 Bowker and Latour, "A Booming Discipline Short of Discipline," 724.

87 D. Howard and M. Longair, "Harmonic Proportion and Palladio's *Quattro Libri*," *Journal of the Society of Architectural Historians* 41 (1982): 116–143.

88 Much of the material in this paragraph is based on a private communication from Geoffrey Broadbent.

Chapter 4 The Field through Time

1 I should warn the reader that this sort of analysis has never been as popular in the English-speaking world as it has been in Europe. Taking the long view, and looking for patterns that span centuries and continents, has usually been regarded as crackpot by American and British historians, although it is the mainstay of many French historians. See the comments on the American reaction to the great French historian Fernand Braudel's work in D. H. Fischer, *The Great Wave* (New York: Oxford University Press, 1996), a rare Anglophone work in this tradition.

2 R. Collins, "A Micro-Macro Theory of Intellectual Creativity: The Case of German Idealist Philosophy," *Sociological Theory* 5 (1987): 48. A complete exposition can be found in Collins's *The Sociology of Philosophies* (Cambridge, MA: Belknap Press, 1998).

3 R. Collins, "Toward a Theory of Intellectual Change: The Social Causes of Philosophies," *Science, Technology and Human Values* 14, no. 2 (1989): 107–140.

4 A. Placzek, "Foreword," in *Macmillan Encyclopedia of Architects,* ed. A. Placzek (New York: Macmillan, 1982), xi.

5 M. Trachtenberg, "Some Observations on Recent Architectural History," *Art Bulletin* 70 (1988): 213.

6 J. F. O'Gorman, "Review of the Macmillan Encyclopedia of Architects," *Journal of the Society of Architectural Historians* 43, no. 1 (1984): 78–79.

7 B. A. Chernow, "Introduction," in *Macmillan Encyclopedia of Architects,* xvi.

8 Not that the *MEA* is without errors: James O'Gorman ticked off the editors for letting an incorrect birthdate get through, and I was about to cite Karel Bazel as the architect who died youngest until I found that his entry had him practicing several years before his recorded birthdate. Such errors, particularly in dates of birth and death, are, alas, a fact of life in such

a large work. Since most of the analyses described in this book rely on large sample sizes, one can only hope that the odd error is insufficient to invalidate the whole.

I read every biography at least twice to hunt out the relevant data. I must confess that I found them a dreary collection of articles. Only once did I find an entertaining biography, that of Stanford White. I was disappointed to discover that it was written by an editor at the *New Yorker*, not an historian.

9   Percentages or proportions are both more illuminating and more comprehensible, but for completeness the raw data is usually presented as figures in brackets hereafter. N.B.: Percentages are rounded, and individual figures may not sum exactly to totals presented in the text because of this.

10 R. K. Williamson, *American Architects and the Mechanics of Fame* (Austin: University of Texas Press, 1991).

11 K. L. Cook, "Laws of Scattering Applied to Popular Music," *Journal of the American Society for Information Science* 40 (1989): 277–283.

12 D. K. Simonton, *Genius, Creativity, and Leadership* (Cambridge: Harvard University Press, 1984).

13 If the fact that there is concentration in the national distribution of the *MEA*'s architects is itself unexceptional, is there any peculiarity in the degree of this concentration? The problem with answering this question is the lack of any reasonable means of saying what would constitute a high or low degree of inequality in the national spread. Studies providing comparable data for other creative endeavors are rare indeed, and only two have examined national distribution over a period as long as the one considered here. Mitsutomo's study of scientists from 1500 onward shows that five nations accounted for 86 percent of the total: the U.S., England, Germany, France, and Italy (Y. Mitsutomo, "The Shifting Center of Scientific Activity in the West," *Japanese Studies in the History of Science* 1 [1962]: 57–75). Simonton's study of visual artists (mainly painters and sculptors) from 1050 onward reveals a similar distribution (D. K. Simonton, "Artistic Creativity and Interpersonal Relationships across and within Generations," *Journal of Personality and Social Psychology* 46 [1984]: 1273–1286). For economics, some data is supplied by B. S. Frey and W. W. Pommerehne, "The American Domination among Eminent Economists," *Scientometrics* 14 (1988): 97–110. In each of these studies, the four largest contributing nations accounted for over 80 percent of individuals. It is clear that the distribution of architects is more egalitarian than that of scientists, economists, or artists in general.

14 Single-family residential buildings include everything from houses to châteaux, where residence is intended for a single individual or family. It excludes apartment buildings but includes palaces. These and other residences of rulers posed a problem, as they could be classed as either residences or buildings of state. Where the building was clearly only for the use of the head of state, such as the White House or Buckingham Palace, it was classified as a building of state. Where it remained in the same family, regardless of changes in their position in the government, it was classed as a residence. Ambiguous cases were classified as residences. The category municipal refers to minor government works, works by a lower tier of government and privately funded public structures such as baths, jails, libraries, town halls, fountains, and a host of other items. Multiple residential buildings are hotels and apartment buildings.

15 Most analyses here use decades as the basic unit of time, rather than pentads. Decades are used when the data is not fine-grained enough to stand a smaller division, as in, for example, national population data through time. Decades begin in years divisible by ten, pentads in years divisible by five. Hence one can refer to the decade "1870" and mean the years 1870

to 1879, the natural way of thinking about it. Some would prefer that the time units be centered on such years, but then we end up using "1870" to mean the period 1865 to 1874.

16 R. Collins, "Why the Social Sciences Won't Become High-Consensus, Rapid-Discovery Science," *Sociological Forum* 9, no. 2 (1994): 155–176.

17 C. McEvedy and R. Jones, *Atlas of World Population History* (Harmondsworth, U.K.: Penguin, 1985).

18 Similar results are obtained if we examine the number of architects per capita of the urban population, defining the latter as the number of persons living in townships of at least 10,000 inhabitants. From 1500 to 1650 Europe proper (not the Western polity used here) supported about ten architects for every million town-dwellers. By 1750 this had risen to about fifteen for each million.

19 For some of the work done on the exponential growth of science, see D. S. Price, *Science since Babylon* (New Haven: Yale University Press, 1961); D. S. Price, *Little Science, Big Science* (New York: Columbia University Press, 1963); D. S. Price, "Ups and Downs in the Pulse of Science and Technology," in *The Sociology of Science,* ed. J. Gaston (San Francisco: Jossey-Bass, 1978), 162–171; B. C. Griffith, "Derek Price's Puzzles: Numerical Metaphors for the Operation of Science," *Science, Technology and Human Values* 13 (1988): 351–360; and S. E. Cozzens, "Using the Archive: Derek Price's Theory of Differences among the Sciences," *Scientometrics* 7 (1985): 431–441.

20 In her innovative study of American architects, Roxanne Williamson almost hit on this when she showed how great American architects spent time in the offices of other greats. But she dodged the social implication of this, and contrived an explanation that avoided at all cost the unwelcome conclusion that one's social background and cultural capital can propel one to eminence. She was left to conclude that architects picked up some "creative spark," a sort of handing down of the divine flame of creativity, in which they were given "courage and self-confidence to be true to one's vision." No doubt, but personal contact with eminent architects also provides symbolic or cultural capital to the protégé in the form of social contacts, modes and manners of social being, and tacit knowledge. Whether it be the passing of a creative spark or networking, the essential mechanism of transmission is the master-pupil chain. See Williamson, *American Architects and the Mechanics of Fame.*

21 Numbers are approximate.

22 P. Bourdieu, *Distinction: A Social Critique of Taste,* trans. R. Nice (Cambridge: Harvard University Press, 1984).

23 From R. M. May, "Models for Single Populations," in *Theoretical Ecology,* ed. R. M. May (Oxford: Blackwell Scientific, 1981), 5–29.

24 See Fischer, *The Great Wave.* He identifies a series of price revolutions in the global economy from the 1200s to the present day, separated by periods of price equilibrium. Two of these, the Renaissance equilibrium of 1400 to 1470 and the Enlightenment equilibrium of 1660 to 1730, match the transitions here. However, it is difficult to construct a causal mechanism linking the two phenomena.

25 J. de Vries, *European Urbanization 1500–1800* (Cambridge: Harvard University Press, 1984).

26 See McEvedy and Jones, *Atlas of World Population History.*

27 See C. M. Cipolla, ed., *The Fontana Economic History of Europe: The Sixteenth and Seventeenth Centuries* (Glasgow: Collins/Fontana, 1973); and J. de Vries, *Economy of Europe in an Age of Crisis 1600–1750* (Cambridge: Cambridge University Press, 1975).

28 The decline in the Modern system after 1920 results from the general decline in the architectural population at about the same time.

Chapter 5 Understanding Architectural Education

1 If we just take American architects as an example, in the mid-1950s only 56 percent of American architects had a degree, very close to the proportion of degreed engineers. As late as 1975 one-quarter of American architects did not have a degree. See R. Collins, *The Credential Society: An Historical Sociology of Education and Stratification* (New York: Academic Press, 1979); J. M. Mayo, "Dilemmas of Architectural Education in the Academic Political Academy," *Journal of Architectural Education* 44, no. 2 (1991): 80–89; and A. Derman, "Summary of Responses to the 1974 AIA/ACSA Teachers Seminar Survey of the Concerns and Interests of Architectural Educators," *Journal of Architectural Education* 28, nos. 1–2 (1975): 10–22.

2 I am indebted to Dr. Sylvia Ficher for emphasizing this point.

3 H. L. Smith, "1984—Architectural Education's Year of Challenge," *Architectural Record*, January 1984, 43; and T. Fisher, "P/A Reader Poll: Education," *Progressive Architecture*, February 1989, 15–17.

4 For examples, see J. Wines, "A Vivid Challenge to the Status Quo," *Architectural Record*, November 1984, 51–57; M. Pawley, "Canterbury: The Architect's Tale," *Architects' Journal*, October 12, 1983, 68–70; R. D. Fox, "A Student's Long Path to Arcadia," *Architectural Record*, April 1984, 53–57; M. S. Stubbs, "Technical Education of Architects," *Architecture*, August 1987, 73–77; T. Fowler, "What Are Students Concerned About?" *Architectural Record*, May 1985, 61–63; R. Gutman, "Education and the World of Practice," *Journal of Architectural Education* 40, no. 2 (1987): 24–25; A. Rapoport, "Studious Questions," *Architects' Journal*, October 26, 1983, 55–57; P. Carolin, "Expectation versus Reality in Architectural Education," in *Strategic Study of the Profession*, ed. F. Duffy (London: Royal Institute of British Architects, 1992), 171–182; and T. G. Heinlein, "Rethinking Architectural Education," *Architectural Technology*, March/April 1981, 12.

5 T. Muir, "All Together," *Architects' Journal*, March 20, 1991, 32–35.

6 See H. N. Cobb, "Architecture and the University," *Architectural Record*, September 1985, 43–51; R. Filson, "Can Schools Span the Gap to Practice?" *Architectural Record*, November 1985, 59–63; and O. J. Mitchell, "ACSA—The Member Schools Should Celebrate Their Diversity," *Architectural Record*, January 1984, 17–18.

7 L. R. Harmon, *A Century of Doctorates: Data Analyses of Growth and Change* (Washington: National Academy of Sciences, 1978).

8 See comments in J. Musgrove et al., "Architectural Research: Problems of Organization and Funding in the United Kingdom," *Journal of Architectural Research* 4, no. 2 (1975): 41–47; J. W. Robinson, "Architectural Research: Incorporating Myth and Science," *Journal of Architectural Education* 44, no. 1 (1990): 20–32; M. J. Malecha, "Architectural Education," *Ekistics*, nos. 328–330 (1988): 121–132; A. Rapoport, "Statement for the ACSA 75th Anniversary (Jubilee) Issue of JAE," *Journal of Architectural Education* 40, no. 2 (1987): 65–66; and T. Woolley, "Why Studio?" *Architects' Journal*, March 20, 1991, 46–49.

9 R. Plunz, "Comments on Academic Research in Architecture in the United States," *Journal of Architectural Education* 40, no. 2 (1987): 62.

10. Musgrove et al., "Architectural Research."
11. M. Bedford and S. Groák, "Current Issues in UK Architectural Education," *Architectural Education* 3 (1983): 7–41.
12. Even so, it is precious little. The construction industry expends a minimal amount on research compared to other industries. It seems to be between one-half to one-tenth the level of other sectors of the economy. See G. D. Oberlender, "Development of Construction Research," *Journal of Construction Engineering and Management* 110, no. 4 (1984): 486–490.
13. J. Templer, "Architectural Research," *Journal of Architectural Education* 44, no. 1 (1990): 3.
14. See Robinson, "Architectural Research."
15. I have omitted reference to design because, while design is regarded as the core of architectural academe, most architectural academics regard "design research" as a ludicrous concept. Design, many feel, is something that is simply done, not researched.
16. W. J. Boyes, S. K. Happel, and T. D. Hogan, "Publish or Perish: Fact or Fiction?" *Journal of Economic Education* 15 (Spring 1984): 136–141.
17. J. P. Bonta, "More on Faculty Publications and P&T Reviews," *Journal of Architectural Education* 39, no. 2 (1985): 28–29.
18. E. L. Boyer and L. D. Mitgang, *Building Community* (The Boyer Report) (Princeton: Carnegie Foundation for the Advancement of Teaching, 1996), 54.
19. Mayo, "Dilemmas of Architectural Education," 80–89.
20. Other arts professionals find themselves in the precisely same position. Art teachers, for example, find no need for input from their colleagues involved in research, and are castigated by those in the commercial world as being insensitive to their needs. See J. LaChapelle, "Conflict between Research and Practice in Art Education: A Sociological Perspective," *Studies in Art Education* 23, no. 2 (1982): 56–64.
21. Italy has not been an important influence in the development of education in the English-speaking world. The art academies of the Renaissance and later ceased to be relevant models after the decline in Italian architecture in the seventeenth century.
22. P. Davey, "Profession or Art?" *Architectural Review,* July 1989, 59–66; and M. Crinson and J. Lubbock, *Architecture: Art or Profession?* (Manchester, U.K.: Manchester University Press, 1994).
23. M. Burrage, "From Practice to School-Based Professional Education: Patterns of Conflict and Accommodation in England, France and the United States," in *The European and American University since 1800,* ed. S. Rothblatt and B. Wittrock (Cambridge: Cambridge University Press, 1993), 142–187.
24. J. Bassin, *Architectural Competitions in Nineteenth-Century England* (Ann Arbor: UMI Research Press, 1984).
25. Crinson and Lubbock, *Architecture: Art or Profession?*
26. T. B. Saunders, "Architectural Education: Germany (with Austria and Switzerland)," *Architectural Record* 13 (1903): 178.
27. T. Bender, "The Erosion of Public Culture: Cities, Discourses, and Professional Disciplines," in *The Authority of Experts,* ed. T. L. Haskell (Blomington: Indiana University Press, 1984), 84–106.
28. See Burrage, "From Practice to School-Based Professional Education."
29. A. Abbott, *The System of Professions: An Essay on the Division of Expert Labor* (Chicago: University of Chicago Press, 1988).

30 Bourdieu's discussion of these sorts of processes can be found in P. Bourdieu, "The Market of Symbolic Goods," *Poetics* 14 (1985): 13–44; and P. Bourdieu, "Intellectual Field and Creative Project," *Social Science Information* 8: 2 (1969): 89–119.

31 J. P. Carlhian, "The Ecole des Beaux-Arts: Modes and Manners," *Journal of Architectural Education* 33, no. 2 (1979): 17.

32 R. Chafee, "The Teaching of Architecture at the Ecole des Beaux-Arts," in *The Architecture of the Ecole des Beaux-Arts,* ed. A. Drexler (London: Secker and Warburg, 1977), 61–110.

33 J. Ben-David, *The Scientist's Role in Society: A Comparative Study* (Englewood Cliffs, NJ: Prentice-Hall, 1971).

34 J. Galtung, "Structure, Culture, and Intellectual Style: An Essay Comparing Saxonic, Teutonic, Gallic and Nipponic Approaches," *Social Science Information* 20, no. 6 (1981): 817–856.

35 V. Clark, "A Struggle for Existence: The Professionalization of German Architects," in *German Professions 1800–1950,* ed. G. Cocks and K. H. Jarausch (Oxford: Oxford University Press, 1990), 143–160.

36 See Abbott, *The System of Professions.*

37 M. Burrage, "Beyond a Sub-set: The Professional Aspirations of Manual Workers in France, the United States and Britain," in *Professions in Theory and History: Rethinking the Study of the Professions,* ed. M. Burrage and R. Torstendahl (London: Sage, 1990), 151–176.

38 See Abbott, *The System of Professions.*

39 See Burrage, "From Practice to School-Based Professional Education"; and R. Gutman, *Architectural Practice: A Critical View* (Princeton: Princeton Architectural press, 1988).

40 See the history in *The Architect at Mid-Century: Evolution and Achievement,* ed. T. C. Bannister (New York: Reinhold, 1954).

41 R. L. Geiger, "The American University and Research," in *University and Society,* ed. M. Trow and T. Nybom (London: Jessica Kingsley, 1991), 200–215.

42 See Ben-David, *The Scientist's Role in Society.*

43 Abbott, *The System of Professions,* 207.

44 Comparing the Design Method movement to the Modern movement, Grant observed that the Moderns had been visionary but impractical, whereas the design methodists had been impractical without being visionary. See D. P. Grant, "Aims and Potentials of Design Methodology in Response to Social Change," *Design Methods and Theories* 20, no. 1 (1986): 389.

45 Quoted in Collins, "The 18th Century Origins of Our System of Full-Time Architectural Schooling," 3.

46 J. Draper, "The Ecole des Beaux Arts and the Architecture Profession in the United States: The Case of John Galen Howard," in *The Architect,* ed. S. Kostoff (New York: Oxford University Press, 1977), 232.

47 S. B. Trowbridge, *Annual Report of the American Academy in Rome* (Rome: American Academy, 1919), 31.

48 J. M. Dixon, "A White Gentleman's Profession," *Progressive Architecture,* November 1994, 55–61.

49 A. Balfour, "On the Characteristic and Beliefs of the Architect," *Journal of Architectural Education* 40, no. 2 (1987): 2.

50 J. A. Davis, *Undergraduate Career Decisions* (Chicago: Aldine, 1965).

51. J. P. Carlhian, "The Ecole Des Beaux-Arts: Modes and Manners," 7.
52. L. L. Willenbrock, "An Undergraduate Voice in Architectural Education," in *Voices in Architectural Education: Cultural Politics and Pedagogy,* ed. T. A. Dutton (New York: Bergin & Garvey, 1991), 100.
53. A full (and early) exposition of Bourdieu's educational theory is P. Bourdieu and J-C. Passeron, *The Inheritors: French Students and Their Relation to Culture,* trans. R. Nice (Chicago: University of Chicago Press, 1979 [1964]).
54. D. White, initial syllabus to "Gender and the Built Environment" (Sydney: University of Sydney, 1995). Note that the disciplines to which White compares architecture are the same as those associated with lesser cultural capital, as seen in table 5.2.
55. J. W. Getzels and M. Csikszentmihalyi, *The Creative Vision: A Longitudinal Study of Problem Finding in Art* (New York: John Wiley & Sons, 1976), 165.
56. It is vulgar to inventory the attributes of cultivation. Perhaps this explains why the approximately 2,900 full-time architectural academics in the English-speaking world seem to have so little to say on the subject: any perusal of the *Journal of Architectural Education* would show that—until recently, at least—only about one-third of its contents, regardless of its excellence, deals in any way with education. We may also understand the sad histories of two journals more specifically devoted to educational theory: *Architectural Research and Teaching,* later the *Journal of Architectural Research,* had a fitful life from 1970 to 1980; the RIBA-sponsored journal *Architectural Education* survived but four issues in 1983–1984.
57. L. B. Alberti, *Dinner Pieces (Intercenales)* trans. D. Marsh (Binghamton: Center for Medieval and Early Renaissance Studies, State University of New York at Binghamton, 1987), 127.
58. Quoted in J. Esherick, "Architectural Education in the Thirties and Seventies: A Personal View," in *The Architect,* ed. Kostoff, 274.
59. See P. Bourdieu and M. de Saint-Martin, "Scholastic excellence and the values of the educational system," in *Contemporary Research in the Sociology of Education,* ed. J. Eggleston (London: Methuen, 1974), 338–371; and P. Bourdieu, *Homo Academicus,* trans. R. Nice (Stanford: Stanford University Press, 1988).
60. S. Kostoff, "The Education of the Muslim Architect," in *Architecture Education in the Islamic World: Proceedings of Seminar Ten in the Series Architectural Transformations in the Islamic World* (Singapore: Concept Media, 1986), 3.
61. P. Bourdieu, "The Scholastic Point of View," *Cultural Anthropology* 5, no. 4 (1990): 380–391.
62. Willenbrock, "An Undergraduate Voice in Architectural Education," 102.
63. K. H. Anthony, "Private Reactions to Public Criticism: Students, Faculty, and Practicing Architects State Their Views on Design Juries in Architectural Education," *Journal of Architectural Education* 40, no. 3 (1987): 2–11, and K. H. Anthony, *Design Juries on Trial: The Renaissance of the Design Studio* (New York: Van Nostrand Reinhold, 1991).
64. Chafee, "The Teaching of Architecture at the Ecole des Beaux-Arts."
65. H. Jacobson, "Peering into the Abîme," *Modern Painters* 1, no. 2 (1988): 54.
66. Anthony, *Design Juries on Trial,* 12.
67. L. J. D. Wacquant, "On the Tracks of Symbolic Power: Prefatory Notes to Bourdieu's 'State Nobility,'" *Theory, Culture and Society* 10 (1993): 1–17.
68. Anthony, *Design Juries on Trial,* 15.
69. Willenbrock, "An Undergraduate Voice in Architectural Education," 107.

70 Ibid., 114.

71 M. Gelernter, "Reconciling Lectures and Studios," *Journal of Architectural Education* 41, no. 2 (1988): 46–52.

72 P. Bourdieu, *Distinction: A Social Critique of Taste,* trans. R. Nice (Cambridge: Harvard University Press, 1984); and J. B. Thompson, "Introduction," in P. Bourdieu, *Language and Symbolic Power,* ed. J. B. Thompson (Cambridge, U.K.: Polity Press, 1991), 1–23.

73 L. J. D. Wacquant, "Towards a Reflexive Sociology: A Workshop with Pierre Bourdieu," *Sociological Theory* 7 (1989): 26–63.

74 From a private communication in 1993 with a student who wishes to remain anonymous.

75 Willenbrock, "An Undergraduate Voice in Architectural Education," 98–99.

76 Anthony, *Design Juries on Trial*.

77 P. Bourdieu, "Manet and the Institutionalization of Anomie," in P. Bourdieu, *The Field of Cultural Production,* ed. R. Johnson (Cambridge, U.K.: Polity Press, 1993), 238–253.

78 S. Timoshenko, *History of Strength of Materials* (New York: Dover, 1983 [1952]).

79 Rapoport, "Statement for the ACSA 75th Anniversary (Jubilee) Issue of JAE."

80 Ibid., 65.

81 See Robinson, "Architectural Research: Incorporating Myth and Science"; and L. N. Groat, "Rescuing Architecture from the Cul-de-Sac," *Journal of Architectural Education* 45, no. 3 (1992): 138–146.

82 See Plunz, "Comments on Academic Research in Architecture"; and Templer, "Architectural Research."

83 J. Meunier, "Paradigms for Practice: A Task for Architecture Schools," *Journal of Architectural Education* 40, no. 2 (1987): 47–49.

84 R. Landau, "Enquiring into the Architectural Agenda," *Journal of Architectural Education* 40, no. 2 (1987): 40–41.

85 Groat, "Rescuing Architecture from the Cul-de-Sac."

86 A number of problems would be solved if it were understood that, in English, the word "architecture" is commonly used to refer to a certain type of building, an occupation, and a discipline, and that these three definitions have only weak linkages outside the conflated use of the term.

87 Calculated by dividing the number of full-time faculty by the number of registered architects in the United States. Data for either of these figures is remarkably hard to obtain. Although the NAARB has published figures for the number of faculty, it is not known exactly how many of these are architects: probably almost all, given the schools' insistence on an architecture qualification as a condition of employment. Counting the number of architects is immensely complicated by the fact of state or regional registration in the U.S., Canada, Australia, Italy, and other countries. Whatever data one uses, a figure of one to two percent is the result.

88 National Science Board, *Science Indicators 1982* (Washington, DC: National Science Board, National Science Foundation, 1983).

89 O. Overby, "From 1947: The Society of Architectural Historians," *Journal of the Society of Architectural Historians* 54 (1990): 9–14.

90 See the two roundtables whose discussions were published in the summer 1996 edition of Harvard's *GSD News*.

91 J. L. Mashburn, "Publication in Architecture," *Journal of Architectural Education* 38, no. 3 (1985): 26–30.

92 G. Broadbent, "Deconstruction: A Student Guide," *Journal of Architectural Theory and Criticism* 1, no. 2 (1991): 10–96.

93 J. P. Bonta, *Architecture and Its Interpretation: A Study of Expressive Systems in Architecture* (London: Lund Humphries, 1979).

Chapter 6 Contemporary Transformations

1 P. G. Rowe, "Introduction," in *Reflections on Architectural Practices in the Nineties*, ed. W. S. Saunders (New York: Princeton Architectural Press, 1996). The last point can be verified by the decisions of those advertising in the architectural journals. Thomas Fisher, former editor of *Progressive Architecture*, has remarked that through the late 1980s to the mid-1990s the main U.S. architectural journals lost considerable income as advertisers moved to target occupations that held key decision-making powers. (This information comes from a personal communication.)

2 M. Bedford and S. Groák, "Current Issues in UK Architectural Education," *Architectural Education* 3 (1983): 7–41; and E. L. Boyer and L. D. Mitgang, *Building Community* (The Boyer Report) (Princeton: Carnegie Foundation for the Advancement of Teaching, 1996).

3 G. Hogben, "Studio Words and Studio Deeds," *Architectural Review*, July 1989, 38–41.

4 This is indirectly supported for architecture by Häyrynen, who notes that female university graduates whose families have the highest cultural capital tend to avoid academia as an occupation; and by Kingsley and Glynn, who note that female architecture graduates rarely become academics. I speculate that female architecture students come from slightly higher strata than their male colleagues. See K. Kingsley and A. Glynn, "Women in the Architectural Workplace," *Journal of Architectural Education* 46, no. 1 (1992): 14–19; and Y-P. Häyrynen and L. Häyrynen, "Career Patterns of Finnish Academics and Intellectuals," *Higher Education in Europe* 18, no. 2 (1993): 59–77.

5 R. Collins, "Changing Conceptions in the Sociology of Professions," in *The Formation of Professions: Knowledge, State and Strategy*, ed. R. Torstendahl and M. Burrage (London: Sage, 1990), 11–23.

6 This is confirmed for architecture in D. Cuff, *Architecture: The Story of Practice* (Cambridge: MIT Press, 1991).See also the long discussion in R. Collins, *The Credential Society: An Historical Sociology of Education and Stratification* (New York: Academic Press, 1979).

7 Boyer and Mitgang, *Building Community*.

8 R. Collins, "Crises and Declines in Credential Systems," in *Sociology since Midcentury: Essays in Theory Cumulation,* ed. R. Collins (New York: Academic Press, 1981), 191–215.

9 P. Bourdieu, *Sociology in Question*, trans. R. Nice (London: Sage, 1993).

10 P. Bourdieu, "The Field of Cultural Production, or: The Economic World Reversed," *Poetics* 12 (1983): 311–356.

11 "Changes Outlined in Euro Report," *Architects' Journal*, November 13, 1991, 5.

12 S. Fuller, "Life in the Knowledge Society," *Theory, Culture and Society* 14 (1997): 143.

13 By 1950 about one-quarter of the American profession was trained by apprenticeship, so we may take the decline of the system to have started about twenty years earlier. See *The*

Architect at Mid-Century: Evolution and Achievement, ed. T. C. Bannister (New York: Reinhold, 1954).

14 S. A. Halpern, "Professional Schools in the American University," in *The American University,* ed. B. R. Clark (Berkeley: University of California Press, 1987), 304–330; K. M. Harman, "Professional versus Academic Values: Cultural Ambivalence in University Professional School in Australia [sic]," *Higher Education* 18 (1989): 491–509.

15 R. Whitley, *The Intellectual and Social Organization of the Sciences* (Oxford: Clarendon Press, 1984).

Index

Abbott, A., 25, 31, 32, 83, 187
Académie des Beaux-Arts, 181
Adorno, T., 44
Age, and achievement, 134
Agents, 49, 52
Ahrentzen, S., 11, 24
AIA Journal, 10, 112, 209
Albers, J., 129
Alberti, L. B., 78, 196
Althusser, L., 38
American Bar Association, 185
American Institute of Architects, 18, 19, 90, 102, 179, 185, 188. *See also AIA Journal*
American Medical Association, 185
American Spectator, 106
Anthony, K., 198, 200
Apprenticeship, 177, 221
Architects. *See also* Architectural education; Architecture; Field of architecture
    activities of, 129–131
    aestheticism and, 88, 92
    character of, 13–14, 74, 84, 152
    lifespans of, 134
    links between, 129
    nationalities of, 129, 133
    original occupations of, 129
    as polymaths, 132
    productivity of, 135
    psychology of, 8–10
    self-promotion of, 120
    social capital and, 120, 177–178
    social space of, 122–123
    stratification of, 94
    subordinate, 144
    symbolic capital of, 95
    tacit qualities of, 80
    taste and, 73–74, 78, 110, 188, 196
    unsociality of, 13, 14
Architects' Journal, 209
Architectural Association, 176, 214, 221, 223
Architectural Design, 119

Architectural education, 169, 221
    academics, 172, 208
    biases in, 189
    conservation function of, 215
    credentialing, 168–169, 217–218
    criticism of, 170–171, 214–217
    functions of, 187
    monoculturalism of, 192
    pedagogy, 204
    practitioners in, 208, 210, 214
    research, 172–173, 207, 222
    schools, 173, 201, 215
    students, 7, 8, 189, 192, 193, 219
        background of, 194
        competition between, 203
        control of, 202
        cultivation in, 196, 198
        development of, 202
        isolation of, 200
        selecting, 191
        symbolic capital of, 193, 198
    subject areas, 198
Architectural Review, 106, 208, 209
Architecture. *See also* Field of architecture
    academic journals in, 209
    competitions, 96, 97
    discipline of, 204–208, 210
    discourse in, 14
    functions of, 213
    historical growth of, 137–151, 212–214
    historical labels, 100
    importance of history to, 125, 152
    market for, 18, 84–86, 98
        natural market of, 86
    occupation vs. field, 3
    other disciplines and, 210
    other professions and, 18, 25, 30
    as profession
        Brain's model of, 22
        firms in, 19, 90, 91, 177
        Gutman's model of, 18
        Larson's model of, 21
        problems of, 12, 18, 21, 25, 30, 212
    resources of, 143–145
    science vs. humanism, 7
    sociological studies of, 17

sociology and, 11–23
studies of practice, 18
universities and, 168, 170–173, 176, 185, 221, 222 (*see also* Architectural education)

Architecture and Urbanism, 209

Aron, R., 40

Art, 15

Articled pupilage, 174

Atelier, 199

Australia, 5, 29, 30, 65, 83, 87

Austria, 133

Auteur theory, 17

Avant-gardes, 100, 103, 114, 115

Avery Periodicals Index, 211

Bachelard, G., 116

Banham, R., 110

Baroque, 20, 151

Baroque transition, 142, 161, 164–165, 167

Barthes, R., 37, 38

Bayley, S., 106

Beaux Arts Institute of Design, 185

Beaux-Arts style, 22, 75, 88, 186, 215. See also Ecole des Beaux-Arts
destruction of symbolic capital, 76

Bedford, M., 172

Benelux countries, 29

Birth dates, 129

Blau, J., 19, 70

Blondel, J.-F., 188

Bonta, J. P., 210

Boullée, E.-L., 210

Bourdieu, P., 3, 12, 36, 42, 48, 52, 53, 91
in architecture, 46–47
and central problem of sociology, 52
and constructivism, 54–55
criticism of, 43, 70
and culture, 68
Derrida and, 45
formal sociology, 49
Foucault and, 42

Heidegger and, 44
Homo Academicus, 43
importance of, 37
in intellectual field, 37
investigating culture, 80
model of dynamics, 98
model of society, 59
polemics of, 41
postmodernism and, 46
science and, 55
style of, 38–39, 41, 42
theoretical overview, 47–48
theory of practice, 56
Veblen and, 44

Boyer Report, 173, 217

Brain, D., 22, 32, 46

Breuer, M., 129

Broadbent, G., 100, 115

Brunelleschi, F., 139

Builders, 20

Buildings, 133

Bund Deutscher Architekten, 28

CAD (computer-aided design), 6, 216, 219, 221

Cambridge University, 174

Canada, 30, 87

Canadian Society for Civil Engineers, 87

Capitalism, 68

Carrying capacity, 151, 159

Castiglione, B., 195

Charismatic inculcation, 197

Chernow, B., 126

Chicago, World's Columbian Exposition (1893), 75

Chile, 30

Choice, 106

Chomsky, N., 38

Cinema, 17

Classes
definition, 65
dominant, 61, 66, 77, 81
movement between, 69

struggle between, 48, 215
  subordinate, 65, 78
Classical tradition in architecture, 21
Cole, S., 13
Collège de France, 46
Collins, R., 15, 16, 124, 155, 216
Consecrated avant-garde, 99, 110
Consecrating institutions, 101
Conservation function, 191, 215
Constructionism, 54
Constructivist structuralism, 52
Cornell University, 113
Countercultures, 79
Craib, I., 42, 50, 51
Credentialing. *See* Architectural education: credentialing
Cret, P., 196
Cuff, D., 13, 19, 91
Cullen, J., 25, 26
Cultural capital. *See* Symbolic capital
Cultural producers, 81
Culture, 37, 38, 44–45, 48, 88, 110, 120, 193
  architectural, 196, 199
  as battleground, 69
  bounding groups, 80
  dominant, 82, 115
  of dominant classes, 70
  functions of, 78
  material, 72
  relationship to, 197
  reproducing class structure, 60
  as social weapon, 73
  structure of the field, 81
  symbolic power in, 61
Cycles, 147, 159, 161

Dada, 103
DADS. *See* University of Sydney
Daly, C., 74
DAPAA. *See* University of Sydney
Davies, S., 107
Death dates, 129

Deconstruction, 54, 112–115, 119, 209, 210
Deconstructivism, 13, 44, 114
Derrida, J., 37, 39, 40, 42, 45, 46, 113, 115, 120, 199
Design studio, 198, 200, 204
De Vries, J., 161, 162
Discrimination, 80
Dixon, J. M., 188
Doctorates, 5, 171, 172, 219
Domination, 24, 48, 76, 87, 98
Domus, 209
Doubling time, 145
Downclassing, 218
Doxa, 56, 61, 110
Drawings, 97
Drexler, A., 112

Early Modern phase, 142, 161, 167
Ecole des Beaux-Arts, 20, 64, 168, 179, 181, 182, 192, 199, 202, 204
Ecole Polytechnique, 204
Economic capital, 48, 60, 62, 64
  competition for, 76
  dominant classes and, 77
  volume of, 67
Education, 129
Educational system, 69
Eisenman, P., 45, 63, 89, 92, 120
Embodied capital, 63, 74
England, 163, 164, 167
Enlightenment, 55
Ethnomethodology, 50, 52, 53
Europe, urban system of, 161–163, 165
European Union, 223
Exponential growth, 145, 151

Family, 58
Fanzago, C., 155
Fathy, H., 155

Field of architecture, 83, 206. *See also* Architecture
    autonomy of, 93–98, 104–105
    changes in, 218–219
    competition in, 99
    as consecrator, 99
    defined, 86
    discourse in, 85
    dynamics of, 95, 98
    forms of capital in, 88–90
    function of, 86–87
    historical dynamics of, 151
    history of, 127
    internal dynamics in, 88
    newcomers in, 99
    power to name, 85
    revolutions in, 100
    schools in, 101
    snobbery in, 87
    structure of, 83, 84, 85
    symbolic capital in, 91, 97, 105, 112, 115
    valued capital, 94

Field of building, 86, 93
Field of culture, 68–71, 74–75, 78–83, 111
Field of mass production, 82, 83, 91, 100
Field of restricted production, 83, 91
Fields, 74–76, 91
Fischer, D., 161
Fischer von Erlach, J. B., 142
Fisher, T., 25, 30
Floruit, 129
Foucault, M., 16, 37, 38, 39, 40, 42, 46, 60, 206
France, 15, 20, 28, 29, 30, 38, 116, 131, 133, 164, 167
    architectural education in, 173
    architectural field of, 222
    cultural studies in, 15, 16
    higher education system, 179
    intellectual community of, 40
    professions in, 175, 179

Frankfurt School, 17, 44
Frederickson, M., 24
Freidson, E., 26
Fuga, F., 155
Fuller, B., 85, 86

Galtung, J., 39, 115, 117
Gans, H., 12
Gender studies, 24
Genius, 146, 152
Genoa, 163
Germany, 28, 29, 105, 116, 117, 119, 133, 162, 173
    architectural students of, 177
    higher education system, 182, 184
    professions in, 175, 184
Ghiberti, L., 139
Ghirardo, D., 45, 120
Giftedness, 194, 195, 198
Gill, B., 178
Glusberg, J., 100
Glynn, A., 24
Grace, natural, 195
Graves, M., 89, 105
Greece, 30, 86
Greenaway, P., 39
Greenspan, D., 107
Groak, S., 172
Groat, L., 11, 24, 206
Gropius, W., 105
Guarini, G., 155
Gutman, R., 12, 18, 86, 185

Habermas, J., 44
Habitus, 11, 44, 57–58, 67, 104, 111, 115, 156, 187, 189, 211
    cultivated, 197, 200
    as a game, 59
    inculcating, 198
    practices and, 76
Hadid, Z., 119
Hare, R. M., 116
Harker, R., 76
Harvard University, 81, 214
Hawksmoor, N., 142
Heidegger, M., 45, 46, 47, 121
Heteronomous stratification principle, 91

Hidden curriculum, 196
Hillier, B., 14, 53
Historical consensus, 139
Holl, E., 155
Holland, 105
Homology of position, 82, 103, 104, 113
Houses vs. homes, 83
Hughes, R., 108
Hungary, 30
Hunt, R. M., 64
Husserl, E., 47, 116
Hysteresis, 67, 159

Immediacy ratio, 152
Inculcation, 196, 197
Industrial Revolution, 20
Intellectual markets, 207
Intellectual production, 177
Intellectuals
    Anglo-American, 39, 115
    European, 39, 40, 116, 117
    social dynamics of, 124
International Style, 103, 105
Investment strategies, 64
Isolates, 155
Italy, 29, 30, 133, 162, 163, 164, 167
    number of architects in, 29

Japan, 27, 30, 39, 119, 133
Jefferson, T., 86
Jencks, C., 101, 105, 119
Jenkins, R., 43, 69
Johns Hopkins University, 113, 186
Johnson, P., 100, 101
Jones, R., 140
Journal of Architectural Education, 23, 205
Journal of the Society of Architectural Historians, 125

Kahn, L., 105
Kant, I., 15
Katsalidis, N., 92
Kingsley, K., 24
Korea, 30
Kostoff, S., 14, 96, 104, 118, 197

Labrouste, H., 181
Landau, R., 73, 206
Larson, M. S., 19, 20, 21, 23, 26, 31, 46, 90, 97
Lash, S., 37
Law, 18, 25, 30, 174
Le Corbusier, 84, 95, 210
Lemercier, J., 166
Lemert, C., 39, 40
Library Journal, 106
Lifestyle, 68
Listener, 106
Logistic growth, 151
London Review of Books, 110

MacKinnon, D., 8, 9, 13, 77, 91, 195
Macmillan Encyclopedia of Architects, 86, 125, 129, 133, 134, 139, 142, 143, 145, 155, 181
    analyzing, 128
    bias in, 126
Major architects, 142, 144, 147, 152, 161
    dynamics of, 153
    growth of, 145
    practitioners and, 146
Malcolm, J., 111
Marchioni, C., 155
Marcuse, H., 44
Marx, K., 47
Marxian theory, 17, 60, 65
Masons, 20
Master-pupil chains, 3, 129, 155, 156, 159, 160, 166, 167, 214
McEvedy, C., 140

McKim, C., 64

Medicine, 18, 25

Meritocracy, 67, 68

Middle Ages, 20

Mies van der Rohe, L., 95, 210

Minor architects, 142, 144, 147, 151, 160
    dynamics of, 159
    practitioners and, 146

Miraculé, 67

Misrecognition, 57, 61

Modernism, 14, 22, 75, 95, 96, 103–107, 112, 120

Modern phase, 142, 151, 161

Morris, W., 96

Museum of Modern Art, New York, 100, 112, 119

Naples, 162

Nation, 106

National Architectural Accrediting Board, 185

National Review, 106

Naturality, 56

Nelson, G., 107, 109, 111, 112

Neoclassicism, 142

New York Review of Books, 121, 209

New York Times, 208

New Zealand, 87

Nice, R., 41

Norway, 29

Objectivism, 50, 51

O'Gorman, J., 125, 126

Ontological gerrymandering, 15

Oscillating growth, 151

Oxford Conference, 176

Oxford University, 81, 174

Palladio, A., 118

Papadakis, A., 119

Paris, 16, 40, 162

Parody, 111

Parvenus, 77

Phenomenology, 50, 52

Placzek, A., 126, 134

Poland, 30, 65

Population estimates, 140

Positivism, 21

Postmodernism, 16

Power, 48, 60, 87

Practices, 48, 56
    habitus and, 76

Presley, E., 79

Priests, 98, 101, 102

Privileged classes. *See* Classes: dominant

Production systems, 207

Professional associations, 90

Professionalization project, 21

Professions. *See also* Architecture: as a profession
    Abbott's model of, 31
    Anglo-American, 23, 27, 28
    concepts of, 23, 31–34
    European, 175, 179
    market monopoly theory, 22, 26, 31
    state, 28
    tacit qualities of, 80

Progressive Architecture, 22, 23, 25, 107, 120, 209

Prophets, 98, 101, 102, 103, 215

Psychology, 8–10, 11, 12, 13, 194, 211

Punch, 107

Rapoport, A., 205, 211

Registration, 85

Relational space, 49

Renaissance, 20, 151, 213

Renaissance network, 166

Renaissance transition, 142, 147

Research, 182

Rococo, 142

Royal Academy of Architecture, 20
Royal Architectural Institute of Canada, 87
Royal Australian Institute of Architects, 96
Royal Institute of British Architects, 176, 179, 185
Russia, 30
Rykwert, J., 106, 109

Sartre, J.-P., 40
Saturation limit, 151
Scholastic inculcation, 197
Schön, D., 53
Science, 93, 110, 152, 207
Scotland, 133
Shaw, G. B., 74
Sheehan, T., 120, 121
Snobbery, 72
Snyder, J., 46
Sobran, J., 106
Social capital, 177, 178
Social pathology, 67
Social psychology, 51
Social space, 65, 67
 bounds of, 124
 structure of, 122
Society of Architectural Historians, 208
Sociology
 Anglophone, 15
 of architecture, 11–23, 89
 of art, 17
 art theory and, 16
 central problem of, 49
 as critique, 11–13
 explanation in, 50
 language in, 42
 objectivity in, 13
 postmodernism and, 55
 of professions, 17, 25–27, 36
 psychology and, 11
 studying, 4
Sorkin, M., 106, 108
South Africa, 79

Spain, 29, 133, 163
Stamp, G., 106
Status groups, 68
Steiner, R., 155
Strategies of capital investment, 64
Stratification principle, 83, 91, 112
Stratification system, 48
Structural constructivism, 52
Structures, 50, 52, 59
Subjectivism, 50, 51
Subordinate architects, 123, 144, 161
Sweden, 65
Symbolic capital, 46, 48, 80, 91, 101, 144, 181, 215
 of academics, 172
 in architecture, 85, 210
 in architecture schools, 187, 188
 of avant-gardes, 110
 conversion of, 64, 81, 220
 and deconstruction, 113
 of the discipline, 206
 economism of, 64
 embodied, 199
 forms of, 62
 model of society, 65
 possession of, 201
 rarity of, 115
 rate of return, 63
 struggles over, 76
 of students, 193
 subversion of, 102
 tacit, 196
 threats to, 111
 transmission of, 124, 155, 167, 168, 187, 197, 213, 214
 valuing, 98
Symbolic resources, 123
Symbolic violence, 60

Talent, natural, 194
Taste, 3, 63, 73–74, 87, 105, 133, 199
 assessing, 199
 defined, 73
 deployment of, 220

embodied, 74
as investment, 111
naturality of, 99
unbuyability of, 91

Telos, 20

Templer, J., 7

Temporal capital, 94

Terminology, 5

Tigerman, S., 166

Times Literary Supplement, 209

Trajectory, 67

Trump, D., 63

Tschumi, B., 119, 199

United Kingdom, 5, 29, 30, 65, 87, 119
architectural field of, 222
architectural publications in, 209
architectural training in, 174, 176
number of architects in, 29
professions in, 174, 184

United States, 18, 22, 62, 65, 119, 131, 133
architectural education in, 173, 219, 223
architectural field of, 222
architectural publications in, 209
architectural research in, 172
classes in, 71
credential inflation in, 218
as cultural democracy, 70
doctoral production, 171
higher education system, 186, 187
number of architects in, 29, 146, 212, 217
number of architecture graduates, 112
professions in, 184, 185
students in, 190

University of Berlin, 182

University of Chicago, 186

University of Liverpool, 176

University of London, 174, 176, 191

University of Pennsylvania, 196

University of Sydney, 189
Faculty of Architecture, 4, 5, 6, 94, 193, 211, 220

Vanbrugh, J., 142

Vasari, G., 3

Vasari database, 129, 134

Veblen, T., 44

Venice, 163

Venturi, R., 88, 105

Vereinigung Freischaffender Architekten, 28

Vidal, G., 63

Viollet-le-Duc, E.-E., 99, 181

Vitruvius Pollio, M., 99, 207

Waters, M., 51

Weak ties, 62

Weber, M., 47, 60, 68, 69

Western polity, 140

White, S., 33, 178

Williamson, R., 90, 178

Wolfe, T., 105–107, 110
critics on, 108

Wren, C., 86, 142

Wright, F. L., 84, 88, 90, 95, 210

Yale University, 113, 214